TACKLING TRANSPORTATION

Edited by

Helmuth Trischler
Stefan Zeilinger
Deutsches Museum, Munich

Associate Editors

Robert Bud
Science Museum, London

Bernard Finn
Smithsonian Institution, Washington DC

Published 2003 by Michigan State University Press, East Lansing, MI 48823-5202

Designed by Jerry Fowler
Printed in England by the Cromwell Press

ISBN 0-87013-659-3
ISSN 1029-3353

Website http://www.msupress.msu.edu

Artefacts series: studies in the history of science and technology

In growing numbers, historians are using technological artefacts in the study and interpretation of
the recent past. Their work is still largely pioneering, as they investigate approaches and modes of
presentation. But the consequences are already richly rewarding. To encourage this enterprise, three
of the world's greatest repositories of the material heritage of science and technology: the Deutsches
Museum, the Science Museum and the Smithsonian Institution, are collaborating on this book series.
Each volume treats a particular subject area, using objects to explore a wide range of issues related to
science, technology and medicine and their place in society.

Edited by   Robert Bud, Science Museum, London
             Bernard Finn, Smithsonian Institution, Washington DC
             Helmuth Trischler, Deutsches Museum, Munich

Volume 1   Manifesting Medicine: Bodies and Machines

            Principal Editor Robert Bud

Volume 2   Exposing Electronics

            Principal Editor Bernard Finn

Volume 3   Tackling Transportation

            Principal Editors Helmuth Trischler and Stefan Zeilinger

Volume 4   Presenting Pictures

            Principal Editor Bernard Finn

Further volumes in preparation, on the themes of:

Environment • War • Space • Music

Contents

Series preface

In the long history of the efforts made by science museums to promote the importance of their collections, the past decade has been among the most exciting. Whereas the competition from non-object-based science centres became ever stronger, interest in using objects to communicate insight into the history of our technological and scientific heritage gained new strength. For millions of visitors, artefacts provide a uniquely attractive and direct link to the past.

Museums also have a research mission. They are a vital force in the community of scholars, especially in the history of technology, and here, too, they have come to be better appreciated. Many outside their walls have come to share the belief that artefacts have played a role which is both inadequately understood and indispensable for a better understanding of historical and cultural change.

Initially, perhaps, it was the insight into technical detail provided by close inspection of the real thing that was generally of greatest scholarly importance. More recently however, studies of experiments and technology have widened the view to the complex role of artefacts within their larger geographical, economic, social and political setting. Rather than being treated in isolation, technological objects and instruments are coming to be seen as material expressions of human culture that shape, mediate and reflect the interactions among science, technology and society. Latter-day onlookers are therefore helped to see not just machines, but also imaginative worlds of the past.

Building on rapidly maturing scholarly interest, three of the world's great repositories of material heritage – the Deutsches Museum in Munich, the National Museum of American History in Washington and the Science Museum in London – are cooperating to support this series of publications. These volumes explore innovative approaches to the object-oriented historiography of science and technology. The series seeks to go beyond a strict technical description of artefacts on the one hand, and an overly broad social history on the other.

Collections reflect local, regional and national traditions and express their cultures and history. This character confers certain constraints, but also advantages. Museums are sensitive to, and reflect, the specific local meanings of objects, but they have the asset, too, of curators whose detailed knowledge of the collections is couched within a wider historical perspective.

Building on these dual strengths, the series is intended to initiate an international discussion which both emphasises local material cultures, and also draws upon recent research in the overall history of science and technology. The authors therefore include curators, but the series attracts into the discussion other scholars from a much wider orbit.

Many people have, of course, been concerned with the problems examined in this series; but all too often this has been in individual or institutional isolation. These volumes engage an international community that is large enough to develop research programmes and debates that will have enduring momentum and excitement.

Situated at the interface between museum, university and independent research organisation, the series addresses professional historians of science and technology, curators, those in charge of the day-to-day administration of museums and those who, so often passionately, simply enjoy visiting. As museums do in general, the series aims to build a bridge between historical research and the use and application of historical knowledge in education and the public understanding of science and technology.

Each volume focuses on a specific field of technology and science in its wider historical context. The first, and larger, part of each volume presents the honed products of presentation and debate at joint conferences. The second part consists of exhibit reviews, critical expeditions into the respective museum's landscape, bibliographical overviews on recent literature, and the like.

The initial collaboration between the three national institutions was made possible by their then directors: Neil Cossons of the Science Museum, Spencer Crew of the Smithsonian Institution's National Museum of American History, and Wolf Peter Fehlhammer of the Deutsches Museum.

Notes on contributors

Michael R Bailey has a DPhil from the Institute of Railway Studies and is an Associate and former Trustee of Manchester's Museum of Science & Industry. Together with John P Glithero he has undertaken investigation, restoration and conservation work on several early locomotives in Britain and Canada.

Colin Divall heads the Institute of Railway Studies & Transport History, run jointly by the National Railway Museum and University of York. His most recent book, written with Andrew Scott, is *Making Histories in Transport Museums.*

John P Glithero is a Chartered Engineer and studied for his PhD at UMIST. Together with Michael R Bailey he has undertaken investigation, restoration and conservation work on several early locomotives in Britain and Canada.

Bettina Gundler is Curator of Road Transport at the Deutsches Museum, Munich.

Peter Lyth is an economic historian, a fellow of the University of Nottingham International Business History Institute and the editor of the *Journal of Transport History*. His latest book, with Philip Bagwell, is *Transport in Britain: from Canal Lock to Gridlock, 1750–2000.*

Gijs Mom teaches at Eindhoven University of Technology and is Programme Director of Mobility History at the Foundation for the History of Technology in Eindhoven. His dissertation on the history of the electric vehicle will be published by Johns Hopkins University Press in 2004.

Kurt Möser is Curator of Road and Water Transport at the Landesmuseum für Technik und Arbeit in Mannheim. He studied at the University of Constance and has taught at the universities of Erlangen, Oxford, New Delhi, and St Gallen.

Andrew Nahum is Senior Curator of Aeronautics at the Science Museum, London. He has published extensively on the history of technology for both scholarly and general audiences. His interest in German aeronautics developed through research for his PhD study at the London School of Economics.

Helmuth Trischler is Head of the research department of the Deutches Museum, Munich, and Professor of History and History of Technology at the University of Munich.

Bill Withuhn has been Curator of Transportation at the National Museum of American History, Smithsonian Institution, Washington DC, since 1983. His first formal proposal for a new and expanded transportation-history gallery was in 1987. A team to implement this was assembled in 1996/97.

Henry Wydler has worked at the Verkehrshaus der Schweiz, Lucerne, since 1970. In 1979 he became Project Manager on the new railway section, opened in 1982, and in 1993 he was appointed Vice-Director and Curator of the air and space section.

Stefan Zeilinger is a Research Fellow at the Deutsches Museum, Munich, and has completed a PhD study on high-speed rail systems in Europe.

Helmuth Trischler

Artefacts and systems in transport: an introduction

Since the early 1990s, transport history has received increasing attention in the world of scholarship. Critical surveys of the recent literature demonstrate that studies in transport history improved in quantity as well as in quality.[1] This trend is manifested by changes in the leading periodical in the field, the *Journal of Transport History*. As an example, consider a recent special issue on 'gender and transport history'.[2]

A number of national as well as transnational networks of historians from various fields have also emerged. 'Lessons from history' is the subtitle of one of these networks, which has brought together historians, economists, politicians and practitioners from more than 20 countries – from Finland to Italy, from Portugal to Estonia, with a particular goal of identifying the historical development of 'a European intermodal transport network'.[3] Others focus on the crucial role of the automobile in the modern consumer society with its high level of individual mobility.[4] The scholars involved in these networks, together with the European Commission, which is funding their research, share the conviction that detailed knowledge and rigorous analysis of concrete historical processes can significantly improve the understanding of current issues involved in the creation of transnational transport networks. Thus, historical knowledge can provide a useful source of orientation in an ever more complex society with an ever-expanding transport system.

The notion of system is at the centre of this fundamental reorientation of transport history. Rather than concentrating on the development of individual modes of traffic, there is an effort to analyse the interrelations of technological, political, economical and cultural factors. Transport is understood as a system of interacting modes (road, rail, inland navigation, air traffic, bicycle, etc.). By including material components and human actors, these systems come close to the sociological actor–network theory, and it is not by chance that one of the creators and a prominent advocate of this theory, Bruno Latour, has tested it with a case study on transport.[5]

Whereas Latour in his works constantly argues for a blurring of the differences between human and non-human actors, other scholars have identified transport history as a perfect test-bed for a separate approach currently popular in the social sciences: according to their understanding, artefacts in transport systems represent the 'cyborgisation' of modern, if not postmodern, society.[6] If we understand a cyborg as 'a *cybernetic organism*, a hybrid of machine and organism', it becomes obvious that the history of transport since the late nineteenth century is more than any other part of society dominated by these hybrids of man and machine.[7] In artefacts of transport, and most significantly in the automobile, the blurring of the boundaries between man and machine has become a ubiquitous phenomenon. The cyborgisation of modern society with the means of transport was already observed in the 1960s, when Lewis Mumford stated that the car 'appeared as a compensatory device for enlarging an ego which had been shrunken by our very success in mechanization'.[8]

Academic historians, philosophers and sociologists of technology may reflect on the crucial importance of artefacts in modern transport systems. But museum people have to cope with problems resulting from the mere existence of these objects. More than in most other fields of technology, transportation artefacts dominate not only the space and imagery in an exhibition, but also the expectations and perceptions of its visitors. People tend to be overwhelmed by the attractiveness of a big steam locomotive, a shiny Mercedes-Benz Silberpfeil racing car, an elegant French Louis XVI stagecoach, a sunken Swedish warship of the eighteenth century or a Second World War jet fighter. Museum curators struggle with the physical dominance of these artefacts: the power of the artefact helps to attract interest, but at the same time endangers its integration into a larger system. One of the great challenges facing a curator is to use these objects in a way that demonstrates the systemic nature of transport.

For historians and curators dealing with transport issues, artefacts are thus of crucial importance in at least two ways. Firstly, they represent visible nodes in the seamless and often immaterial networks that provide mobility for goods, information and people. These nodes materialise as means of transport. Artefacts such as cars or mountain bikes are highly charged with human emotions; they are manifold coded components of complex systems. For a better understanding of these hidden elements of physical artefacts, historians and curators of transport have to apply a multi-perspective approach in their research, embracing a variety of theories of historical change. The controversy over historical interpretation of the bridges built by the famous New York architect and regional planner Robert Moses in the 1920s underlines the importance of open-minded scholarship, which allows for constant reinterpretation. In a seminal article Langdon Winner saw Moses' low bridges, which enabled private cars but not buses to reach the attractive area of Jones Beach on Long Island, as the materialised expression of a deliberate policy to segregate the black lower classes from the white middle classes. More recently Steve Woolgar and Geoff Cooper have rewritten the creation of Moses' bridges as a history full of contingencies, and Bernward Joerges has tried to offer a middle-way interpretation of Moses' artefacts, situated between political control and pure contingency.[9] Whatever the 'right' interpretation might be, bridges are important nodes in transport systems – and beyond their character as aesthetical manifestations of engineering ingenuity they are highly valued symbols of humankind's will to bridge gaps in society.

Artefacts, secondly, enable us to identify the material culture of mobility. The history of technology has undergone a change of paradigm. It is more and more shifting the focus from the production to the use of artefacts. As we have learned from recent studies, technology most often is not shaped at the 'consumption junction', the interface between producers and consumers.[10] As a consequence, historical research more and more emphasises that technological artefacts are not primarily ready-made products, springing from the drawing boards of engineers and designers. They generally result from users' choices, and they are reproduced by the consumers themselves, as the history of transport most significantly shows. More than most other classes of artefacts, cars, bicycles and boats represent identities of individual persons. Furthermore, an individual not only chooses a vehicle to express an identity, but often makes changes in it to satisfy particular needs or ideas. Thus, artefacts of transport reflect modern consumer societies, and the careful examination of these artefacts sheds light on the emergence of modernity.

The authors of this volume tackle the interrelations between artefacts and systems in transport from a variety of angles. Gijs Mom's essay is an intriguing case study on the evolution of the automobile. Even more, it is an important contribution to the theoretical debate on the process of technical change. Based on a careful rereading of the vast literature on technical evolution and change, the author favours an approach which looks at interactions between alternative technologies. In his case of the early automobile, the two main alternatives were the gasoline car and the electric car. The article shows that artefacts were the medium through which innovations and technical knowledge were transferred between these two competing subsystems of automotive transportation. But it was technical properties and applicational functions, rather than the artefacts or parts of the artefacts, by which technology was transferred. This form of interartefactual transfer of technologies can be observed in three crucial elements of the maturing automobile: the battery, the tyre and the transmission. In all three cases, the modern gasoline car, driven by a combustion engine, profited from successful technical solutions, which were taken from the electric car. Mom calls this distinct form of technology transfer the 'Pluto effect', which was based on the seemingly anthropological wish of engineers to keep up with the latest state of the art in their field.

A different form of learning through carefully studying an artefact is demonstrated by Michael R Bailey and John P Glithero. Their case study in industrial archaeology has chosen one of the icons in the history of railway transport: Robert Stephenson's *Rocket*, which paved the way for a century and a half of steam locomotive development. By combining the examination of conventional archival material, i.e. written sources, with a complete dismantling of all parts of the locomotive, the authors try to reconstruct the biography of this individual artefact. As with the biography of a historic person, the two authors aim at finding out as many details about the life of their subject as possible. And as in conventional biography the 'life' of *Rocket* spans different phases: its youth, when it was designed and constructed; its period as an adult, when it was operated for inter-city traffic and later for linking several collieries in Cumberland; its old age, when it was displayed in exhibitions as a masterpiece of railway construction. But in contrast to a traditional biography, the body was not buried or burned; it has remained and serves as an important source for the biographer. By carefully examining and reporting all the modifications and improvements which *Rocket* experienced in its working life, the artefact sheds more light on the rapid development of locomotive engineering in the second third of the nineteenth century. The method of industrial archaeology thus provides an efficient tool to understand better technological change in one of the most important fields of industrialisation. It also enables the authors to come up with a qualified and convincing statement in museological controversy: how should an artefact be displayed? After discussing the advantages and disadvantages of all potential options for display, they propose a mixture of two forms: one side of the locomotive should be fitted with replica components enabling the visitor to follow its working life; the other side should be left in its present form representing the end-of-service condition of *Rocket*.

Automobiles are integral parts of the large technological system of road transport, and they are machines of individual owners or users. This dialectics of large systems and individual artefacts becomes most clearly visible in the driver's workplace and on the dashboard in the interior of a car. The driver's workplace serves as an interface between the systemic and the artefactual elements of automotive traffic. Similar to the keyboard of the personal computer, the workplace and dashboard allow the driver to communicate with the larger system. But unlike the keyboard of a PC, which is highly standardised and follows the model established by the typewriter,[11] car interiors show large variations in time and space. In his essay, Kurt Möser follows the development of car interiors from the open car of the early twentieth century to the enclosed automobile of the late twentieth century. He interprets it as an ambivalent process. On the one hand, the interior was a highly artificial environment, a 'technotop' in its best sense.

On the other hand, drivers were keen to convert the interiors of their cars from technotops into living-room-like environments, which met their individual demands as users. The ambivalence helped to bridge the opening gap between the systemic restrictions of road transport and the individualistic self-perceptions of their users. Here, a careful examination of existing historical artefacts allows us to gain new insights into the emergence of the modern consumer society and its ambivalences – and the museum with its stores full of relevant first-hand sources is the obvious place to undertake research.

The history of Anglo-American relations in high technologies in the twentieth century is a mixture of conflict and cooperation. Peter Lyth's essay concentrates on the crucial two decades after the Second World War, when Britain lost its position as the international leader in aviation technology. The critical artefact in this shift of technological leadership was the de Havilland Comet, the world's first civil aircraft driven by a jet engine. The British decline in aviation technology culminated in the misfortune of the Comet as a commercial airliner. The last attempt of Britain as an 'air-minded nation'[12] to challenge American technological dominance centres around the efforts to catch up in jet engine development, the most significant innovation in the history of long-distance transport. The turbojet airliner became the main artefact of a rapidly expanding large technological system, which revolutionised commercial air transport. It not only allowed airlines to grow by expanding their networks all over the world, it also helped to create international tourism, one of the fastest growing industries in the second half of the twentieth century.

Like its transatlantic allies, Britain profited from the 'intellectual reparations' Germany had to pay at the end of the Second World War. Special intelligence forces shipped tons of paperwork from German research centres to Britain. Among other technical innovations, these materials contained the swept-wing design concept, which revolutionised aviation technology in the postwar period. Leading German aerodynamicists and aircraft specialists such as Karl Doetsch and Dietrich Küchemann followed. The latter became a leading figure at the Royal Aircraft Establishment at Farnborough and a key member of the team that designed Concorde, Britain's most spectacular contribution to aviation technology since 1945. In his essay, Andrew Nahum stresses the importance of these German inputs for the British innovation system in the early postwar years. But, like Peter Lyth, he underlines the decline of British aviation industry in the long run. With orders from even British Airways, the national flag carrier, going to the United States, Britain's aircraft industry soon lost its leading position in the market.

Transport museums themselves are the subject under research in the contribution by Colin Divall. Recent scholarship has identified the museum as a cornerstone for the formation of the knowledge society in which we live today. Museums are archives of shared knowledge within and across nations; they represent the collective mind of societies. During the Enlightenment, more and more collections and museums emerged, mostly founded by European court society. After the French revolution, bourgeois society transformed the museum into a public institution. Not surprisingly, formats for transport museums emerged and expanded along the lines of industrialisation, when the mobility of goods and people became a key issue. Often, exhibitions – most prominently London's Great Exhibition of 1851 – stimulated the founding of these museums, which usually were devoted to one single mode of transport. It is important to note that the modern transport museum, combining artefacts and systems and telling stories about the social effects and implications of travel and transport, is a very young member of the worldwide family of museums. But its roots date far back into the nineteenth century. To trace these roots is not only an important exercise in the constant process of professional reassurance and self-reflexivity. It can also stimulate dialogue within the museum community and between museums and the public regarding how arte-facts and systems of transport should be combined in future exhibits.

Three major museums of transport communicate their approaches in this volume: the Deutsches Museum with its ambitious attempt to create an 'intermodal' branch museum on land transport; the National Museum of American History of the Smithsonian Institution in Washington DC with its new long-term exhibition on the history of transport; and the Swiss Transport Museum in Lucerne.[13] Not by chance, the museums in Munich and Washington are following the systemic approach, which has become a key issue in historical studies on transport. Furthermore, both aim at contextualising the artefacts by telling meaningful stories. Artefacts are used as a means to communicate the results of latest research in the history of transport, to which the two museums prominently contribute with the work of their curators and researchers. Evidently, the world of museums and the community of historical scholars are closely connected: as Bettina Gundler and Bill Withuhn show, academic scholarship and museums have the same understanding of the subject under research and display, and they share the arsenal of theories and methods to perform historical studies. The museum at the lake of Lucerne, which Henry Wydler portrays as a hybrid of museum and science centre, is somewhat different. Whereas the two other museums have suffered from budget cuts during the last few years,[14] the latter institution has been forced to balance a budget with almost no public funding. This heavy constraint has limited the space for manoeuvre in realising ambitious exhibitions and in performing extended research activities alike. The museum's management tries to follow a middle way by strengthening the ties to the academic landscape on the one hand, and by meeting the customers' interest in 'edutainment' on the other.

Notes and references

1 For Germany see especially Merki, C M, 'Die verschlungenen Wege der modernen Verkehrsgeschichte. Ein Gang durch die aktuelle Forschung', *Schweizerische Zeitschrift für Geschichte*, 45 (1995), pp444–57; Schmucki, B, 'Automobilisierung. Neuere Forschungen zur Motorisierung', *Archiv für Sozialgeschichte*, 35 (1995), pp582–98; Kühne, T, 'Massenmotorisierung und Verkehrspolitik im 20. Jahrhundert. Technikgeschichte als politische Sozial- und Kulturgeschichte', *Neue Politische Literatur*, 41 (1996), pp196–229; Hascher, M, and Zeilinger, S, 'Verkehrsgeschichte Deutschlands im 19. und 20. Jahrhundert. Verkehr auf Straßen, Schienen und Binnenwasserstraßen. Ein Literaturüberblick über die jüngsten Forschungen', *Jahrbuch für Wirtschaftsgeschichte* (2001), pp165–83.

2 See especially the article of the guest editor, Margaret Welsh, 'Gendering transport history: retrospect and prospect', *Journal of Transport History*, 23 (2002), pp1–8.

3 'Towards a European intermodal transport network: lessons from history', started in 2000 as COST Action 340, running until 2004; for the research agenda see http://www.cordis.lu/cost-transport/src/cost-340.html.

4 'European Mobility. Automobile European scenarios' is part of the ESF project 'Tensions of Europe: technology and the making of twentieth-century Europe', which runs in its first phase from 2000 to 2003; for the research agenda see http://www.histech.nl/tensions/.

5 Latour, B, *Aramis or the Love of Technology* (Cambridge, MA/London: 1996)

6 Schmucki, B, 'Cyborgs unterwegs? Verkehrstechnik und individuelle Mobilität seit dem 19. Jahrhundert', in Schmidt, G (ed.), *Technik und Gesellschaft, Jahrbuch 10: Automobil und Automobilismus* (Frankfurt am Main/New York: 1999), pp87–119

7 Haraway, D, 'A cyborg manifesto: science, technology, and socialist-feminism in the late twentieth century', in Haraway, D (ed.), *Simians, Cyborgs and Women: The Reinvention of Nature* (London: 1991), pp149–81, p149

8 Mumford, L, *The Highway and the City* (New York: 1964), p244

9 Winner, L, 'Do artifacts have politics?', *Daedalus*, 109 (1980), pp121–36; Woolgar, S, and Cooper, G, 'Do artefacts have ambivalence? – Moses' bridges, Winners' bridges and other urban legends in STS', *Social Studies of Science*, 29 (1999), pp433–49; Joerges, B, 'Brücken, Busse, Autos und andere Verkehrsteilnehmer – Zur Repräsentation und Wirkung städtischer Artefakte', Schmidt, G, (ed.), note 6, pp197–218

10 Schwartz Cowan, R, 'The consumption junction. A proposal for research strategies in the sociology of technology', in Bijker, W E, Bijker, T P, Hughes and Pinch, T J (eds), *The Social Construction of Technological Systems. New Directions in the Sociology and History of Technology* (Cambridge, MA/London: 1987), pp261–80; see also Wengenroth, U, 'Technischer Fortschritt, Deindustrialisierung und Konsum. Eine Herausforderung für die Technikgeschichte', *Technikgeschichte*, 64 (1997), pp1–18

11 Cf. the seminal article of Paul David, 'Clio and the economics of QWERTY', *American Historical Review*, 74 (1985), pp332–7.

12 Edgerton, D, *England and the Aeroplane. An Essay on a Militant and Technological Nation* (London: Houndsmills, 1991)

13 During the conference at the Deutsches Museum on which this volume is based, Nicholas Néiertz, from the Musée des Arts et Métiers, presented a paper on the plans for the transport section arising from the complete renewal of this museum of science and technology in Paris. The author left the museum before the exhibition was finished, and the management of the museum decided not to publish the paper. An overview of what has been achieved by the Musée des Arts et Métiers can be found in the museum's catalogue; see also http://www.arts-et-metiers.net/.

14 Bunch, L G, 'If you ain't got the dough, re, me, boys: the impact of funding and politics on American museums', in Henke, K-D, Dienel, H-L, Molella, A P (eds), *Research Budgets in an Age of Limits. Basic Science – Health – Culture* (Baden-Baden: Nomos, 2000), pp147–51; Trischler, H, 'Budget cuts in museums in Germany. Comment on Lonnie G. Bunch', *ibid.*, pp152–6

Gijs Mom

Conceptualising technical change: alternative interaction in the evolution of the automobile

At their first appearance, innovations are less valuable for their immediate advantages than for their potential for future development and this second quality is always very difficult to assess.[1]

The analysis of competing technologies in their earliest phase of development is often based on the assumption of equal initial opportunities and mutual exclusiveness, as well as mutual exchangeability for all alternatives concerned. This assumption has been especially popular in the realm of automotive technology, where, most importantly, the electric vehicle has been and still is considered to be a promising, 100-per-cent alternative to the mainstream internal-combustion-engined vehicle. This has led, among electric vehicle proponents then and now, to very optimistic expectations about new transportation paradigms, often followed by deep disappointments when such expectations did not materialise.

Such hopes are often based on strategies to influence the moment, if not the entire process of so-called 'lock in' of the preferred technology as the dominant design. However, as I will show in the following contribution, such approaches are based on meso-level analyses (characterised by an ex-post determination of 'winners' and 'losers', 'superior' versus 'inferior' technologies) and on a concept of artefacts as mutually exclusive monolithic entities engaged in a mostly rather limited set of interartefactual relationships. As such, these approaches underestimate both the crucial uncertainty of the choice process by contemporaries, not endowed with the hindsight of the historian, as well as the extremely complex and only partly quantifiable character of interartefactual interaction.

In this contribution an alternative approach is offered, based on a contextual and evolutionary perspective on sociotechnological choice.[2] First, some preliminary remarks about evolutionary technical change will be offered, introducing a new 'field theory' of technical change.[3] Second, three detailed cases from the history of automotive technology will be presented, applying these theoretical notions. Third, on the basis of these cases a special type of interartefactual technology transfer will be hypothesised, called the 'Pluto effect'.

9

Interaction and the diffusion of technology

The classical answer to the question of how technological change works when artefacts compete is a reference to the phenomenon of substitution, as a special case of the diffusion of innovations.[4] According to the 'bible' of the diffusionist school, Everett Rogers' *Diffusion of Innovations*, this phenomenon – covered in more than 4000 publications since the 1920s – is probably the most thoroughly researched topic in the social sciences. From the point of view of the historian of technology, who is primarily interested in the (actual as well as perceived) possibilities of historical actors, there are several drawbacks to this approach.[5]

First, this approach, which treats innovation diffusion as basically a process of communication and of knowledge *about* technology, implicitly seems to favour a linear one-to-one replacement concept of substitution. In most cases the entity to be replaced is simply the previous non-existence of the innovation before adaptation, but in more sophisticated models the innovation (an artefact or a process) is placed in opposition to an 'older' technique that is treated in the same manner, i.e. as an unchanged and unchangeable entity.[6]

Second, many diffusion and substitution studies are finalist and deterministic in scope, because they intrinsically depend on hindsight knowledge.[7] As long as diffusion does not reach saturation (as seems the case again and again in automobile diffusion), the fixing of a saturation level (necessary to draw the logistic or S-curve as a quantitative representation of this process) leads to severe misjudgements, as the history of predictions of national car fleets clearly shows. The finalist character becomes especially apparent when substitution processes are characterised by long periods of coexistence of two (or more) competing technologies. The supposedly transitional character of these processes is based on the juxtaposition of 'old' and 'new' technologies and on an implicit assumption that 'new' is 'superior' to 'old' and in the end will 'win'. This might be true in some clear cases of obsolescence of 'old' technologies such as gas lighting versus electric lighting, or sailing ships against steam ships (although many knowledgeable contemporaries judged otherwise), but what about examples of seemingly continuous coexistence, like the telephone versus the cordless version, or personal computers and laptops, or even such cases as the fountain pen versus the typewriter or the PC, or coffee and tea, Pepsi-Cola and Coca-Cola, steel and aluminium, newspapers and the Internet, bicycles and automobiles in the city, automobiles, trains and aeroplanes between cities, subsonic and supersonic flight for long-range transport, and electric versus petrol/diesel vehicles? Despite the overwhelming proliferation of case studies it seems that in many cases the enormous variety of alternative technologies has been reduced to a set of clear-cut dual (and in some cases triple or quadruple) competition during the phase of 'early adoption', mostly resulting in the 'locking in' of a 'dominant design'.

If diffusion and substitution analysis cannot cope with the complexities of artefact interaction, two other traditions of research within the historiography of technology promise to offer more insights into our problem: micro-level studies into the process of technological choice, and meso- and macro-level studies into the evolutionary aspects of technological change.

The sociotechnical dilemma of interartefactual choice

Technology changes through the activities of people in their capacity as producer, legislator, user or non-user, and their organisations. In most cases of technical change a multitude of solutions exist (or are thought to be possible), and people have to *choose* in order to bring about innovation.

In general historiography a lot of research has been done on the phenomenon of technical choice,[8] although the dominance in this domain of economic historians has led to a questionable emphasis on costs and prices. The implication of this type of approach often is that user preferences follow a mainly rational and quantifiable path. Since (mainly Schumpeterian) criticism of neoclassical economics (which treated economic agents as having perfect information and, being perfectly rational, permanently seeking to maximise their satisfaction as consumers and to maximise their profits as firms) has gained momentum, several corrections of the concept of well-informed, perfectly rational choice have been put forward.[9]

This was all the more necessary, as a new technology can hardly be compared with the alternative(s) it is meant to replace on the basis of cost data alone, for the simple reason that these data are not available as long as this new technology is not embedded in a user culture. Instead, a set of selection criteria is badly needed. Also, expectations play a decisive role here, not only in terms of the economic advantages of the new technology in the long run, but also in terms of the new functions this technology promises to provide. Thus, it is by no means clear at the moment of innovation on what criteria the choice in favour of an alternative technology should be based. In fact, while the artefact is being 'invented', the use of it has to be 'invented' as well. A classical example is the American telephone, which was introduced as a 'better telegraph' for business applications, but became a medium for social communication, especially in the hands of female users.[10]

'Most inventions are relatively crude and inefficient at the date when they are first recognized as constituting a new invention,' economic historian Nathan Rosenberg remarked. 'They offer only very small advantages, or perhaps none at all, over previously existing techniques.' This raises the question, obviously, why producers and users should opt in favour of a new technology, especially if one takes

into account that innovation is not restricted to new technologies
at all. 'There is much evidence', Rosenberg asserted elsewhere, 'to
suggest that historically, the *actual* improvements in old technologies
after the introduction of the new were often substantial and played a
significant role in slowing the pace of the diffusion process' of the new
technology [italics in original]. Classic examples are the water wheel,
which underwent major improvements during the century it competed
with Watt's steam engine, and the wooden sailing ship's sequence of
important technical changes long after the introduction of the iron-
hull steamship. Yet, 'it is a very general practice among historians to
fix their attention upon the story of the new method as soon as its
technical feasibility has been established and to terminate all interest
in the old. The result [...] is to sharpen the belief in abrupt and
dramatic discontinuities in the historical record.'[11]

However, the evolutionary approach, within economic history, of
seeing technological change as basically a stochastic process, seems to
lay too much emphasis on the aggregate level, with the population of
the artefact (or the process) as the unit of analysis. And although it has
become customary within the history of technology to shy away from
the fundamental discussion about the very nature of technology, it
seems worthwhile to lend an ear, not only to economic historians, but
to the philosophers of technology as well, especially since they started
to perform an 'empirical turn'.[12] According to this relatively new field
of thinking, artefacts are characterised by their 'dual nature' of both
'intrinsic' and 'relational' characteristics, the first being influenced by
engineers and producers, the second by users. We will have to come
back to this very important distinction later.

Evolutionary technological change
Rosenberg's implicit plea for an evolutionary approach to looking
at technological change is appealing indeed.[13] Thus, 'biological
concepts of selection, adaptation and mutation can be twinned with
their economic counterparts, competition, imitation and innovation.
In this regard selection and adaptation are different mechanisms for
reducing variety while mutation is a mechanism for generating variety.'
Formulated in a more structural way: Darwinian theory as applied
to the evolution of technology is founded 'on the basic assumption,
that in a self-contained system *mutations* occur in the genotype as
spontaneous, non-predictable changes, followed by a *selection* at the
phenotype, a choice which is independent of internal and external
conditions in accordance with the increase of reproductive changes
of the mutant within the system. This approach allows us to describe
the emergence of new forms and parallel developments, as well as the
trailing along of dysfunctional elements or the complete dying out
of a species.' [Italics in original.] If, as Amartya Sen states, 'natural
selection is, in fact, choice through *selective extinction*', [italics in

original] then the role of 'failures' and 'technologies in decline' (and their analysis) in the history of technology becomes crucial indeed.[14]

German historian Wolfgang König rightfully remarks that a serious theory of the history of technology, like one of general history, has to combine 'history as action' and 'history as a stream of events' ('Geschichte als Geschehen'), ontogeny (the making of the artefact) and phylogeny (the making of the family of species), agency and structure. And although, according to nineteenth-century zoologist and evolutionist Ernst Haeckel, 'ontogeny recapitulates phylogeny', it is worthwhile to distinguish clearly between micro- and macro-level developments.[15]

At the ontogenetic level, the Darwinian distinction between the phenotype of an organism (its morphological and behavioural characteristics) and the genotype (its structure embodied within the DNA) can be fruitfully adapted to the history of technology. According to Darwinian theory, only the phenotype is susceptible to influences from the environment and the changes caused by these influences are not transmitted to the offspring.[16] On the other hand, several scholars have used the concept of the genotype to identify comparable phenomena in the social world, such as know-how in general, the pool of dominant competence of organisations, routines and decision rules, or 'deep structure'.[17]

According to this approach, to which I adhere in this essay, technology is *not* treated as a mere knowledge concept. Analogous to the distinction between phenotype and genotype, for a given point in time and a given locale, an inventory of alternatives can be constructed, a kind of 'artefactual whole', consisting of two different phenomena: a set of concrete artefacts on the one hand, and, on the other, their abstract historical structure, which not only encompasses structural knowledge (the 'state of the art') but also can be viewed as an aggregate of all existing artefacts, reduced to their common structural denominator.[18]

Apart from being 'frozen, materialised information', technology is also about *doing* things (behaviour), as much as it is a set of artefacts.[19] Like biology, the history of technology is 'a discipline where data come from observation rather than experiment', and in such a discipline, according to biologist Stephen J Gould, 'taxonomy is essential, because rather than a mindless process of allocation of objects into self-evident pigeon-holes, it becomes a theory of causal ordering'. Moreover, artefacts are not mere emanations of a structure, of a genotype: they have a certain relative autonomy, and are susceptible, according to John Odling-Smee, to 'ecological inheritance' or to an 'organism–environment coevolution'.[20]

If, as Hodgson explains, 'phylogeny is the complete and ongoing evolution of a population', then the concept of population can be of much help, viewed as the aggregate of members of a species. For instance, in the history of transport, especially of individual transport vehicles like the automobile, it is often difficult to characterise the specific, localised car technology of a certain period. Cars are designed, produced and used in makes and models and although it is often done, direct generalisations on the basis of specific case studies are hampered by the fact that what is true for one market segment or geographical setting does not hold in another. How does one decide, for instance, whether front-wheel drive in automobiles was 'superior' to rear-wheel drive when both types of drive-train configurations coexist to this day? How should the technology of *the* car of, say, the 1950s, be characterised if users could still choose between these alternatives? The concept of population implies that not only average or typical artefacts are important but also their distribution. Also, this clarifies why an artificial juxtaposition of 'good' and 'bad' technologies is absurd. For the 'species' automobile consists of different 'subspecies' like front-wheel and rear-wheel drive cars, which should be analysed within their specific contexts of application.[21]

The field approach

In order to allow for these nuances in the intricacies of technical change, I use the field metaphor, borrowed from electromagnetic theory. Applied to automotive history the 'field of application' comprises the areas of actual use and prototypical, real-world experiments of a vehicle type (a passenger car, a truck, a racing car) in a certain stage of its development and at a certain geographical location. So, the contents and dimensions of such a field are historically determined, depending on 'distortions' by neighbouring fields, and the field of application itself influences its surrounding fields. In the field of application the sociotechnological choice takes place. The field of application can also be called the 'functional field', because it is the function as realised by using the artefact, which enables the building of this field.[22]

The 'field of expectation' is where the historical actors' technical and social fantasies and images of future applications are embedded. According to some historians of technology, it is a crucial field, because here the subjective impulses of action are formed. These constitute an important motor behind the technical change, in that they influence choice behaviour, of producers and users alike. The field of expectations is often very wide: it contains prototypical near-reality ideas about artefacts and their possible applications, but also science-fiction-like constructs that are not even intended to be realised, but which nonetheless influence other, more realistic fantasies. In the history of technology this field is often restricted to a prevailing field of expectations, a kind of commonly held mainstream conviction among opinion leaders about the desired route of development. In the German sociological approach to technology, the prevailing fantasy is indicated by the term 'Leitbild', a translation of the English 'image' and a subjective form of Kuhn's 'paradigm'. But the field of expectations can also be split into opposing fields, such as in the case where a 'gasoline culture' was relatively separated from a 'subculture of the electric vehicle'. As long as the description is restricted to these fields, the options are inexhaustible. No wonder, then, that much of the social-historical research remains caught up in this domain.[23]

In between the two fields of expectations and of applications exists a cluster of fields that function as a kind of filter, a lens, a restriction of the fantasised possibilities. This cluster consists of sociocultural, technical, political, and economic fields that enable or constrain, help expand or block the field of applications. Although in the contextualist history of automotive technology we intend to develop, all these fields have to be taken into account, for reasons of simplicity we concentrate on the technical field, without, however, excluding from our analysis important parts of the other fields in this cluster. In the technical field the conversion of the fantasised schemes and expectations into a concrete artefact takes place. The size of the technical field also determines the ease with which the conversion of a desired artefact into a realised artefact is possible (feedback also occurs here: fantasies are adapted and, conversely, changing fantasies lead to changes in artefacts).

The size of the technical field is determined by 'technical boundaries' that assume a different character, depending on the 'distortion' by other fields. For example, my research makes it plausible that the lead battery formed the technical boundary of the first-generation electric car. The 'width' of the technical boundaries in this case can be expressed quite accurately in the life span of the battery, which restricted the application of the electric vehicle to certain niches. For the second-generation electric car, however, this technical boundary changed significantly: the life span no longer presented a problem. Instead, the boundary was formed by a problem of materials and maintenance, which made the battery too expensive for private use, at least in Europe.[24]

If the technical field is too small for the application concerned, I call such a field 'closed'. If this is the result of a technical cause, the field is (for the moment and in the location under investigation) 'absolutely closed'. Once opened, the field's boundaries are also subjected to social negotiations: even though an artefact may 'function' in a strict technical sense (that is, realise the technical properties expected from it), it still may end up in a museum as a 'failed innovation'. Society, or part of it, may decide that the price for such functioning is too high, not only in a financial, but also in a sociocultural sense. This recently seemed briefly to be the case with the internal-combustion-engine car in California.[25]

The notion of fields also implies that different types of 'failures' can be at work in the history of technology, which are often not sufficiently distinguished in transport historiography. One could, for instance, want a vehicle speed of 200 km/h in 1895, or a diesel engine in a passenger car around the beginning of the twentieth century. But the 'failure' of such an alternative is different from the failure of the American electric truck after the First World War. In terms of the field notion: in the first case the technical field was absolutely closed, in the second case it was relatively, or conditionally, closed. In the one case we deal with a frustrated illusion, in the other with a realistic alternative. In the latter case even further distinctions are possible. For, already in those days, the desire for an electric city car was more realistic than that for an electric touring car. In terms of the field notion: the technical boundaries were too narrow for the field of application of the touring car, but for the city car they were not. The technical properties of the lead battery and the pneumatic tyre were the cause of this.[26]

Assessing technical wishes and fantasies, and the ensuing attempts at realising them, is not an easy task. Here it occasionally seems necessary to be 'smarter than the contemporary actors'.[27] The task cannot be carried out by social science per se, as out of necessity it has to rely on the (conscious) mental history of such actors. If the sources do not contain any criticism of an alternative, the historical sociologist cannot determine whether the alternative was a realistic one. He must enter the 'black box' all by himself and hope that he will not find it empty.[28] That is also the reason why in the recent technological history of the car, so many 'alternatives' have cropped up, the exact status of which (a fantasy or a realistic alternative) is not clear. Yet this distinction is crucial, because without such a distinction an unfounded 'faith in technology' is strengthened, which is of no avail to anyone, including social scientists.[29]

System and structure

Studying the 'artefactual whole' within the three fields of expectation, technology and application should go beyond the hotchpotch of varieties and possibilities, and beyond the fuzzy image of 'the automobile'. It is therefore worthwhile to systematise 'the artefact' into a hierarchical classification, a taxonomy of the population of concrete artefacts. In the same vein it is worthwhile to systematise the internal structure of the abstract automobile, in order to be able to analyse technological change at a sufficiently deep level. Although sometimes, for a given geographical area and a certain point in time, contemporary handbooks and overviews in the trade press offer such systematisations, it is mostly the task of the historian of technology to construct (at least a part of) them. For instance, the invention of the electric starter motor has often been referred to as the innovation that sounded the death knell of the electric vehicle. But the Model T (which represented nearly half of all cars sold in the USA and Canada in 1914)[30] did not contain such a starter. Besides, the American electric vehicle witnessed a second revival (both as a passenger car and as a truck) just when the Model T started to appear on the market. The hierarchical classification of both external and internal automobile systems can prevent automobile historians from making such mistakes.

If written sources are not available (in the case of the very early electric vehicles, for instance, because the technical field was so variegated that any systematisation seemed futile) such internal classification can also be accomplished by performing a kind of 'automobile archaeology,' analysing preserved artefacts in museums. Not only a technical analysis is possible here (especially when a curator decides to take the artefact apart for the purpose of restoration), but even an analysis of early driving experience, at least as far as ergonomic aspects are concerned. It is, for instance, interesting to learn from a kind of 'test tube' approach (giving information which often can be drawn from the written sources only by a very critical text analysis) that early electric vehicle users had 'gear-shifting' problems comparable to those of their petrol-car-driving colleagues, because early speed choice in urban traffic was realised by constantly shifting between two adjacent controller positions. Such phenomena, which only very rarely reveal themselves in the sources (perhaps because they were experienced by contemporaries as 'natural', 'inevitable' properties of electric vehicles), reduced the user-friendliness of the electric vehicle to a much lower level than one is inclined to think from hindsight, an opinion which probably is based on driver experience in some *modern* electric vehicles with their continuously variable speed change.

A question that has not yet been answered by means of this model is: how then can we investigate the technical field? One should realise that the field of application does not overlap with 'society' or any (automobile) part of it. Neither is the technical field another term for the collection of all cars. The field notion does not coincide with a realistic entity, but it is an aid, an abstraction of a realistic phenomenon, in which a classification has been introduced. Figure 1 gives an example of only one small part of 'the automobile' (the transmission), and can be read as a static overview of most of the alternatives in a certain phase of automotive history.

Figure 1 already implicitly indicates that for a history of technology, in the majority of the cases, it is insufficient to treat the technical artefact as if it is a monolithic entity. Such an artefact, in this case the complex and 'typical' artefact 'automobile', consists of components that have been combined in a meaningful way to perform a technical property (for example, the turning of the wheels) or a user function (driving a car, for instance). Because of the meaningful grouping of the components an artefact can be seen as a system. In this system a

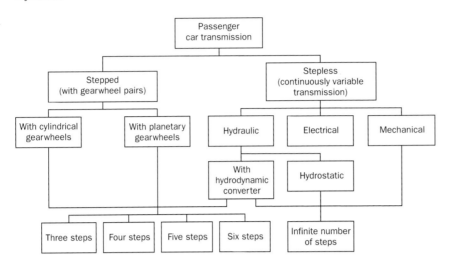

Figure 1 A static overview of the alternative types of transmission in a certain phase of automotive history.

hierarchy of components can be observed, for example, because one component fulfils a general function (such as a gearwheel) and another plays a role, more tailored to the specific function of the artefact (such as a piston of a car engine).[31] Figure 2 gives such a 'structural model' of 'the automobile' for a certain phase of the history of automotive technology, again completed up to the level of the basic components of the transmission only.

Figure 2 A 'structural model' of 'the automobile' for a certain phase of the history of automotive technology.

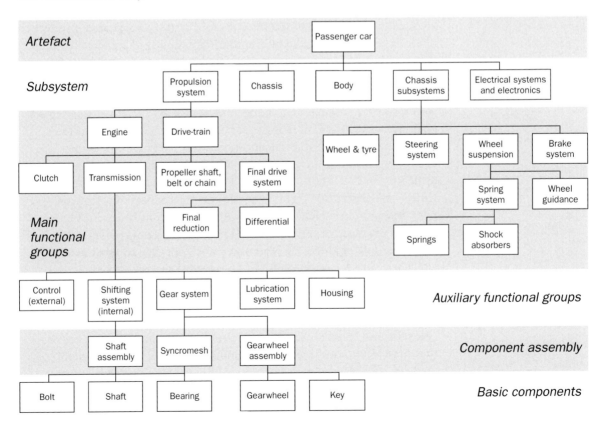

The automobile structure, as depicted in Figure 2, is an abstraction, just as 'the automobile' (and thus 'the electric car') does not exist, except as a form of knowledge.[32] An important part of the confusion about the reasons for the failure of the electric car has originated here. However, such explanations are useless if there is no fundamental distinction between geographical location, historical phase, and especially application or market segment. A different application (at the fire department, the post office or a taxicab company) implies a different function (as fire-extinguishing 'machine', as parcel delivery van or as taxicab). This function is enabled by a different technical property (quick starting, advantageous stop-start behaviour, cleanliness and user-friendliness) integrated in a different vehicle type (as 'special vehicle', as light commercial vehicle or as adapted passenger car). Where one automobile type failed, another was successful. This also implies that the notions of 'success' and 'failure' only make sense if they are differentiated as to application, function, and vehicle type. Moreover, for each of those three phenomena they should be distinguished temporally and geographically. The 'failure of the electric vehicle' in the current discussion often concerns the privately owned passenger car. However, this discussion is far too limited and leads to a serious distortion of the history of electric road-vehicle propulsion. The notion of automobile structure has to enable a technical comparison between these different types of vehicle.

From this it follows that the automobile structure as abstraction is not a timeless notion either. It often varies by geographical region and changes over time. Components are removed, new ones are added, and in general their function is subjected to a process of continuous, incremental change. The 'trick' of the modern history of technology is to relate such processes to social processes of change. An example of such a dynamic structure change in the electric vehicle is the switch from a dual-motor system to a single-motor system. This switch took place very irregularly, differing by vehicle type and by geographical region.

Interactions between alternative technologies

Up to now, hierarchical classification and taxonomy have resulted in two static images of artefactual variety, which one could call the 'structural model of the population' and 'structural model of the artefact' respectively, or, for that matter, 'phenotypical and genotypical hierarchical classifications'.[33] The first of these models or classifications contains (a selection of) the alternatives for a certain period and locale. The question, then, remains, how these alternatives interact. As in economic history and evolutionary theory, in the history of technology different types of interactions between alternative technologies can be distinguished. Maynard Smith distinguishes between three types: competition (where each species has an inhibiting effect on the other), commensalism (where each species has an accelerating effect on the other) and predation (where the 'predator' inhibits the 'prey' from developing, whereas the 'prey' has an accelerating effect on its 'predator'). In the course of time several other interaction modes have been added to this set, resulting quite recently in a 3 x 3 matrix of nine possible modes.[34]

The essence of evolutionary development of technology suggests that no alternative is exactly equal to other alternatives. In reality, these (often tiny) differences are a reflection of a different use (or of a fantasised, intended use) and as such are a representation of different needs and desires. The idea of a 'trajectory' or a 'paradigm' thus tends to lay too much emphasis on the meso- and macro-level, whereas a more thorough investigation into artefactual variety would suggest that internal characteristics at the local and the micro-level prefigure events at higher levels: no 'closure' without an equivalent change at the level of the artefact and at the level of the individual user and producer. This seems to me the real challenge of a history of technology: to find these small interartefactual varieties and to explain them in their context, i.e. their different fields of application. In order to do so, all possible and actual alternatives have to be included in the 'artefactual whole', which should be analysed as such.

Variety plays a role at two levels of an artefact: its technical characteristics (properties) and its performance characteristics (functions), the first being directly influenced by engineers, the second only indirectly. It is here that the users come into play: they generally do not influence the inner structure of an artefact directly, but they *can* have a direct impact on the artefact's functions, by applying it in a different way, not foreseen by the producer or the designer.[35] As it follows from our evolutionary approach that the original set of technical properties enable this new function in only a restricted way, it is to be expected that, consequently, the newly realised function entails changes at the level of the technical properties.

When taking a closer look at the substitution process at the micro-level, in many cases one alternative appears to have more chances of success in one field of application, whereas the other alternative has more chances in another application field. As has been said above, this makes the general idea of technological 'failure' highly questionable. When alternative technologies compete for dominance, this creates a feedback mechanism, a kind of interartefactual transfer of technology and knowledge.

Mostly, if at all, this process has been described as a flow from 'new' to 'old' technologies, the most famous example being the interaction between sailing ships and steam ships, between wooden ships and ships with an iron hull. In a tiny, hardly noticed contribution to a magazine on physics, W H Ward coined the phrase 'sailing-ship effect' to describe the phenomenon 'that the sailing ship developed fastest while it was being supplanted'. Parts of this development were direct borrowings from the steamship, but there were also intrinsic improvements of sailing ship technology per se, resulting in improvements in sailing qualities and, hence, enabling the sailing ship to compete in one of the crucial areas (transport speed). This made the choice in favour of the 'new' technology less straightforward than it seems from hindsight, or, for that matter, from a birds-eye view generated by an S curve.[36]

In an effort to integrate this phenomenon into his evolutionary theory of technological development, Hans-Dieter Hellige proposed the term 'mimicry', which describes the effect of less-successful species trying to imitate some properties of the more-successful ones in order to survive the evolutionary struggle for dominance. All these, and similar, approaches seem to start with the implicit assumption of an uphill (and desperate) battle for the 'old' technology. The 'inevitability' of the negative outcome for the 'old' technology is remarkable, as full substitution seems to be an exception rather than the rule.[37] In the case of Ward's sailing-ship effect this is all the more remarkable, because at least until the mid-nineteenth century (and in some applications until the end of the century) the sailing technology was the dominant one. In particular, the mimicry metaphor suggests that for the 'inferior' technology to stay alive it is necessary to deceive the selecting agents, so that they *perceive* this technology as being a 'winner'. Instead, it seems more appropriate to take a different starting point and analyse competing technologies as a part of the abstract, artefactual 'whole' as explained above.[38]

A multitude of cases, in economic history as well as management and organisation studies, has been unearthed in which interartefactual transfer phenomena took place (see Table 1).[39] However, many of these studies have been undertaken with the hindsight knowledge of the eventual 'winner' in mind, thus 'black-boxing' a lot of the processes which took place among alternative technologies. It is especially difficult, if not impossible, to draw from these cases details about the exact nature and direction of interartefactual transfer. Moreover, if these studies contain any indication of *functional* transfer (as opposed to transfer of component or general technological knowledge), the multidimensional interaction between the alternatives is mostly reduced to one or two performance characteristics (such as speed for land vehicles or production numbers for processes).[40] Therefore, the following section presents three detailed examples from automotive technology history, explicitly studied to enable an analysis of these microprocesses. These examples are: the electrochemical battery as an energy source for early electric vehicle propulsion, the role of the electric vehicle in the introduction of pneumatic-cord tyres, and the postwar competition between different transmission configurations for automotive purposes.

Table 1 Examples of functional transfer between interacting artefacts and processes

Mainstream	Alternative	Functional transfer	Properties to enable this transfer	Did mainstream disappear?
Icebox	Electric refrigerator	Long-duration cooling	Better insulation	No (camping ice boxes)
Plate camera	Celluloid roll-film	Amateur use	Ligthweight plate camera, developing and printing outfit for amateurs	Yes
Steam locomotive (USA)	Diesel–electric locomotive	Lower fuel consumption	Steam-turbine/mechanical and electric hybrids	Yes
Natural fibres	Synthetic fibres	Ease in manufacturing	Grading wood and cotton filters to uniform fibre length; fibre coating	No
Cast-iron engine blocks	Aluminium engine blocks	Fuel economy	Thin-wall cast-iron blocks	No
Gas illumination	Electric incandescent lamp	More and more pleasant light, energy consumption	Gas mantle	Yes
Mechanical watch	Electronic watch	Purchase price, ease of handling	Fine-mechanical precision techniques	No (expensive niche)
Vacuum tube	Solid-state semiconductor	Less bulky, less heat build-up, lower costs	More complicated design to allow for more applications	No (specialised niche)
Sailing ship	Steam ship	Higher speed, smaller crews	More sails by smaller crews, faster hull	No (pleasure boating)
Piston-engine aircraft	Jet-engine aircraft	Higher speed, greater cruising altitude		No (business and pleasure niche)
Cardboard packaging	All-plastic bottle	Ease of handling, production costs	Wax coating replaced by plastic coating, fold-away spout replaced by screw-in plastic cap	No
Magnetic disc	Optical disc	More storage capacity	Enhanced storage capacity of magnetic disc	No
Netscape web browser	Microsoft PC operating system	More user functions	More user functions	No
Refined gasoline	Gasoline with tetraethyl lead (TEL) dope	Possibility of developing high-performance engines	More aromatic compounds to enhance knock resistance, other dopes like ethanol and tertiary butyl alcohol (TBA)	No

(Sources: see note 39)

Interaction among alternatives: batteries

The first example is the energy source of early electric vehicles: the electrochemical battery. During the first half of the nineteenth century, the lead–acid cell (consisting of a sulphuric acid electrolyte and a lead/lead oxide electrode pair) had been developed as a laboratory device. In 1859, the Frenchman Gustave Planté developed the lead cell into a sturdy device for stationary applications. The Planté battery was heavy, because the electrodes were 'formed' out of solid lead, a process in which a chemical conversion occurs on the lead surface by repeatedly charging and discharging it. The process is reversible, so that electrical energy can be derived from it by connecting a 'load' (a lamp, an electric motor). In 1880 another Frenchman, Camille Faure, developed the predecessor of the grid-plate battery, which could accommodate a prepared lead paste. This led to a growing interest in battery traction, because the same amount of energy could now be obtained from a much lighter battery. The first mobile tests took place on the basis of the Faure concept, for example in Paris. There, Nicolas-Jules Raffard started a series of experiments in 1881 on a converted horse streetcar, accompanied by a lot of publicity.[41]

In Germany, the Kölner Akkumulatoren-Werke (KAW) was the company that, together with Accumulatorenfabrik AG (AFA), initiated an 'anti-Faure reaction', a response to the problems with bonding of the active mass in the lead grids. After the Faure patents expired in 1896, however, KAW grew to become the most important German producer of the grid-plate battery, owing to its involvement in the first electric-car experiments. Meanwhile, AFA developed its own version of the Planté concept: the large surface plate. This plate combined the advantages of the Planté and Faure concepts by consciously sacrificing the active mass during the first discharges. But this did not happen until the thick, grooved positive plate had continued formation by means of this mass. Heavy, but durable: that became the product philosophy of AFA, the main competitor of KAW. In the early 1890s the former company grew into the major battery producer when it started a strategic cooperation with Siemens and AEG.[42]

Moreover, because of its monopolistic position in the stationary-battery market, AFA, for the first time in history, could put the problematic life span of the lead battery on the agenda. Inspired by an initiative of the British Electrical Power Storage Company (EPS), it initiated a 'revisions organisation'. For an annual subscription of 5 to 10 per cent of the purchase price, trained engineers periodically monitored and overhauled the battery installation, exchanging defective plates with fresh ones. This passed an important part of the trials (and the costs) of new designs on to customers, but also offered them the opportunity to calculate depreciation and maintenance accurately and in advance. So, this fundamental predictability of battery life was not brought about using intrinsically perfect construction, but using monitoring by specialists. This principle was later adopted in electric vehicle fleets and even functioned as a model for the car system in general by delegating maintenance to a specialised garage infrastructure. In the terms of the field notion: because the technical field was conditionally closed for this application, AFA decided to expand the field of expectations by taking maintenance into its own, specialised hands. This is a clear example of how a technical constraint can be bypassed by remedial action in the field of application. Although a *perpetuum mobile* cannot be made to work by changing the application field, an unacceptably short battery life span apparently can. At any rate it made the battery a reliable source of energy for stationary purposes (especially in power stations). Thus, the life span of the batteries was extended by continuous renewal of faulty plates, which themselves had a short life. It was a new idea in the machine-building industry, as well as in the electrotechnical industry, where responsibility for the product ended after its sale.[43]

The British EPS company was the first battery producer to successfully exploit the Faure patent. The active mass was placed in holes in the lead grid. Between 1888 and 1901 the energy density of EPS's grid-plate batteries increased from 7.6 to 25 Wh/kg (Faure's battery had a density of 7 Wh/kg). Whereas in the earliest experiments the batteries accounted for half of the vehicle mass, for the second generation this was around 25 per cent, and sometimes even less.[44]

So, it was by no means a coincidence that the second German battery-tram boom started in Hagen, Westphalia, where AFA was located after 1887. The boom also reached Bremerhaven, Charlottenburg near Berlin, Hanover, Dresden, Ludwigshafen, and Karlsruhe. Berlin had by far the largest battery-tram fleet, with 335 cars in 1901.[45] AFA's main competitor was the KAW, which supplied its light grid-plate battery to Bremerhaven. After the Faure patents expired in 1896, the KAW was to grow into the most important German supplier of the grid-plate battery, owing to its involvement in the first electric-car experiments.

After trams powered by overhead wire won the battle for dominance in the urban transport application field, battery producers began to look for alternative uses for their product, especially in the United States, where the Electric Storage Battery Company (ESB) became the major battery producer. Founded in 1888, this company had monopolised the American battery market by buying many hundreds of patents, including those on the grid-plate principle.[46]

When, from about the mid-1890s, development of the 'horseless carriage' started to gain momentum, the struggle between the three propulsion alternatives (steam, petrol and electricity) was fought first and foremost within the application field of the taxicab. An American electrotechnical trade journal wrote in an editorial at the end of 1901: 'The development of the electric automobile has proceeded to that point where it is safe to say that the machine is practically perfect, if – and the if is a large one – the proper accumulator can be discovered.' For all involved, it was clear that such a battery could only be realised by a different combination of electrodes instead of the lead/lead oxide couple, and it seemed that Thomas Edison was going to provide it. In 1901 Edison announced in a press campaign that he was about to put a battery on the market with an energy density that was twice as high as had been achieved before. A similar initiative to perform a miracle took place in France, where in 1903 Jeantaud proposed a lead battery based on a highly controversial new material which he called 'allotropic lead', of which the name *le Messie* (the Messiah) spoke for itself. During the following two years Jeantaud further developed his battery into a prototype, for which he claimed an energy density of no less than 41.2 Wh/kg and which he dubbed '*E I t*', the electrotechnical product of voltage, current and time that together deliver 'energy'.[47]

Whereas Jeantaud's hopes did not materialise, in 1904 Edison put his alkaline battery (the so-called Type E) on the market, the result of three years of very thorough developmental work, preceded by an extensive study of patent literature. The idea behind this battery type was not new: the French electric vehicle builder Louis Kriéger, for instance, had taken out a patent on a similar concept in 1901. This type of battery was based on the insolubility of the electrodes in an alkaline electrolyte and the fact that this electrolyte did not participate in the electrochemical reaction between the electrodes. In principle this required a much smaller amount of electrolyte than for the lead battery, of which the electrolyte accounted for a quarter of the total battery mass. In combination with the application of electrode materials with a lower density, the hope for a much higher energy density for the battery seemed justified indeed.[48]

The Swedish inventor Waldemar Jungner, who developed a comparable concept, founded the Jungner Accumulator Company in the spring of 1900. When Jungner made a deal with AFA shortly after, Edison began to feel threatened. Moreover, in the meantime a world cartel in the field of the lead battery had been formed, led by AFA and ESB. Edison, whose most important patent dated from 6 February 1901, established the Edison Storage Battery Company in May of that year. In the following decade Edison's publicity campaign swept through the electrotechnical and automobile trade press of the Western world with great intensity, and even generated newspaper articles.[49]

It is not surprising that the lead-battery manufacturers looked upon these developments with anxiety. ESB, for example, released the Exide battery in 1900, with wooden separators between the lead plates. This allowed the plates to be densely packed without risking a short circuit, so that a higher energy density was possible – just as in the Edison alternative, but realised using different technical means. It is likely that this important development of the lead battery was prompted by Edison's simultaneous attempts to achieve a higher energy density using the same idea of a smaller distance between the plates in his alkaline battery.[50]

At the 1905 Berlin automobile exhibition, ESB's German cartel partner AFA saw that there was a new wave of interest in electric cars and that KAW was surfing along on this wave with its lighter grid-plate batteries. AFA therefore sought advice from its American counterpart. In the meantime ESB had managed to improve its design, so that the short-circuit problem (in the old lead battery caused by the active mass falling from the plates) had largely been solved. By 1904 virtually all American battery manufacturers had adopted wooden separators. Alarmed by the German competition and encouraged by the establishment of large taxicab companies in Berlin, AFA then developed a relatively light battery (the Ky type) in little over two-and-a-half years. The company had taken great care that the lead plates were not so thin that the life span would be too much affected.[51]

The field of expectations regarding the further expansion of the electric vehicle's range received another boost when Edison, after he had taken his Type E alkaline battery off the market because of technical problems, launched a new alkaline type (Type A) in the winter of 1908/09. Based on Edison's patent of 1905, the 'Improved Edison' was now equipped with a robust positive tubular plate. With an energy density of about 28 Wh/kg, the life span was several times that of the lead battery. The Edison battery formed a serious threat to the (lead) battery monopoly of ESB. In response, ESB developed a version with thinner plates (the 'Hycap', launched in 1910) with an energy density of 18.5 Wh/kg (increasing to 24 Wh/kg while in operation). Finally, a 'Thin-Exide' was put on the market with an energy density of between 20 and 26.5 Wh/kg. This type was probably launched as a reaction to the 'Philadelphia thin-plate battery', produced by one of the few remaining competitors, the Philadelphia Storage Battery Company. It offered 40 per cent more range compared with the conventional grid-plate battery. This was the result of the application of an oversize lead plate with a fine grid structure, the 'diamond grid'. The shorter life span of the thin plates (expressed in the number of charging/discharging cycles) was compensated by the high energy density. On balance, this turned out to be more maintenance-friendly, because each cycle enabled a longer range. Apparently, the quality of grid technology had meanwhile improved so much that a mutual comparison based on maintenance costs made sense. Thus, a newly defined technical field had emerged in comparison with the situation of a decade ago, when, during the famous lead-battery contest in Paris in 1899, the life span of the thin-grid plates appeared to be an insurmountable barrier.[52]

So fierce was the competition between Edison and ESB in the electric-truck battery market that both companies employed spies in each other's factories. In the end ESB opted for the tubular-plate technique too. After all, this technology had proved to be one of the better concepts at the Paris lead-battery contest. ESB subsequently obtained the rights to the Phénix battery with tubular-plate technology, in 1906. With engineer Edward W Smith in charge and in cooperation with the American Hard Rubber Company, the extrusion technique (as applied by this company) for the production of fountain pens was adapted to manufacture of lead batteries. The hard rubber tubes placed around the lead pins of the positive plate had to prevent the loss of active mass. At one stroke, the life span of the positive plate no longer was the determining factor of the life span of the lead battery. ESB even had to make a slightly thicker version of the negative plate, so that the life span of this plate would become equal to that of the positive plate.[53] The result was the Ironclad battery.

The rivalry between ESB and the Edison Storage Battery Company was particularly important, because a choice in favour of the alkaline type – owing to its different voltage and different charging characteristic – made application of the lead–sulphuric-acid type impossible, unless one opted for two different charging units. Whereas the lead battery remained dominant in the passenger car, in 1913 a third of all electric trucks were provided with an Edison battery. The General Motors Truck Company, for example, charged 30 to 40 per cent more for an electric truck with an Edison battery than for a truck with a lead battery. The price difference became smaller as the truck became heavier, providing a further incentive for the use of the Edison battery in heavy trucks.[54]

When we try to summarise the main developments in the 'artefactual whole' of electrochemical battery technology in the application field of the automobile during its first two decades, it is clear that the competition between the alternatives was focused on a limited set of user functions. Apart from a customer wish for a more sturdy battery with enough longevity to guarantee a profitable taxicab business, there was a general tendency towards development of a relatively light battery. The technical property to be developed to enable this reduced weight was smaller plate distance, a property which, compared to the lead–acid battery, was an 'intrinsic' characteristic of the Edison battery because of its lesser need for liquid electrolyte. ESB (and AFA) countered this threat in two ways: first by inserting wooden plates between the lead plates, and then by simply copying the tubular-plate concept from its competitor, thus combining smaller plate distance with greater robustness. So, for the same user function, different properties were implemented. In the end, the competitive advantage of the Edison battery was decreased to such a degree that the lead battery was not dethroned from its dominant market position, although the Edison alternative was to stay on the battery scene as a successful device for certain specialised application fields. Figure 3 schematises this development.

Interaction among alternatives: tyres

The second example concerns the development of the pneumatic automobile tyre. While proponents of electric propulsion boasted of its greater reliability, mainly because of the development of a sturdy and reliable battery, the petrol car seemed to escape all engineering rationality by embedding itself in a male 'sports' culture of technical challenge and adventure. As analysed elsewhere, the petrol car thrived as an 'adventure machine', not only in time and space (as a fast car

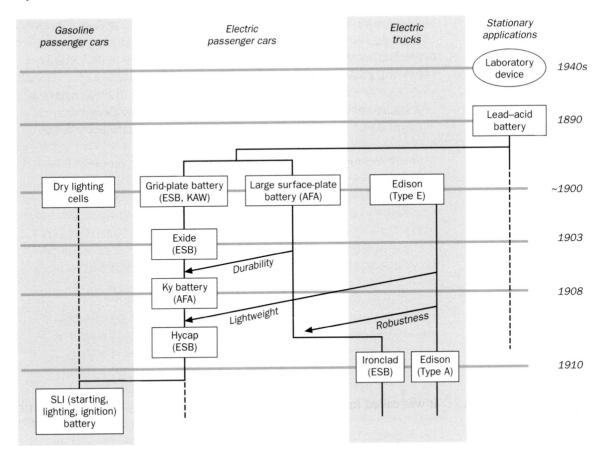

Figure 3 A scheme for the 'artefactual whole' of electrochemical battery technology in early automobiles and trucks.

that enabled one to drive wherever one wanted), but also in a technical sense.[55] Frequent but easily detectable defects were as much a part of this male subculture (because they offered a technical challenge) as racing and touring. But in the midst of the race to dominance of the petrol car as an 'adventure machine,' mainstream car culture seemed to hit boundaries that threatened to jeopardise its further expansion. This became quite clear during the 'crisis of 1907', which represented a whole lot more than just an economical disturbance of a growth phenomenon. This crisis can be typified as a catalyst of the developments that would lead to a radical change in the technical, the applicational, as well as the expectational fields of the automobile. As a consequence, the crisis would have an important impact upon the interaction between the electric and the petrol car.

A part of this crisis was the speed crisis, very concretely expressed in a technical crisis of the pneumatic tyre. As the utilitarian aspect of the automobile gradually became more important, the social function of its technical unreliability changed, and thus the way in which automobile users perceived the nuisance of tyre trouble. The reason for this change in the field of expectation was the expansion of the original very 'well-to-do' user group towards a group of entrepreneurs and professionals such as physicians, military officers and lawyers, who increasingly sought to deploy the automobile both for pleasure and for utilitarian purposes such as visits to patients, driving to work or delivering goods. In this expanded field of application, the tyre, as well as being a large expense item, now also became a source of irritation that questioned the usefulness of 'the automobile' for daily business. Thus, the technical field of the petrol car threatened to become too narrow for the changing, new field of application.

What exactly was the weak spot of the pneumatic tyre that had made the tyre problem expand into a full-blown crisis? The crucial problem was the translation of bicycle-tyre technology into that of the automobile. Here, not only did the higher axle load and the higher speed play a role, but in particular so did the greater lateral load on the tyre, at the spot where the tyre bead grips the rim edge. The first pneumatic tyres were made of natural rubber, enriched with zinc-oxide powder and at first strengthened by linen, but soon – under the influence of American tyre manufacturers – by 'Sea Island' cotton. Such tyres were so soft that they ripped open very easily, but this also made them easy to remove from the rim for repair. In 1904 the removable tyre, the so-called 'clincher tyre', was part of the standard equipment of the American automobile.[56]

The crossed textile fabric for strengthening the tyre (the 'canvas' as it was called in Britain) had an unfortunate property. As the pneumatic tyre repeatedly flattened (when in contact with the road surface) and recovered its original form, a 'scissor-like action' developed between the cotton threads that led to the heating of the rubber and so to a much greater chance of damage occurring. This effect became a problem when the structure – borrowed from the bicycle tyre – had to carry a much greater mass. According to Michelin the wear and tear of the pneumatic tyre increased with the third power of the axle load.[57]

For the lighter petrol car a return to the hollow solid-rubber tyre seemed possible in this period. For these cars the switch was not so radical, because the pressure of the pneumatic tyres of the first automobiles was at least twice as high as it is nowadays, in order to limit distortion on the road surface. So, the tyre crisis mainly affected the heavier petrol cars that cruised the country roads at high speed. This may well have been an extra incentive for petrol-car manufacturers to focus on producing city cars. The tyre crisis, which was as much of a cultural as of a technical nature, started in France as a result of a fatal car accident involving the Marquis d'Audiffret-Pasquier in the summer of 1904. It instigated an overwhelming number of letters to the editors of the leading car magazines complaining about the 'killer tyres'. The examples of near-fatal tyre blowouts filled the pages of the automobile magazines for weeks on end. At that time Michelin started to increase its publicity activities by writing weekly columns for these magazines.[58]

Between 1906 and 1909 at least 140 proposals were published for replacing the 'Achilles heel of the automobile' (as a German magazine called the pneumatic tyre) with a mechanical suspension system, either in the hub, or as replacement for the spokes or the tyre around the wheel rim. In automotive historiography, especially its nostalgic variety, such 'elastic wheels' are often set aside as curiosities. But from the relief expressed in the rubber-trade journals after the apparent failure of such innovations, it can be deduced that the tyre industry really felt threatened by what was essentially a technical crisis. At the beginning of this crisis 'De Cadignan's elastic wheel' – one of the best-known innovations of this period – was introduced, equipped with coiled springs instead of spokes. A rubber-trade journal suggested that this design should worry the pneumatic-tyre industry: 'We have here a serious competitor for the pneumatic tyre and our manufacturers had better not neglect this.' It is noticeable that such proposals were made in relation to those for the installation of shock absorbers: for the first time wheel suspension was approached as a system. Here, the compromise between comfort and safety required complex solutions like spring–absorber combinations. The shock absorbers stayed, but the elastic wheel did not. Apart from the fact that it broke down easily, it had a major disadvantage that the pneumatic tyre did not have: small, high-frequency vibrations in the elastic wheels provided an upward acceleration of the compartment where the driver was sitting. The pneumatic tyre, on the other hand, 'absorbs the obstacle', as a relieved rubber-trade journal formulated it, referring to the well-known Michelin slogan that had been known for several years by then. For heavy trucks with a speed lower than 30 km/h elastic wheels may have been useful, but for the passenger car they were not.[59]

And so, convergence of the technical fields of the petrol and electric passenger car took place, as illustrated dramatically by the development of tyre technology. The manufacturers, who were afraid to offer a pneumatic tyre for electric cars, put solid rubber tyres on the market made with special resilient rubber compounds. Such expensive 'cushion tyres', made of very pure Pará rubber, often had a special shape, so that their geometry also supported the elasticity of the tyre: a deep incision was made in the middle of the tyre that ran along its entire circumference. The tyre walls were also given incisions. In this way, the tyres could be compressed more deeply than a tyre with the same rubber mass but a circular cross-section. However, the cushion tyre had two major disadvantages. First, it was not as resilient as the pneumatic tyre. Second, it reacted more slowly to tiny bumps in the road, so that at high speeds the wheel experienced an upward acceleration. So, as the speed of the electric car increased, it could not cope without the pneumatic tyre either, just as its heavy petrol rival could not.[60]

As the cotton carcass of the tyre could only be woven in a cylindrical shape, the fabric folded around the rim when it was being mounted on it. This caused an irregular tensile stress in the carcass and thus an irregular resilience. Moreover, the pneumatic tyres for petrol cars, with their sturdy walls and thick tread, caused far too much wastage of energy for them to be applied to the electric car. Therefore, special thin-walled pneumatic tyres were developed with a coarse-meshed carcass fabric and a thin tread. These, however, were very sensitive to a tyre pressure that was either too high or too low, and thus impinged on the barrier of a maintenance-friendly car culture, especially in the United States. The special tyres for the electric passenger car suffered from the scissor-like effect of the crossing cotton threads, causing rapid heat build-up. Thus, high resilience and high durability came into conflict, so that regular maintenance became a crucial factor here, just as for the lead battery. Such tyres were not very strong, but they were very expensive, because 'absolutely the best cotton' and the purest natural rubber had to be used.[61] In other words: the technical field seemed to be absolutely closed for the application of sturdy and not-too-expensive pneumatics on both the electric and the petrol alternatives. But in this case there was a way out of the dilemma, and the role of the electric vehicle appeared to be crucial.

The solution consisted of a typical crossover phenomenon: the conflict between resilience and durability had been solved for the bicycle by the application of the so-called cord tyre. In the cord tyre's construction, two layers of rubberised parallel cords were placed across each other. The textile threads were not crossed, but rolled into a cord and vulcanised in the rubber side by side, at a non-perpendicular angle with the rim edge. This was done after each layer of cords had been separately rubberised first in order to further lower the frictional heat build-up. London Palmer Tyre Ltd produced the best-known cord tyre. John Fullerton Palmer patented it in America in the fall of 1892 and six months later in Britain. This type became the standard in bicycle-tyre technology.[62]

The electric car served as a guinea pig in the translation of this technology into automotive technology. Goodyear wrote in a retrospective account: 'The early *cord tires* were used only on electric vehicles, where the demand was for a tyre of extreme resiliency so as to get the maximum mileage per battery charge. Many designs were tried and discarded, but always Goodyear had a *cord tire* of some design to offer the electric vehicle owner. It took years to attain the desired combination of resiliency and long tire life, but always *cord fabric* was the carcass material used in the experiments.' [italics in original][63]

Almost all large tyre manufacturers tried to put such tyres on the market, but usually without enduring success. Petrol cars were not equipped with them, even though they increased vehicle speed and improved ride quality, as the early applications in racing proved. 'But these tires will puncture more easily, are more difficult to repair, and in the end will not give as low a tire mileage cost as the gasoline type of tire,' said P W Lichfield, operations manager of the Goodyear Tire and Rubber Company in Akron, Ohio. Lichfield explained the situation very clearly: the normal, state-of-the-art petrol car tyre was designed for low mileage costs, but because of the narrow energetic margins for 'long-distance electric tyres', the petrol car tyre could not be applied to electric cars. The price the electric-car owner had to pay for it was high. The petrol car had so much reserve energy, that extra energy loss from using the conventional fabric tyre did not present a problem, especially in the United States, with its low fuel prices. The petrol-car driver could use an electric tyre if he wished, but the electric-car owner did not have a choice.[64]

The rolling resistance of the cord tyre was only three-quarters of that of the tyre with a cotton carcass. So, it will come as no surprise to learn that early in 1915 a cord tyre was launched that was also suitable for petrol cars: Goodrich's Silvertown cord tyre. All the racing cars that reached the finish in Indianapolis that year were equipped with these, based on the Palmer patents. By the end of 1915 the first cord tyres appeared on the expensive petrol passenger cars, which marked the beginning of the large-scale commercialisation of what in later automotive technology would be called the bias-ply tyre. The Silvertown was the first sturdy tyre, in which resilience was not sacrificed to increase tyre life. The introduction of the cord tyre during the First World War – and its general application from the beginning of the 1920s – solved the problem of internal overheating. Its increased sturdiness also enabled a considerably lower tyre pressure, which improved comfort, especially as it absorbed small bumps in an otherwise smoothly asphalted road surface.[65]

Like the development of the battery, this development can be schematised into a sort of 'pneumatic tyre lineage' (Figure 4). Here again it is clear that the technical alternatives were competing on user functions, such as tyre costs, comfort and user-friendliness. These functions were enabled by technical properties, such as longevity, resilience and sturdiness. The combination of these functions was only possible with a cord-tyre concept, which was developed for electric vehicle use, through petrol-car racing, from mainstream bicycle-tyre technology. Only a decade later the petrol passenger car took over this technology from the electric alternative.

Interaction among alternatives: transmissions
A third case of this interartefactual functional transfer is not taken from the struggle between electric and petrol automobiles during the early phase, but from postwar developments in transmission, during a period when petrol propulsion had long been the dominant propulsion technology. Here, the mainstream consists of the gearbox

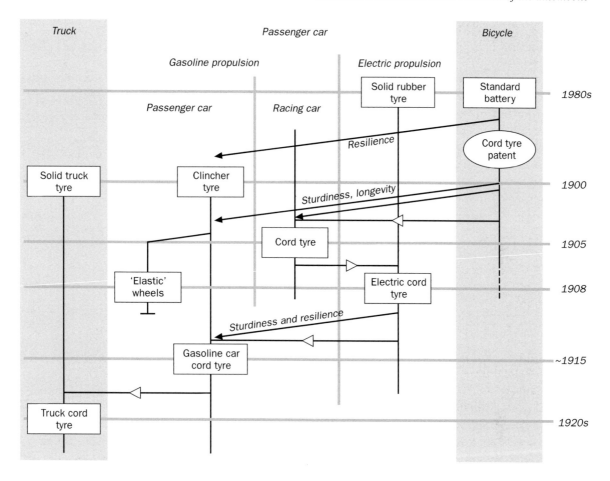

| Truck | Passenger car | | | | Bicycle | |

Figure 4 A scheme for the 'artefactual whole' of tyre technology in early automobiles and trucks.

with manual gear shifting (in Europe) and the automatic transmission (in the United States and Japan), which was developed shortly before the Second World War. However, a third alternative had been lingering on since the early days of automotive history: continuously variable transmission (CVT), characterised by a stepless gear-change function. This function has always been the ideal transmission for many automotive engineers, who have designed numerous technical solutions, such as friction-wheel transmissions, variable-pulley transmissions and even highly complicated systems with levers and beams. Some of these appeared in production cars, but they never made it to appreciable series production until the Dutch firm Van Doorne's Transmissie sold a system on the basis of a metal 'push belt' to some Japanese and US car companies.

After the 'push-belt CVT' and a German competitor based on a metal chain were developed, an interesting process of functional transfer between the three alternative systems occurred. First, both automatic transmission and CVT pushed manual transmission towards having more steps and automatic gear shifting. Then, especially in Europe, manual transmission inspired both the alternatives to integrate

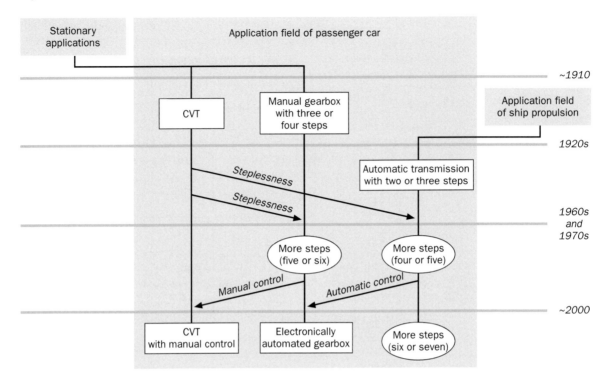

Figure 5 The changing use of transmission technologies in postwar passenger cars.

a manual gear-shifting function into their designs. It is remarkable that this transfer was purely on a functional basis, because the technical properties to enable these functions where quite distinct for all three alternatives. Simulation of the stepless function (intrinsic in the CVT) in the automatic and the manual transmission was achieved by adding more gearwheel pairs, while the manual shifting function (intrinsic in the manual gearbox) was provided in automatic and CVT transmission by electronic simulation. Thus, no 'technology' in the strict sense was transferred here, only user functions, realised by totally different technologies (Figure 5).

The Pluto effect

In all three examples analysed here, a transfer mechanism between interacting alternative technologies plays a role which does not involve a transfer of technology per se. This mechanism seems to be more general than the sailing-ship effect, because it involves many more phenomena and directions of exchange, and not just an uphill battle of an 'old' technology which is bound to die out in the long run. Therefore I have given this mechanism a new name: the 'Pluto effect'. This description enables better analysis of the phenomenon that technologies in interaction tend to 'steal' each other's properties and functions in order to make it less desirable for designers, manufacturers or users to choose a new technology. In doing so, however, they strengthen the case of the dominant technology,

especially if this technology tends to have a 'built-in' capacity of quasi-
universal adaptation. It is important to stress here that the Pluto effect
covers a transfer of (technical) *properties* and (applicational) *functions*,
and not necessarily, or primarily, a transfer of artefact parts.

The name Pluto refers to the dog in the Walt Disney cartoon.
The dog, harnessed to a cart, runs after a sausage held in front of his
nose, but never reaches his target. In this metaphor the coachman
represents the prevailing technology or its actor(s) and poor Pluto the
alternative technology or its actor(s), the sausage functioning as 'the
lure of the (Schumpeterian) innovative laurels'.[66] Pluto literally runs
after a 'flying target'. One often tends to forget, however, that it is
Pluto who enables the movement of this seemingly constantly receding
target. Only by means of Pluto will the 'coachman', handling the stick
with the sausage, reach his goal. On the other hand, if the coachman
does not manage to present to Pluto a target worthy of pursuit, the
mechanism comes to a halt. A sausage which is held too far in front of
Pluto, or which does not look appetising, discourages him in his
efforts. If the sausage is too close he will swallow it and will choose his
own route; then, Pluto will become the dominant 'prime mover'. The
introduction of the Pluto effect in the analysis of technical change has
to counterbalance the 'closure' principle in the social science
approaches, which puts too much emphasis on spectacular changes
that are easy to trace. It reappraises the equally important incremental
changes that also continue *after* closure.[67]

The Pluto effect fits into the field concept in that it bridges the gap
between the genotypical and the phenotypical parts of both the
technical and the application field, as well as bridging the gap between
both fields themselves. It also suggests a possible connection between
the ontogenetic (development of the artefact) and phylogenetic
(development of the population) aspects of technical change. As such,
it differs in several respects from the research tradition of artefact
interaction.

First, the Pluto metaphor does not approach this competition as
an uphill battle by the alternative technology against the dominating,
mainstream technology, as the desperate swan song of a vanishing
technology. Indeed, in automotive history this interpretation is also
possible. Note, for instance, the emergence of the hood in electric-
vehicle technology around 1910, when its manufacturers tried to
mimic the hood of the petrol car, which hid the combustion engine
and which represented the very essence of what the petrol car was all
about. Note also the introduction of electric racing cars as early as
1898/99 and the marketing of slender electric touring cars during the
First World War in the United States that were no longer recognisable
as electric – a nice example of 'mimicry'.

But the Pluto effect appreciates the flow of properties in just
the opposite direction. It describes the 'stealing', if you like, by the

dominant technology of certain properties and functions, proposed by the alternative technology, which form a constant threat to the dominance of the mainstream technology. A good example outside the realm of electric-vehicle technology is the introduction of the gas-turbine car by the British company Rover after the Second World War. Although, like the electric vehicle, this alternative can also be analysed as a 'failure' (because it did not become the universal vehicle type), the Pluto effect resulted in the addition of the turbo generator to modern combustion-engine technology. This gave, exactly as was the intention of the gas-turbine proponents, a decisive boost to the performance of petrol and diesel cars. Thus, a boost *function* and a rotating-pump *property*, and not a component, moved across at the level of the abstract artefact.[68]

In other words: making use of the Pluto effect seems to be necessary for the dominant technology to remain dominant, and, as such, it is comparable to the concept of 'repressive tolerance' in the social sciences (Marcuse's 'incapsulation' of protest movements by the system).[69] In fact, Nathan Rosenberg, in his analysis of technical diffusion, has already drawn our attention to this question, although he narrowed his answer down to the economic consequences of a higher efficiency which would result from this process. 'The imminent threat to a firm's profit margins which are presented by the rise of a new competing technology seems often in history to have served as a more effective agent in generating improvements in efficiency than the more diffuse pressures of intra-industry competition. Indeed, such asymmetries may be an important key to a better understanding of the workings of the competitive process, even though they find no place in formal economic theory.'[70]

Second, because it favours continuity over discontinuity, the Pluto effect directs our attention to incremental instead of paradigmatic changes and, as such, necessitates a thorough knowledge of the technology under investigation. However, although the analogy with evolutionary theory would suggest that interacting technologies would behave like plants and animals (or better, their selfish genes), in their long-term struggle for survival, it must obviously be remembered that artefacts do not produce their own offspring. Therefore, changes in them do not necessarily need to be incremental in character and, thus, do not seem to be always the result of a random process of infinitesimal mutations. For instance, although biological evolutionary theory denies the possibility of inter-species breeding, 'crossover' phenomena are not uncommon in the history of technology. A porcupine does not develop a long neck because it sees a giraffe eat leaves from a tree, whereas an engineer can take over whole concepts from a threatening, alternative technology.[71] Nor does the Pluto effect necessarily describe conscious processes of imitation, as the 'mimicry' metaphor would suggest. Most changes described by the Pluto effect cannot be explained by direct copying, but rather by a general attitude of engineers to keep constantly in touch with the 'state of the art', which functions as a basis of inspiration for similar solutions.

Third, the Pluto effect seems to favour technologies with a built-in potential for 'universality' or, more accurately perhaps, 'multifunctionalism'. How exactly this works has yet to be established, but it seems that the broader the field of application (and, as a result of this, the lower the production costs because of economies of scale), the greater the chances of one of the alternatives becoming dominant. The same conclusion was drawn by Devendra Sahal in his study of the diffusion of the agricultural tractor: 'It seems that the greater variety of tasks to which a design has been adapted, the more likely it is to serve as a guide to the general direction of technical advances.' This is also true if no single artefact becomes dominant. In that case, all alternatives seem to tend towards 'functional convergence', brought about by different technical 'styles' for different classes of artefacts. This seems to be the case not only with the petrol vehicle, but also with, for instance, the digital computer.[72]

And, fourth, the Pluto effect tends to make relative the concept of technological failure. The history of automotive technology provides many examples of outright successes for the electric vehicle, which makes the concept of 'failure', from a historian's point of view, nothing more than an empty ex-post statement. Instead, alternative technologies, as concrete emanations of an abstract artefactual 'whole', can be analysed as a 'materialised' or 'frozen criticism' of the mainstream technology. As such, artefacts can be exhibited not only as windows onto a culture, but also as a comment (or even a criticism) on it. In this respect, the nearly continuous presence of the electric propulsion alternative for the dominant internal combustion engine technology is a clear case in point.

The Pluto effect, as a mechanism governing interartefactual technology transfer, enables the analysis of technological changes at the level of artefacts, but it does not replace the explanation of these changes. How a certain artefactual structure is changed remains to be explored.

The analysis of several historical examples reveals that if one considers the electric vehicle as the other universal possibility, one cannot escape the conclusion that the electric vehicle failed utterly. This conclusion, however, seems only 'logical' if one adheres to the idea that all alternatives inherit the same application potential. This helps to explain why, among many proponents of the modern as well as the earlier generations of electric vehicle, the belief in the coming of the 'miracle battery' is and was so very strong. This belief was planted in the minds of engineers as well as the public during the early years of American automobilism, when Thomas Edison proposed his alkaline battery on the basis of nickel–iron. It is still haunting automotive engineering circles, as well as science, technology and society scholars alike, when they invest their hopes of a miracle in the new, high-energy batteries or fuel cells. In another setting I have analysed Edison's proposal as the ultimate attempt to give the electric car all the properties from the petrol car that it lacked so shamefully, as an attempt to change the direction of the Pluto effect in favour of the electric vehicle.[73] In fact, the early attempts to develop hybrid alternatives can also be analysed from the same perspective, and it is remarkable how social scientists, after they have been disappointed by the 'failure' of the modern electric vehicle, now turn their attention to the hybrid as the new promising alternative. As such, the hybrid can be seen as a new version of the 'miracle battery', except that this new attempt to reverse the direction of the Pluto effect relies on the help of the internal combustion engine. It is, moreover, not difficult to predict that once the fuel cell becomes smaller and cheaper, interest will shift back again to the fully electric alternative.

However, using the Pluto metaphor in the sense I explained earlier can offer a more benign interpretation of these historical examples. The Pluto effect can explain why the electric car was highly successful without ever reaching dominance in the market place. From this perspective, the closed-body concept, the electric starter motor, the quieter running of the combustion engine, its growing reliability in order to become a city vehicle at the end of the first decade of the twentieth century, and, indeed, the resilient but sturdy pneumatic tyre: all these characteristics can be traced back to the electric and early hybrid vehicles. It must be stressed here that the petrol car manufacturers started to 'steal' from electric vehicle technology from the moment that they wanted to prove the universality of their product by developing it in such a way that it also became useful as a city vehicle (say, from about 1907). On the other hand, the 'theft' of these characteristics lessened the impetus towards a paradigmatic change to another propulsion systems for land vehicles. In this sense, the car of today is an 'electrified car', pushed, by virtue of the Pluto effect, ever further to the limits of its possibilities of technical change.[74] As such, the electric vehicle, as a constant threat to the mainstream technology, was an outright success. There is no reason to believe that this mechanism has lost much of its power in the meantime. The electric vehicle as a 'car of tomorrow', as a powerful fantasy, has had a long tradition indeed, and may well continue in the years to come.

Notes and references

1 Cipolla, C M, 'The diffusion of innovations in early modern Europe', *Comparative Studies in Society and History*, 14 (1972), pp46–7

2 I am also indebted to Henk van den Belt and Johan Schot for their critical reading of earlier versions of the manuscript, as well as to the editors of this book. The empirical basis for this contribution was an in-depth analysis of the early competition between electric and petrol vehicles in several countries. For a shortened and revised version of the original Dutch publication, see Mom, G, *The Electric Vehicle: Technology and Expectations in the Automobile Age* (Baltimore, MD: forthcoming).

3 The 'field' concept was touched upon in Mom, G, 'Das "Scheitern" des frühen Elektromobils (1895–1925). Versuch einer Neubewertung', *Technikgeschichte*, 64 (1997), pp269–85.

4 According to Grübler, A, *The Rise and Fall of Infrastructures: Dynamics of Evolution and Technological Change in Transport* (Heidelberg: 1990), p42, technological change is not a consequence of diffusion but of substitution. For a comparable reduction of technological change to substitution see Linstone, H A and Sahal, D (eds), *Technological Substitution; Forecasting Techniques and Applications* (New York: 1976), pxiii.

5 Rogers, E M, *Diffusion of Innovations* (New York: 1995); Mahajan, V and Peterson, R A, *Models for Innovation Diffusion* (Beverly Hills, CA: 1985), p7

6 Recently, more sophisticated models have been developed which analyse 'multilevel', 'multimode' or 'multidimensional' substitution, although they keep treating the technologies in question as monolithic entities. See Pistorius, C W I and Utterback, J M, 'Multi-mode interaction among technologies', *Research Policy*, 26 (1997), pp67–84; Tilton, J E, 'Material substitution; the role of new technology', *Technological Forecasting and Social Change*, 39 (1991), pp127–44; Girifalco, L A and Simozar, S, 'Multi-level technological substitution: application to steelmaking', *Journal of Resource Management and Technology*, 14 (1985), pp45–54; Ayres, R U and Ezekoye, I, 'Competition and complementarity in diffusion; the case of octane', *Technological Forecasting and Social Change*, 39 (1991), pp145–58. These studies all build upon an older tradition, initiated by Devendra Sahal and his school. See, for instance, Nawaz Sharif, M and Kabir, C, 'System dynamics modeling for forecasting multilevel technological substitution', in Linstone, H A and Sahal, D (eds), *Technological Substitution*, pp21–45; Sahal, D, 'The multidimensional diffusion of technology', *ibid.*, pp223–44.

7 The most extreme position was taken by IIASA researcher Cesare Marchetti who, somewhat ironically (I hope), commented upon his own research on the automobile in Italy from the 1950s that the diffusion curves presented such a perfect 'fit', that further explanation was superfluous. See Marchetti, C, 'The automobile in a system context; the past 80 years and the next 20 years', *Technological Forecasting and Social Change*, 23 (1983), pp3–23. Marchetti speaks of 'a very high level of determinism, most probably due to strong and efficient social feedback loops' (*ibid.*, p3), a phenomenon which he calls 'homeostasis'.

8   Even theoretical efforts to reconcile quantitative diffusion theory and individual choice behaviour (represented typically by the work of Michael Sonis) have to rely on assumptions that tend to blur the actual 'functional flexibility' (see below) of artefacts. For instance, artefacts have to be 'mutually exchangeable' and 'mutually exclusive' in order to be allowed to enter into Sonis' sophisticated model of substitution. In reality, for both cases the opposite is true and it is one of the main aims of this contribution to show that it is the fundamental non-exchangeability and the partial overlap of functional spectra of artefacts which drive incremental evolutionary technical change. See Sonis, M, 'A unified theory of innovation diffusion, dynamic choice of alternatives, ecological dynamics and urban/regional growth and decline', *Ricerche Economiche*, 40 (1986), p700.

9   For a typical critique of neoclassical economics, see Nelson, R R and Winter, S G, 'Neoclassical vs. evolutionary theories of economic growth: critique and prospectus', *The Economic Journal*, 84 (1974), pp886–905.

10 Fischer, C S, *America Calling: A Social History of the Telephone to 1940* (Berkeley: 1992)

11 Nelson, R R and Winter, S G, 'In search of useful theory of innovation', *Research Policy*, 6 (1977), pp47–8; Rosenberg, N, 'Factors affecting the diffusion of technology', *Explorations in Economic History* (1972), pp10, 23; Rosenberg, N, 'On technological expectations', *The Economic Journal*, 86 (1976), p531 (emphasis in original). However, Rosenberg also uses the (at the time unproven) 'total superiority of the internal combustion engine' (*ibid.*, p532) to explain the 'failure' of the electric vehicle.

12 Kroes, P and Meijers, A (eds), *The Empirical Turn in the Philosophy of Technology* (Amsterdam: 2000)

13 It must be stressed that evolutionary change does not necessarily equal gradual change. Economic evolutionary theory resolves this by introducing the concept of 'punctuated equilibria', which enables quasi-static analysis. See Mokyr, J, 'Evolutionary biology, technological change and economic history', *Bulletin of Economic Research*, 43 (1991), p141. A whole body of literature on technological change has been built on this 'punctuated equilibrium' hypothesis, with the history of the American automotive industry as an exemplary case. See, for instance, Abernathy, W J, *The Productivity Dilemma: Roadblock to Innovation in the Automobile Industry* (Baltimore, London: 1978); Abernathy, W J, and Utterback, J M, 'Patterns of industrial innovation', *Technology Review*, 81 (1978), pp41–7; Anderson, P, and Tushman, M L, 'Technological discontinuities and dominant design: a cyclical model of technological change', *Administrative Science Quarterly*, 35 (1990), pp604–33.

14 Metcalfe, J S and Gibbons, M, 'Technological variety and the process of competition', *Economie appliquée*, 39 (1986), p493; Poser, H, 'Evolution – ein neues disziplinübergreifendes Paradigma?' in König, W (ed), 'Umorientierungen: Wissenschaft, Technik und Gesellschaft im Wandel', (Frankfurt am Main: 1994), p168 (my translation); Sen, A, 'On the Darwinian view of progress', *Population and Development Review*, 19 (1993), p125

15 König, W, 'Geschichte als Geschehen und als Tat. Projektion und Realität am

Beispiel der frühen Eisenbahngeschichte', in Dienel, H-L and Trischler, H (eds), *Geschichte der Zukunft des Verkehrs: Verkehrskonzepte von der Frühen Neuzeit bis zum 21. Jahrhundert* (Frankfurt am Main, New York: 1997), p130; Huxley, J, *Evolution in Action* (New York: 1953), p13

16 Odling-Smee, J, 'Biological evolution and cultural change', in Jones, E and Reynolds, V (eds), *Survival and Religion: Biological Evolution and Cultural Change* (Chichester: 1995), pp1–43

17 Saviotti, P P and Metcalfe, J S, 'Present development and trends in evolutionary economics', in *id.* (eds) *Evolutionary Theories of Economic and Technological Change* (Chur: 1991) pp5–14. According to the most knowledgeable (in terms of the theory of biological evolution) economic evolutionist Joel Mokyr, 'for the distinction to make sense, we have to assume that the knowledge required to produce an artefact and the artefact itself are separate entities,' which implies a departure from the merging of the two in the theory of social construction of technology. See Mokyr, J, 'Evolution and technological change: a new metaphor for economic history?' in Fox, R (ed), *Technological Change: Methods and Themes in the History of Technology* (Amsterdam: 1996), p67.

18 Chanaron, J-J, *Innovation technologique et développement économique: cours d'économie appliquée* (Grenoble, n.d. [1991]), p199. Referring to Gibbons, Metcalfe and others, Chanaron distinguishes between 'régime' (such as 'bande magnétique') and 'configurations' ('stéréo 8', 'cassette compacte', 'bande traditionelle'). For a definition of the state of the art, see Vaughn Koen, B, 'The engineering method', in Durbin, P T (ed.), *Critical Perspectives on Nonacademic Science and Engineering* (Bethlehem: 1991).

19 The 'frozen' metaphor is borrowed from: Hård, M, *Machines are Frozen Spirit: The Scientification of Refrigeration and Brewing in the 19th Century – A Weberian Interpretation* (Frankfurt am Main, Boulder, CO: 1994).

20 Gould paraphrased by Mokyr, J, note 17, p69; Odling-Smee, J, note 16, pp16–17.

21 Hodgson, G M, *Economics and Evolution: Bringing Life Back into Economics* (Cambridge: 1993), p40; Saviotti, P P, 'The role of variety in economic and technological development,' in Saviotti, P P and Metcalfe, J S (eds), *Evolutionary Theories of Economic and Technological Change* (Chur: 1991), p195

22 MacKenzie, D, 'How do we know the properties of artefacts? Applying the sociology of knowledge to technology', in Fox, R (ed.), *Technological Change: Methods and Themes in the History of Technology* (Amsterdam: 1996), p247

23 Koolmann, S, *Leitbilder der Technikentwicklung: Das Beispiel des Automobils* (Frankfurt am Main, New York: 1992); Schmucki, B, *Der Traum vom Verkehrsfluss. Städtische Verkehrsplanung seit 1945 im deutsch-deutschen Vergleich* (Frankfurt am Main, New York: 2001)

24 Mom, G, note 2

25 The introduction of a measure of 'closedness' (not to be confused with the 'closure' concept from economic and social theories) of the technical field meets the justifiable wish of Walter Vincenti to devise some 'kind of hierarchy of real-world constraints, depending on degree of directness and restriction'.

As examples of absolute boundaries, Vincenti mentions *perpetuum mobile* and gravitation in the design of airplanes. See Vincenti, W, 'The technical shaping of technology: real-world constraints and technical logic in Edison's electrical lighting system', *Social Studies of Science*, 25 (1995), p565.

26 For a taxonomy of failure factors, see Braun, H-J, Introduction, *Symposium on 'Failed Innovations', Social Studies of Science*, 22 (1992), pp217–26. For an analysis of the influence of 'failures' on technological change, see McCray, W P, 'What makes a failure? Designing a new national telescope, 1975–1984', *Technology and Culture*, 42 (2001), pp265–91; Petroski, H, 'The success of failure', *ibid.*, pp321–8.

27 Hellige, H D, 'Von der programmatischen zur empirischen Technikgeneseforschung: ein technikhistorisches Analyseinstrumentarium für die prospektive Technikbewertung', *Technikgeschichte*, 60 (1993), p193

28 Winner, L, 'Upon opening the black box and finding it empty: social constructivism and the philosophy of technology', *Science, Technology, and Human Values*, 18 (1993), pp362–78

29 König, W, 'Technik, Macht und Markt. Eine Kritik der sozialwissenschaftlichen Technikgeneseforschung,' *Technikgeschichte*, 60 (1993), p253 (my translation)

30 Epstein, R C, *The Automobile Industry: Its Economic and Commercial Development* (Chicago, New York: 1928), p242

31 Bayla Singer also concludes that in historiography the car is still too often thought of as a monolithic, undifferentiated entity: 'We need some additional vocabulary …. Historians have not provided such a vocabulary, perhaps because of their customary focus on case studies.' See Singer, B, 'Automobiles and femininity', *Research in Philosophy and Technology*, 13 (1993), p37. The classification, and the basic knowledge about the construction of the car, in this and the following paragraphs has been taken (with a few changes) from Mom, G (ed), *De Nieuwe Steinbuch: De Automobiel: Handboek voor Autobezitters, Monteurs and Technici* (Deventer: several volumes since 1986).

32 Max Weber called such an abstraction an 'ideal type', which 'belong(s) to the world of ideas' and is 'inductively abstracted from reality' (quoted by Hård, M, note 19, p35). Hård distinguishes between 'ideal type' and 'archetype', which, unlike the former, actually exists in historical or contemporary reality, and functions as an exemplar (*Vorbild*) in a Kuhnian sense (*ibid.*, pp36–7, 50–1). For the purpose of the theory, as developed in the text, I need a third category, the 'average type', which describes the common denominator of all concrete artefacts at a certain 'punctuated equilibrium'. The latter is constructed from existing structural components of these artefacts, but, like the ideal type, it mostly has no equivalent in artefactual reality. Whereas the ideal type is often to be found in contemporary handbooks, the average type mostly has to be constructed by the historian, based on the population concept of artefactual variety and its distribution. For instance, while the Ford Model T may have functioned as an archetype (as a light but sturdy, cheap, high-wheeled family car) during the period between 1910 and 1925, and may have been treated by contemporaries as an important constituent of the ideal type as analysed in technical handbooks and trade and engineering magazines, it certainly did not

coincide with the average type of car during that period. This becomes clear if the historian of automotive technology constructs the latter type for this period, and discovers that the Model T's planetary gearbox, its flywheel-system with electricity generator and its lack of an electric starter motor until the end of the second decade of the twentieth century, are no part of this average.

33 For a similar (but mathematically inspired) approach, see Foray, D and Grübler, A, 'Morphological analysis, diffusion and lock-out of technologies: Ferrous casting in France and the FRG', *Research Policy*, 19 (1990), pp535–50.

34 Saviotti, P P and Metcalfe, J S, note 17, p16. Chanaron expands the predator–prey relationship with the notion of 'parasitism' and replaces commensalism by symbiosis or mutualism and cooperation (which favours both species in both cases); see Chanaron, J-J, note 18, p228. For another taxonomy (the artefact as independent, complementary, contingent or substitute) see Mahajan, V and Peterson, R A, *Models for Innovation Diffusion* (Beverly Hills, CA: 1985), pp39–40. Also see Hellige, H D, note 27, pp207–8, who distinguishes between complete substitution (slow and fast), displacement into niches, permanent competition (De Laval's action turbine versus Parsons' reaction turbine, petrol versus diesel engines in cars), and coexistence (AM and FM modulation in radio technology).

35 For an example in automotive history ('Dial-a-Ride'), conceived as a correction to the general negligence of the user in diffusion theory, see Rice, R E and Rogers, E M, 'Reinvention in the innovation process', *Knowledge: Creation, Diffusion, Utilization*, 1 (1980), pp499–514.

36 Ward, W H, 'The sailing ship effect', *Bulletin of the Institute of Physics and Physical Society*, 18 (1967), p169

37 Bayus, B L, Kim, N and Shocker, A D, 'Growth models for multiproduct interactions: current status and new directions', in Mahajan, V, Muller, E and Wind, Y (eds), *New-Product Diffusion Models* (Boston, MA), p150

38 Hellige, H D, note 27, p207

39 A selection of studies with a broad empirical basis, giving examples from a large variety of artefact classes and production processes, includes: Utterback, J M and Kim, L, 'Invasion of a stable business by radical innovation', in Kleindorfer, P R (ed.), *The Management of Productivity and Technology in Manufacturing* (New York, London: 1985), pp127–9 (eight pairs of competing technologies, from ice boxes v. refrigerators to vacuum tubes to solid-state semiconductors); Foster, R N, 'Timing technological transitions', *Technology in Society*, 7 (1985), pp127–41 (cotton v. rayon v. nylon v. polyester pneumatic-tyre cords); Pistorius, C W I and Utterback, J M, note 6 (11 pairs of examples); Bayus, B L, Kim, N and Shocker, A D, note 37, pp150, 153 (cardboard milk and juice packaging v. all-plastic bottles, magnetic v. optical disc, Netscape Internet browser v. Microsoft PC operating system). See also Table 1.

40 For a similar view that it is function rather than technology per se which is transferred, see Sahal, D, *Patterns of Technological Innovation* (London: 1981), pp195–7, 311.

41 Lockert, L, *Les Voitures électriques*, Vol. 4 (Paris: 1897), pp125–30. For the overall narrative of this episode, see Mom, G, note 2.

42 Mom, G, 'Das Holzbrettchen in der schwarzen Kiste: die Entwicklung des Elektromobilakkumulators bei und aus der Sicht der Accumulatoren-Fabrik AG (AFA) von 1902–1910', *Technikgeschichte*, 63/2 (1996), pp119–51; Schallenberg, R H, *Bottled Energy: Electrical Engineering and the Evolution of Chemical Energy Storage* (Philadelphia: 1982), pp90–7; Müller, A, *25 Jahre der Accumulatoren-Fabrik Aktiengesellschaft 1888–1913* (Berlin: 1913), pp38–47

43 Wade, E J, *Secondary Batteries: Their Theory, Construction and Use* (London: 1908), p254

44 David, Ch., 'Die Accumulatoren auf der Pariser Weltausstellung', *Centralblatt* (1 August 1900), p262

45 Bauer, G (ed), *Berliner Strassenbahnen* (Berlin: 1987), pp20–2; Hilkenbach, S and Kramer, W, *125 Jahre Strassenbahnen in Berlin* (Düsseldorf: 1990), pp12, 13, 16; Prasuhn, P H, *Chronik der Strassenbahn* (Hanover: 1969), p19; Hendlmeier, W, *Von der Pferde-Eisenbahn zur Schnell-Strassenbahn* (Munich: 1968), pp24–6

46 Schallenberg, R H, note 42, pp201–22

47 'The automobile', *Electrical Review* (16 November 1901), p598; 'A new departure in storage batteries', *Horseless Age* (17 April 1901), pp52–3; 'Another departure in storage batteries,' *Horseless Age* (12 February 1902), p194; Hospitalier, E, 'L'Accumulateur E.I.t.', *La Vie automobile* (11 February 1905), pp81–3; Rosset, G, 'L'accumulateur E.I.t. au plomb allotropique', *La Vie automobile* (25 February 1905), pp122–4

48 *Industrie Electrique* (10 February 1905), p49

49 'Storage battery traction', *Electrical Review* (8 June 1901), p715; 'Annual Meeting of the American Institute of Electrical Engineers', *Electrical Review* (25 May 1901), pp665–9

50 Schallenberg, R H, note 42, p371

51 'A review of the storage battery situation for the year 1904', *Electrical Review* (14 January 1905), p67

52 'Thin plate lead battery', *Central Station* (December 1910), p174; Skinner, J M, 'The Philadelphia thin plate battery', *Central Station* (March 1913), p289; Skinner, J M, 'Thin plate battery truck in service', *Central Station* (March 1916), pp238–41; 'Vehicle batteries', *Commercial Vehicle* (February 1910), p76

53 Schallenberg, R H, note 42, pp270–1, 284–6; 'The December meeting of the Electric Vehicle Association of America', *Central Station* (January 1911), p191; Ford, B, 'The "Ironclad-Exide" battery', *Central Station* (February 1911), p226; 'The "Ironclad-Exide"', *Central Station* (January 1911), p200. The German AFA shortly afterwards launched a virtually identical battery, called 'Panzerbatterie', see Schallenberg, R H, note 42, p271.

54 'The electric truck: a sketch indicating the development and present status of this modern successor of the horse' (Pontiac, MI: 1912); Cushing, H C, Jr and Smith, F W, *The Electric Vehicle Hand-Book* (New York: 1913), p13 (advertisement)

55 See, in general, Mom, G, note 2.

56 'Tissues pour pneumatiques', *Le Caoutchouc & la gutta-percha* (15 March 1907), p902; Lord Montagu of Beaulieu and McComb, F W, *Behind the*

Wheel: The Magic and Manners of Early Motoring (New York, London: 1977), pp70, 76; 'Tires at the New York automobile show', *The India Rubber World* (1 February 1904), pp159–60

57 Weber, C O, 'Technical notes on motor tyres', *The India Rubber World* (29 February 1904), pp79–80; Tompkins, E, *The History of the Pneumatic Tyre* (Birmingham: unpublished, 1981), p21; French, T, *Tyre Technology* (Bristol, New York: 1988), pp14–15; Petit, H, 'Comment on doit se conduire avec les pneus', *La Vie automobile* (13 April 1912), p235

58 Baudry de Saunier, L, 'La mort par le pneumatique!', *La Vie automobile* (2 July 1904), p417–18, and follow-up articles: (9 July 1904), pp441–3; (16 July 1904), pp453–5; (30 July 1904), pp488–90; (6 August 1904), p505

59 Baudry de Saunier, L, 'La roue élastique', *La Vie automobile* (8 April 1905), pp216–19; Overnoy, L, 'La roue élastique de Cadignan', *La Vie automobile* (15 October 1904), pp668–9. For an overview of 140 designs between 1906 and 1909, see Rutishauser, J, *Roues élastiques* (Paris: 1941). The Achilles heel quote is from 'Die Pneumatikfrage bei künftigen Konkurrenzen', *Allgemeine Automobilzeitung* (Berlin) (17 November 1905), p28; 'serious competitor' from 'La roue élastique de Cadignan', *Le Caoutchouc & la gutta-percha* (15 February 1905), p52; spring–absorber combinations are described in 'Les roues élastiques rivales des pneus', *Le Caoutchouc & la gutta-percha* (15 December 1905), p380; 'absorbs the obstacle' is from Mortimer-Mégret, 'La vie en auto', *Le Caoutchouc & la gutta-percha* (15 January 1910), pp3603–4.

60 Petit, H, 'Les pneus à cordes', *La Vie automobile* (4 May 1912), pp282–3; 'Les succès des pneumatiques Palmer', *Le Caoutchouc & la gutta-percha* (15 March 1913) p7132; Norton, S V, 'Relation of tires to the efficiency of electric vehicles', proceedings of the *39th NELA Convention*, Chicago, IL, 22–26 May 1916, accounting section sessions, papers, reports and discussions, pp93–104; Watson, W H L and Mitchell, R J, 'Electric automobiles in England', *Electric Vehicles* (US) (July 1913), p107

61 'Tires for electrics', *Electric Vehicles* (US) (July 1913), p90; Graves, H, 'Special features of tires for electrics', *Electric Vehicles* (US) (August 1913), pp129–30

62 Tompkins, E, note 57, p22

63 'The first ten years', unpublished manuscript, Box 2-5, Goodyear archives, Akron University, OH

64 Lichfield, P W, 'History of the pneumatic tire design', *Electric Vehicles* (US) (June 1914), p236

65 Brewster, T D, 'Cord tires for passenger electrics', *Electric Vehicles* (US) (March 1915), pp111–12; Palmer, J F, 'Construction of cord tires', *Electric Vehicles* (US) (August 1915), pp67–9; Epstein, R C, note 30, p107

66 Silverberg, G, 'Adoption and diffusion of technology as a collective evolutionary process', *Technological Forecasting and Social Change*, 39 (1991), p74

67 Hans-Joachim Braun has repeatedly pointed to the existence of this mechanism; see, for example, 'Gas oder Elektrizität? Zur Konkurrenz zweier Beleuchtungssysteme, 1880–1914', *Technikgeschichte*, 47 (1980), pp1–19. In a way, the Pluto effect has already been formulated by Wolfgang König: 'On

the one hand, the "new" will be designed after the "old", which it aims to supplant, and in doing so will integrate elements of the "old", on the other hand it adapts itself into the continuing environment of the "old", likewise taking over elements of the "old".' See König, W, note 29, p248.

68 Mom, G, 'Gasturbine als alternatieve voertuigaandrijving', *Polytechnisch Tijdschrift, Editie Werktuigbouw* (November 1991), pp44–7. In fact, the transfer process was even more complicated, because the gas turbine was proposed because of concerns about shortages of fuel (especially high-quality petrol) and about the environment. After these concerns had waned, the turbogenerator was integrated in mainstream internal-combustion-engine technology in order to increase performance. As with many other automotive components, however, the turbogenerator can also be used to achieve lower fuel consumption and emissions, an approach that became customary in automotive technology only two decades later.

69 Indeed, the Pluto effect is not restricted to the material world. It can be seen at work in the historiography of technological change (the integration of the constructivist thesis within diffusion theory) as well as in culture (the integration of pop music in the Catholic Mass, to attract youth). See Bardini, T, 'Diffusionisme, constructivisme et modèle technique: ébauche d'une approche communicationnelle du changement technico-social', *Technologies de l'information et société*, 5 (1993), p376; Pleij, H, *De Sneeuwpoppen van 1511: Stadscultuur in de late Middeleeuwen* (Amsterdam: 1998), p33.

70 Rosenberg, N, 'Factors affecting the diffusion of technology', note 11, p26

71 For a conceptualisation of the crossover phenomenon in the history of technology, which introduces the concept of 'hybridization' as a characteristic of technological change, see Kirsch, D A, *The Electric Vehicle and the Burden of History* (New Brunswick, NJ: 2000).

72 Sahal, D, 'Alternative conceptions of technology', *Research Policy*, 10 (1981), p20; Hughes, T P, *Rescuing Prometheus* (New York: 1998), p31

73 Mom, G, 'Inventing the miracle battery: Thomas Edison and the electric vehicle', *History of Technology*, 20 (1998) pp40, 43

74 I am aware of the fact that it is very difficult to define the 'technological potential' of a given technology, without falling into the trap of historical hindsight. For the analytical usability of this concept (in this case even accompanied by a conviction of the 'inevitability' of the choice in favour of the technology with the highest 'potential') see Foster, R N, note 39.

Michael R Bailey and John P Glithero

Learning through industrial archaeology: the Rocket *locomotive project*

Introduction

In the quest for greater understanding of the history of engineering and technology, the artefacts in the world's museums of science, technology and industry provide a most important resource. A thorough survey of these artefacts, together with historical and technical research surrounding their history, can advance our knowledge of the development of materials, manufacturing methods and maintenance practices. The importance of this resource is apparent because engineers and technologists often failed to record their approach to design and manufacturing methods, and their understanding of materials. Furthermore, the accumulated knowledge and skills of the tradesmen were rarely recorded, being transmitted from master to apprentice, each generation developing the skills of its forebears.

Recent calls to pursue a greater understanding of artefacts, through survey,[1] have led to several research studies in the 1990s, some leading to conservation and restoration projects by the authors, summaries of which have recently been published.[2] The most comprehensive of these studies was carried out by the authors at the National Railway Museum in York during 1999, on George and Robert Stephenson's *Rocket* locomotive of 1829 (Colour plate 1). This preceded its return to the Science Museum in London for display in its new *Making the Modern World* gallery. The study was supervised by Richard Gibbon, Head of Engineering at the National Railway Museum, and its findings were set down in a comprehensive and fully referenced report to the Museum, which has been published in full.[3] The manner in which the study was conducted, and its principal findings, form the present case study of learning through industrial archaeology.[4]

Background

Although *Rocket* is one of the world's best-known locomotives, rightly perceived as being the progenitor of main-line railway motive power, its interpretation has been limited to its success at the 1829 Rainhill Trials, and to its being the first locomotive fitted with a multitubular boiler. *Rocket*'s importance as an artefact is much wider, however, as it was:

- an important example of a prototype locomotive manufactured during the time of rapid design evolution and component development between 1828 and 1830

- designed and manufactured during the period of transition between the millwright-based manufacturing practice of the early locomotive builders and the factory-based practice that developed from the late 1820s

- the first example of a machine able to convey people at a sustained speed in excess of that which was possible by animal power

- the earliest surviving example of a locomotive which was maintained and modified by railway and contractor teams charged with keeping a fleet of main-line locomotives in service

- employed as a test-bed for dynamic and thermodynamic experiments, at a time of high expectation that further traction improvements, beyond reciprocating engines, were possible.

The research study sought to build on the work undertaken during the 1920s by the three respected locomotive historians, E A Forward, J G H Warren and C F Dendy Marshall.[5] Their work had formed the basis for the design of the replica built in 1929 for Henry Ford (on display in the Henry Ford Museum in Dearborn, Michigan), three later museum-displayed replicas of *Rocket*, and the fifth, operable, example, built in 1979 under the supervision of Michael G Satow, which is regularly steamed at the National Railway Museum.[6]

Although several components were removed in the years immediately after its withdrawal from service, the remains of *Rocket* represent a physical 'chronicle' of engineering design and maintenance practices between 1829 and 1840. To develop a more comprehensive understanding of the technological context in which *Rocket* was built and later modified, its design and manufacturing features, and its operating and maintenance history, the study was carried out through the combination of three disciplines:

- **Industrial archaeology**, being a comprehensive survey and systematic paper-and-photographic recording of the form, dimension and material of surviving components

- **Engineering**, being the determination of the reasoning behind the locomotive's design and the manufacturing method of each component

- **History**, being a comprehensive archival study to ascertain the events and decisions taken during the locomotive's career, and the context in which they occurred.

The survey was carried out in four phases, namely component removal, systematic recording, historical assessment and reassembly. From this survey, component and arrangement drawings were prepared using computer-aided design software. The drawings included all fittings and redundant holes and marks, as well as dimensions. The likely history of each component was sought using the drawings and the photographic record, in conjunction with the findings of the historical research.

Historical context

Rocket's importance as an artefact reaches far beyond its status as the well-known locomotive that won the Rainhill Trials, and the perception of it as the progenitor of the main-line railway locomotive. An understanding of *Rocket*'s specific place in locomotive development and the origins of main-line railway operation provided a background against which the findings of the survey were assessed and a guide to consideration of the artefact's future display and interpretation.

Rocket was manufactured by Robert Stephenson & Co. in Newcastle upon Tyne in 1829 during an intense period of locomotive development. This was necessary to advance its capabilities from those of the slow and relatively unreliable 'colliery' type used in the coalfields of the North East, to those of a machine capable of meeting the much greater speed, load-haul and reliability requirements of main-line operation. In the 33-month period between January 1828 and September 1830, locomotive technology advanced from the colliery type to the prototype *Planet*, the first class adopted for main-line operation.

The stimulus to this development programme was the strong advocacy for the use of locomotives by George Stephenson (1781–1848), Chief Engineer of the Liverpool & Manchester Railway.[7] The building of the railway required Stephenson's almost full-time attention, however, and thus his son, Robert Stephenson (1803–59), began a programme, at their Newcastle factory, to accelerate locomotive development towards the requisite main-line standards.

Robert Stephenson's programme, conducted in consultation, through correspondence, with his father, was a systematic appraisal of component and material improvement, rather than the incremental and empirical approach hitherto taken. This significant change to the method of technological progress saw improvements to the boiler, steam pipe, transmission and suspension. Improved materials were particularly required to fulfil the increasing dynamic and thermodynamic requirements of the developing locomotive. During the development programme, the Stephensons manufactured several experimental locomotives for customers in Britain, France and the United States, each of which incorporated innovations.

Rocket was an important example of this programme, designed to meet the weight, performance and other specifications determined for the Rainhill Trials.[8] As well as being the first locomotive to be fitted with a multitubular boiler and separate firebox, it also incorporated the most successful components already developed by the programme, namely the steel leaf spring and direct drive between piston and wheel crank using a crosshead, slide bars and connecting rod.

The *Planet* class, the prototype of which was delivered to Liverpool shortly after the opening of the line, incorporated significant improvements over the earlier locomotives, including *Rocket*, and became the first class of main-line locomotives used on several of the world's earliest main-line railways. The post-Rainhill improvements included:

- improved steam generation, by the adoption of a greater number of tubes of smaller diameter providing a larger heating surface, and the provision of a smokebox, improved blast pipe and firebox integrated within the boiler barrel

- increased thermal efficiency by the incorporation of a dome and internal steam pipe and the use of inside cylinders

- improved dynamics through the provision of horizontal inside cylinders, a substantial outside frame and the use of a leading carrying axle

- improved adhesion by the use of driving wheels at the rear of the locomotive, adjacent to the firebox.

Rocket was retrospectively fitted with some of these improvements when opportunity arose, but, after 1833, it was no longer economic to make further modifications. *Rocket* and its sister locomotive *Invicta*[9] are thus important artefacts that reflect the design and material achievements from this era of rapid technological progress.

Rocket is also important in representing one of the earliest achievements of mechanical design engineering. At the beginning of the development programme, Robert Stephenson recognised the need to introduce a design capability to provide a much-improved size and weight envelope within which components would be manufactured and fitted.[10] Innovations were incorporated within this envelope, whilst meeting a stipulated weight limitation and using different materials according to component specifications. This contrasts with earlier locomotives that had been developed and assembled in accordance with the long-established machinery and engine-fitting practices of millwrights and engine-wrights, and of other tradesmen working to their overall schemes. For these locomotives, schematic preproduction drawings only were produced, and neither general arrangement nor component drawings were prepared.[11]

Further improvements on later locomotives, including *Rocket*, were made possible by improved components and arrangements incorporated into more detailed drawings. By the summer of 1830, the

Planet-class locomotives had significantly better power-to-weight ratio within the strict axle-load limitations.

Operating speed on locomotive-hauled railways prior to the Rainhill Trials was typically 5 to 8 mph (8 to 13 km/h). *Rocket* incorporated significant dynamic improvements as well as the ability to generate more steam. It was 'made expressly for 12 miles an hour' when hauling a load of three times its own weight, and achieved this speed on its initial trial outing at Killingworth.[12] At the Rainhill Trials, *Rocket* exceeded the expectations for main-line locomotives when, with its assigned load, it achieved runs of between 14 and 24 mph (23 and 39 km/h).[13] At the conclusion of the trials it ran, without a load, at 35 mph (56 km/h),[14] thus trebling the previous maximum speed for a locomotive. For the first time, a speed had been achieved which exceeded that which could be achieved on horseback, which sent the symbolic message that the world was approaching an era in which it would no longer be dependent on horses for long-distance travel.

Rocket was the first locomotive to be adopted for main-line railway service, and its preservation therefore provides an excellent opportunity, through survey, to understand early main-line maintenance and repair practices, particularly for the boiler and wheels. The higher main-line operating speeds, for which the locomotives proved capable, subjected them to dynamic forces well beyond previous experience. This was compounded by material unreliability and the inadequacy of some initial fitting practices. The intensity of service on the railway was also much greater than had been anticipated, limiting the maintenance time for locomotives.[15]

The problems of maintaining an adequate locomotive fleet led the railway from 1832 to develop a much higher capability for maintenance in its locomotive running sheds, with correspondingly less dependence on outside firms. As experience grew, the sheds were better equipped, becoming the progenitors of the latter-day large railway workshops. The *Rocket* survey identified replacements, modifications and repair work of the railway's early maintenance teams, providing wider evidence relating to their developing role.

The majority of *Rocket*'s time with the Liverpool & Manchester Railway was spent on works trains and other secondary duties. It was involved in four serious accidents, the first being the well-known fatality to the Liverpool Member of Parliament, William Huskisson. Damage was sustained in accidents at Chat Moss in October 1830, Olive Mount cutting in January 1831 and on the Wigan Branch Railway in November 1832. The necessity to return to Liverpool for repairs on each occasion provided the opportunity to modify *Rocket* with the improved features.

Rocket was demonstrably better than its competitors at the Rainhill Trials, and the Stephensons' development programme for the reciprocating locomotive went on to produce significant improvements in both performance and efficiency with the *Planet* design. There was, however, an anticipation that 'further improvements' could be made, and for the more promising ideas locomotives were made available for testing purposes.[16] Following its withdrawal from regular services in 1833, *Rocket* was employed as a test vehicle for at least two of these schemes, including an unsuccessful rotary engine experiment, proposed by Lord Dundonald. As an artefact, the locomotive therefore takes on a further significance in providing an opportunity, through survey, to obtain a better understanding of these alternative technologies.

In 1836 *Rocket* was sold to the Earl of Carlisle, whose independent Naworth railway system linked his several collieries in Cumberland. It was retired from service by the colliery lessee, James Thompson, in about 1840, but was retained out of sentiment rather than scrapped. In 1862, Robert Stephenson & Co. prepared it for exhibition at the Patent Office Museum, latterly the Science Museum, at which site *Rocket* has been subsequently displayed.

Three contemporary drawings of *Rocket* were consulted during the survey. The first, retained in the Science Museum, depicts *Rocket* as it looked when sold by the Liverpool & Manchester Railway in 1836, by whom it was prepared in recognition of its historical association with the line. The second, privately-owned, drawing became known about as the result of the project research work. Watermarked 1839, it depicts the locomotive as it looked when withdrawn from service, and is almost identical to another drawing, retained in the National Railway Museum, but which does not have a watermark (Colour plate 2).

Survey methods and techniques

Following a review of the benefits of dismantling, selected components were carefully removed, with minimum risk to the artefact. Only those components that were to be of benefit to the survey were selected for removal. Photographs were taken of each assembly before dismantling. Easing oil was applied prior to removal of nuts and bolts, and brass shims were used within the jaws of spanners to avoid marking their heads. Components were carefully cleaned, labelled and weighed prior to survey (Colour plate 3).

A systematic programme of photographic recording and detailed examination was undertaken for each component, in order to ascertain:

• its material

• its dimensions

• the method of manufacture, machining and fitting

• the presence and dimensions of rivets, studs, bolts and nuts

• the presence and dimensions of redundant holes

• the presence and likely purpose of fitters' marks.

From this survey, drawings were prepared for each component, showing all fittings, redundant holes and marks, as well as dimensions, to aid assessment of component history. In conjunction with the research into the locomotive's career, the drawings and photographs provided an understanding of the likely history of each component, including an assessment of dynamic and thermodynamic characteristics. On completion of the report, all components were reassembled and restoration carried out to the limited surface areas that had been affected.

Figure 1 Rocket *in its original form as derived from the survey evidence.* (*John P Glithero*)

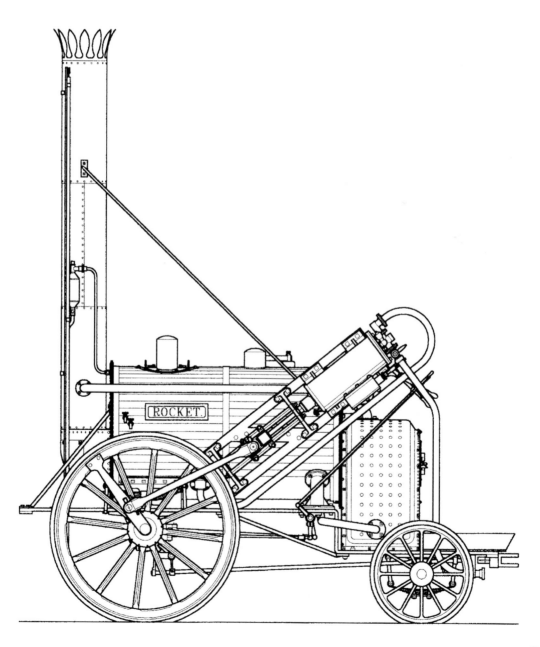

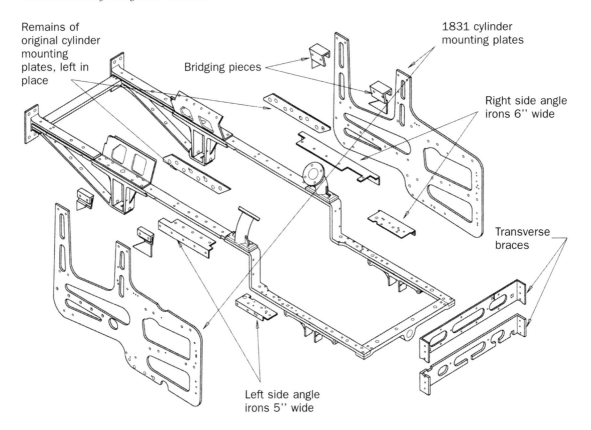

Remains of
original cylinder
mounting
plates, left in
place

Bridging pieces

1831 cylinder
mounting plates

Right side angle
irons 6″ wide

Transverse
braces

Left side angle
irons 5″ wide

Main survey findings

The evidence from the survey now provides a clearer understanding
of *Rocket*'s as-built form and of the design processes with which it was
made. From this evidence, Figure 1 is now believed to represent its
original appearance. Its arrangement was developed from the earlier
prototype locomotives, notably the *Lancashire Witch*, which operated
on the Bolton & Leigh Railway. The chosen four-wheel option limited
its weight to 4½ tons.

   The original main frame of rolled iron bar survives (Figure 2).
The driving wheels were made of wood, but were fitted to a 3¼-in.-
diameter axle, to minimise the weight. It is most likely that straps, to
accommodate the crank bosses, had been fitted between the naves and
the rims. Cast-iron horns, bronze bearings and steel springs were used,
their original location being identified on the frames.

   The original boiler barrel and tube plates have survived, and
provide evidence of several missing fittings. A weighted safety valve
had been fitted to the top of the rear plate, while a second, 'lock-
up' safety valve was fitted into the door of the inspection hole in the
leading plate.

   The novel firebox, made necessary by the multitubular boiler, was
formed from two copper plates into a 'saddle'-shaped crown and sides.
To provide a 3-in. stayed water space, the outer plate was made in an

*Figure 2 Example of a
survey drawing: exploded
view of structural
components.
(John P Glithero)*

54

'ogee' form, while the inner plate remained flat. Although the saddle was removed during the 1840s, the evidence from the frame and back plate confirms that it was out of true both in plan and end views, other fittings being correspondingly asymmetrical.

The surviving regulator valve originally drew steam directly from the upper boiler space, resulting in 'priming', which was accentuated by *Rocket*'s speed and the gradients on the Liverpool & Manchester line. This necessitated a low water level in the boiler, confirmed by stopped-up sight-glass and gauge-cock fitting holes. The cylinders and driving motion were originally set at 38° to the horizontal, as confirmed by the surviving members of the original cylinder-mounting frames. The locomotive would thus have been unsteady in its first months of operation. It is most likely that slip-eccentric valve gear, fitted to the original driving axle, was similar to the surviving fittings on *Invicta*.

The progress made in locomotive technology in the year after the Rainhill Trials was rapid and far-reaching, and *Rocket* was fitted with some of these improvements when the opportunity arose. One such innovation, first fitted to *Invicta*, was a steam 'riser' inside a boiler-top dome, and steam pipe directing dry steam to the regulator that largely prevented priming. In October 1830, following its derailment near Chat Moss, *Rocket*'s inspection-hole door was replaced with a new fitting incorporating a dome, and a riser and steam pipe fitted internally. This allowed the water level to be raised by 3 in., as confirmed by a second set of sight-glass and gauge-cock fitting holes. The displaced second safety valve was refitted towards the rear of the boiler. The evidence thus discounts the long-held perception that *Rocket* had been fitted with a dome when first constructed. The original firebox back plate was replaced by the surviving wrought-iron water-jacket back plate, fitted within the rear of the saddle, and providing evidence of its form.

Rocket was then rostered for passenger duties, but in January 1831 it was badly derailed in Olive Mount cutting, Liverpool, and further repairs and modifications were undertaken. To reduce the locomotive's instability, the cylinders and motion were relocated to a near-horizontal position. The original cylinder-carrying frames were cut away, and large wrought-iron plates substituted (Figure 2). The plates, stiffened across the rear of the firebox back plate with transverse braces, made the routing of the valve gear more difficult. To overcome this, the cylinder and valve chests were exchanged side for side and inverted.

The leading end of the frame was badly bent in the accident and appears to have been straightened by cold hammering resulting in the breaking of the left side member. The frame was strengthened at the leading end, to which was fixed an oak buffer beam and draw eye. New wooden driving wheels were made, fitted to a 4-in.-diameter axle, which appear to be the surviving wheel set (Colour plate 4). The wheels have cast-iron naves keyed to the axles with rectangular steel keys. The wooden spokes and felloes are in line rather than the concave form of conventional road carriages. Wrought-iron rims were secured with bolts, and wrought-iron tyres shrunk onto the assembled wheels. The surviving slip-eccentric valve gear was probably fitted to the 4-in. axle at this time.

In November 1832, *Rocket* was involved in a collision with a coal train near Wigan. The repairs appear to have included the remaking of the right-side driving wheel, the spokes and felloes of which show differences from those of the left-side wheel. The opportunity was taken to replace the boiler tubes, rebore the cylinders and provide new pistons, fitted with brass rings and steel springs.

The October 1834 trial saw rotary engines fitted to *Rocket*'s driving axle. It is assumed that steam for the engines was drawn through the front tube plate, with steam pipes routed to the driving axle. There is a blank flange on the upper part of the front tube plate covering what was probably a steam-pipe opening, and which may well be the only surviving evidence of the trial.

Rocket was out of use for many months before being restored for sale by the Liverpool & Manchester Railway, and it would appear that the surviving smokebox was fitted at this time. The Naworth colliery workshops fitted supplementary buffers, beneath the main buffer beam, for use with the coal wagons. The leading end of the locomotive had, however, sustained a further collision, which left the main and supplementary frames buckled, and the buffer beam sloping (Colour plate 1).

Several prominent components were removed after withdrawal, and, in 1862, Robert Stephenson & Co. prepared *Rocket* for display at the Patent Office Museum by erroneously replicating several of the missing components. It remained on display in this condition for thirty years, but in 1892 the carrying wheel set was replaced. With greater curatorial involvement with the artefact in the twentieth century, the replicated components were removed, as were the supplementary buffers and braces. The last modification to be undertaken, in 1935, was the fitting of the surviving replica chimney.

Interpretation

It is clear that visitors find difficulty in understanding *Rocket*'s surviving components and the dynamic and thermodynamic principles that lay behind them. There is, firstly, a preconception arising from the visitor's expectation to see the locomotive in its 'as-built' condition, with livery being only a small part of this expectation. The position of the cylinders, the addition of the smokebox, and the lack of several prominent components all contribute to the interpretative problem. More importantly, one of the basic messages that visitors find difficult to understand, and which applies to many artefacts in technical museums, is that machinery has undergone modification and improvements during its working life, arising from operating experience and advancement in technology and material knowledge. This difficulty will increase as the proportion of visitors with memories of working steam locomotives diminishes.

From both the historical and interpretative standpoints, therefore, mechanical artefacts should be displayed in their end-of-service condition, incorporating the evidence of the improvements made during their working life. They should be accompanied by interpretative material to enable the visitor to understand the technological progression during the life of the artefact and the reasons for the improvements. This is particularly true of *Rocket*, whose modifications form an important part of its history. In the absence of an interpretative strategy, however, the locomotive now has a derived rather than planned appearance, which neither relates to its end-of-service configuration nor fulfils visitor requirements.

This recent survey of the locomotive and the resulting increase in knowledge about it therefore provide the opportunity for an improved interpretation for the Museum visitor. The contemporary drawings have provided new evidence towards a more comprehensive understanding of *Rocket*'s form at the end of its service. From them, it is now possible to consider a strategy for its future interpretation, by offering the opportunity to re-create those components that would enhance the visitor's understanding of the locomotive.

The debate concerning an improved interpretation needs to take account of both the importance of the surviving components as historic artefacts for the discerning visitor to see and understand, and the need to develop the locomotive's display for the benefit of the majority of visitors. There are, thus, four basic options for its display, with several variations according to circumstance:

1 Continue to display the locomotive in its current form, without alteration.

2 As 1, but with the replacement of the erroneous replica chimney and trailing wheels with correct versions based on the contemporary drawings.

3 Replicate some of the missing components to combine the advantages of showing both the remains and providing an improved interpretation.

4 Replicate all of the missing components, based on the contemporary drawings, and fit them to the locomotive to restore it fully to its end-of-service appearance.

Option 1 would not take advantage of the greater knowledge about the locomotive that is now available, while option 2 would at least correct the errors made during the locomotive's time in the Science

Museum. The extent to which it would be desirable to replicate missing components is itself conditioned by interpretative opportunities and the need to meet the needs of the discerning visitor.

It was therefore recommended that partial replication of the locomotive should be undertaken, based on both the contemporary drawings and the evidence obtained from the survey. The important principles of this strategy are:

• It should be fully reversible, thus ensuring that further changes could be made, should additional evidence become available.

• It should not in any way be damaging to the remains.

• The replica components should be made, as far as possible, from the same materials as the original ones.

• The components should be fitted to the remains using surviving holes and studs, with replicated bolts and nuts.

• The components should be stamped with the Museum name and date to clarify their origin for future generations.

• Full records of the changes should be kept.

There are a number of variations to partial replication, but to stimulate the debate about its extent, it was proposed that, in addition to replacing the chimney and trailing wheel set, one side of the locomotive should be fitted with replica components, leaving the other side in its present form. This would provide the visitor with the opportunity to view the locomotive, from either side, both in its end-of-service and preserved conditions.

With the assistance of textual, model and diagrammatic displays, *Rocket*'s progression from its 1829 to its 1840 configurations, based on the findings of the survey, could thus be fully explained to future generations of Museum visitors. The extraordinary international interest that the locomotive has generated over the years has led to the production of several working and non-working full-scale replicas. These have all related to *Rocket*'s 'as-built' form, and have been made out of the strong desire to interpret the technology of the locomotive at the Rainhill Trials. These have increased knowledge of the locomotive's original arrangement, component design and assembly, as well as its operating and maintenance characteristics, and have also served to accentuate the perception that the locomotive was the progenitor of main-line motive power.

Conclusion

Rocket's survival is remarkable both because of its public 'persona' as of one of the world's most historic industrial artefacts, and because it is an engineering 'time capsule'. Its components are a combination of the changing design, material and manufacturing characteristics of locomotive technology at the dawn of main-line railways. The authors' published report developed the study's findings, with sections on the condition of each component and the evidence regarding service wear and maintenance procedures. Such detail has provided a special insight into the locomotive's manufacture and operating life. The findings are now available not only to scholars of early railway technology, but also to museums of science and industry around the world. The principles that have been applied to the *Rocket* project may equally be applied to other industrial artefacts.

The knowledge gained from this project demonstrated the benefits of such a detailed survey, combined with intensive archival research. This has both enhanced understanding of the technology of the early main-line railway era and set aside some of the misperceptions of previous historical accounts. This greater understanding of the rapid development of the skills and knowledge of both engineers and artisans relates as much to material, manufacturing and component capabilities and limitations, as to the arrangement, assembly and maintenance of the whole machine. The evidence has further provided a better understanding of the decision-making processes towards the application of developing dynamic and thermodynamic knowledge.

It is a characteristic of all machinery that modifications are made during its working life, taking advantage of technological advances and improved materials, manufacturing and maintenance techniques. The findings of artefactual research projects thus provide opportunities for improved interpretation of these techniques and their evolution. Such interpretation may include partial replication of missing components to enhance the understanding of the whole artefact for both museum students and general visitors. Textual, model and diagrammatic displays should complement such restoration through sequential presentations of the artefact's progression, with explanations for the improvements and their benefits.

With artefacts being presented in their final form after a lifetime's work and incorporating all modifications, research projects may provide sufficient evidence to determine their original form. A beneficial form of interpretation for much-altered artefacts, such as *Rocket*, is therefore full replication, especially working examples. Such replication projects can, of themselves, enhance knowledge of arrangement, assembly, operating and maintenance characteristics of long-disused machinery. The challenge for museums is therefore to develop the most appropriate artefactual displays that allow visitors to interpret their historic machinery and the technological advances that they represent.

Notes and references

1 Cossons, N, 'An agenda for the railway heritage', in Burman, P and Stratton, M (eds), *Conserving the Railway Heritage* (London: Spon, 1997), p10; Bailey, M R, 'Learning through replication: the *Planet* locomotive project', *Transactions of the Newcomen Society*, 68 (1996–97), p109

2 Bailey, M R and Glithero, J P, 'Learning through conservation: the *Braddyll* locomotive project', in Dollery, D and Henderson, J (eds), *Industrial Collections: Care and Conservation* (Cardiff: Council of Museums in Wales and the United Kingdom Institute for Conservation, 1999), pp27–39; Bailey, M R and Glithero, J P, 'Learning through restoration: the *Samson* locomotive project,' proceedings of the conference *Early Railways* (London: Newcomen Society, 2001), pp278–93

3 Bailey, M R and Glithero, J P, *The Engineering and History of* Rocket: *a survey report*, (London: Science Museum, 2000)

4 This paper has been derived from a similar paper published in Cossons, N (ed.), *Perspectives on Industrial Archaeology* (London: Science Museum, 2000), pp163–73.

5 Warren, J G H, A *Century of Locomotive Building by Robert Stephenson & Co. 1823–1923* (Newcastle upon Tyne: Andrew Reid, 1923), pp175–227; Dendy Marshall, C F, 'The Rainhill Locomotive Trials of 1829', *Transactions of the Newcomen Society*, 9 (1928–29), pp78–93; 'Memorandum on the replica of the "Rocket"', limited-circulation report, R Stephenson & Co. Ltd, 1929

6 For a list of all known full-size replicas of *Rocket* see Bailey, M R and Glithero, J P, note 3, p176.

7 Bailey, M R, 'George Stephenson – locomotive advocate: the background to the Rainhill Trials', *Transactions of the Newcomen Society*, 52 (1980/81), pp171–9; Rolt, L T C, *George and Robert Stephenson: The Railway Revolution* (Longman, 1960 and subsequent editions)

8 Bailey, M R and Glithero, J P, note 3, pp171–3

9 Preserved by the Transport Trust and displayed at the Canterbury Heritage Museum.

10 Bailey, M R, 'Robert Stephenson & Co. 1823–29', *Transactions of the Newcomen Society*, 50 (1979–80), pp123–7

11 The earliest known surviving preproduction locomotive drawings are those showing alternative parallel-motion schemes for the first locomotives made by R Stephenson & Co., n.d. but *c.* 1824, and annotated in George Stephenson's hand. They are in the collections of Tyne & Wear Museums, ref. TWCMS: C6181.

12 Stephenson, R and Locke, J, *Observations on the Comparative Merits of Locomotive & Fixed Engines as Applied to Railways & c.* (Liverpool: 1830), p27

13 *Ibid.*, p79

14 *Ibid.*

15 'Report of the Board of Directors', *Fifth Annual Meeting of the Liverpool & Manchester Railway,* Liverpool, 28 March 1831

16 Minutes of the Board of Directors of the Liverpool & Manchester Railway 1823–30, Public Record Office, ref. RAIL 371/2, *passim*; Minutes of the Sub-Committee of Management of the Liverpool & Manchester Railway 1831–33, Public Record Office, ref. RAIL 371/8, *passim*.

Kurt Möser

The driver in the machine: changing interiors of the car

This article is based on a curious observation, namely that automobile historians have paid much more attention to the exterior of the car than to the interior. The technology of the car as a whole and the design of the body shell have been extensively researched,[1] whereas the passenger compartment has received little attention.[2] This seems inappropriate, since the interior is as highly designed as the exterior, but has some more significant features and functions. Explaining the development of the interior helps us to understand the attraction of motor vehicles as part of the road transport system. Moreover, a history of the interior helps to explain the history of the antisystemic image of cars which was important for the diffusion of individual road vehicles.

The automobile can be understood on the one hand as a part of the complex system of road transport, and on the other hand as an 'individual machine', which comprises several subsystems. The functions of the transport system and the images of their functions differ considerably, though. Driving a car in the traffic of today is to participate in a highly organised and regularised and therefore restricting system, whereas the ideas and desires of drivers mostly preserve an older image, derived from the European romantic movement, of 'lonely and free' driving. The interior of the car reflects clearly this discrepancy.

My approach tries to aim at functional development, not so much at the style and design of the interior. The dashboard and the 'cockpit', being part of the passenger's compartment, can be interpreted as a 'user surface' of a complex mobility machine. It is perhaps the most significant interface between man and a machine – certainly with a machine which is in the most widespread use and excites sentiments in a most extraordinary way. Unfortunately, the complete history of the interior and the 'sub-histories' of components and functional devices such as the gear sticks or the driver's seat have not been written yet. But I will attempt to outline briefly some significant changes in the interior of the car and in the relationship between driver, passenger and the 'speed machine'. I will concentrate my remarks on the German car culture, which in several respects is different from other European car cultures or from that in the United States. The German motoring culture caught on later and favoured different, generally smaller, types of cars.[3] Motorcycles were more common until the 1930s. Many developments pioneered by American manufacturers (e.g. powered windows) were adopted later, while some significant interior features were introduced in German models first.

It is obviously rather risky to span more than a century of development in a short text. This article should therefore be regarded as a summary of the issues to be explored in a future programme of scholarship. It could also be read as a sketch outlining the contents of an exhibition on the subject. Such a potential exhibition could offer a different view on automobiles. In most museums or exhibitions, these vehicles, representing the intersection in the relationship between the system of road transport and the user, are presented as integral objects like sculptures. Therefore the focus is on their exterior (and often on their technology). By concentrating on the interior of cars, a rather neglected but nevertheless significant element of car culture would come into view.

Two separate functions of the driver: working a machine and driving on the road

In the early car – up to about 1910 – the tasks of controlling a machine and of driving a vehicle were clearly separated (Figures 1–5).

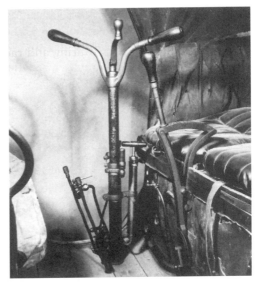

Figure 1 A typical 'workplace' of an early motor vehicle. Lubricators and pressure pumps to be actuated by the driver are prominent on the wooden dashboard. The equipment for producing acetylene for lighting purposes has to be watched. Levers for gear shifting and braking do not disguise their connection with the mechanical core of the driving machine. There is no windscreen. (Beaulieu)
Sedgwick, M, Early Cars (London: 1972)

Figure 2 The workplace of a steam car, made by Schöche, c. 1900. Steering is not yet performed using a steering wheel. The reversing lever is prominent, as is the manual water feed pump. Another typical feature is that driver and passengers face each other, with the driver sitting in the rear. Frankenberg, R v and Matteucci, M, Geschichte des Automobils (Künzelsau: 1973), p45

Figure 3 Functional separation I: The driver's position has rudimentary protection from the weather, but it is mainly open. Passengers in this British Talbot car, c. 1910, are provided with a coach-like closed compartment. Sedgwick, M, Early Cars (London: 1972)

Touring and racing cars especially were strictly 'two-person affairs'. The mechanic had to watch the gauges in order to scan the state of the engine. He had to work the lubrication system, to control or even maintain the pressure in the petrol tank, and he had to have an eye on the temperature of the water cooling system. An early Austrian article refers to the driver being 'scared about the oilers which must be actuated, small holes having to be greased, carburettor levers having to be handled'.[4] The necessary variation of the ignition timing, which had to be done by hand, was a task often shared between driver and co-driver. The co-driver's main task was maintenance and repairs. Even *Herrenfahrer*, gentlemen drivers, usually had a mechanic with them. When touring, his presence was often felt. Eugen Diesel, the son of the inventor, reported in his book[5] *Autoreise 1905* the complete dependence of the touring party on the mechanical ability, as well as on the mood, of the paid mechanic with whom they had to share their journey.

The driver himself was considered to be overtaxed by performing both the functions of driving and of controlling the machine. Often he was neither qualified nor willing to act as his own mechanic. The early petrol car owners had to be wealthy persons who did not feel inclined to tinker with a complex, greasy and often dangerous mechanical device. The division of labour in the early motorcar is evident in the dashboard layout: the gauges were in the middle so they could be read by both persons (Figure 6).

Lozier-Fahrzeuge in der Innenstadt von London

In contrast, the rear part of the car interior was kept free of visible mechanics. This was space for the passengers who were supposed not to interfere with the mechanics or the driving at all. Here the 'creature comforts' such passengers would expect were fitted: upholstery was more opulent, fabrics prevailed instead of the more workmanlike leather, rugs were present and armrests were common. Since the bodywork of early cars was commissioned by coach makers, all the comfortable features which had been developed in the course of the nineteenth century were incorporated in the passenger compartments of motorcars too. To underestimate the standard of engineering in horse-drawn vehicles at the beginning of the twentieth century would be a mistake. State-of-the-art interiors of quality coaches were highly developed and gave their passengers a comfortable ride.

The passengers in the rear of the car had a view similar to the passengers in coaches. It was a panoramic view, looking at the landscape as it unfolds.[6] This view, which does not look directly onto the oncoming road, was sometimes aided by longitudinal or even backwards seating for the passengers. The interior arrangement of early cars thus allowed two types of views to be established: whereas the driver and co-driver looked straight onto the road and into the landscape, the passengers in the rear seats viewed the landscape in a sideways fashion, preserving the older type of view associated with

Figure 4 Functional separation II: The driver is wearing a worker's flat cap, but the passengers in the rear are clearly upper class. Neubauer, H-O, Die Chronik des Automobils *(Gütersloh, Munich: 1994), p31*

Figure 5 Shared tasks: The driver of this typical two-person racing car is Louis Renault at the Paris–Madrid race (1903). His mechanic has a lower position, literally as well as socially. Frankenberg, R v, Matteucci, M, Geschichte des Automobils (Künzelsau: 1973), p130

journeys by rail or by horse-drawn coach. Moreover, the early car had clearly separated interior spaces: there was a front–rear separation between driver(s) and passengers, and the front driving position was also split longitudinally into a driver's and a mechanic's 'workplace'.

One of the attractions of early electric cars, apart from their easy starting and driving, was the relative lack of the controls and mechanical devices which were so obtrusive in early petrol cars.[7] A driver of an electric car was able to concentrate his attention on driving, instead of on minding a machine. A contemporary German science-fiction writer, intent on identifying the most advanced road vehicle, saw this as a main attraction of electric cars, securing their future: 'It will only require a short span of time until the intelligent mechanic will come down from the box of his petrol coach and give space to the simpler coachman, who will be able to steer his electric vehicle through the dense street traffic careless of the car mechanism.'[8]

When taking a leap forward to the late-twentieth-century car, it is evident that Hans Dominik's early vision of 'de-mechanised', simple driving has come true – but in the form of the petrol car. One of the functions of early driving has more or less disappeared. Most of the engine's systems are now fully automatically actuated and require hardly any attention by the driver. She or he does not have to deal with ignition timing, lubrication or fuel-supply pressure any more.

The driver has been relieved of the machinist's tasks and the driving function has properly been 'liberated'. A motorcar is no longer 'served' – it is driven.

This development is typified by changes in the types of gauges fitted to cars (Figure 6). In general, two groups of gauges, serving different purposes, are evident: gauges for monitoring the 'driving machine', and gauges supporting proper driving. The car of the 1920s had many of the former – voltmeters and ammeters, oil pressure gauges and water thermometers. Experience and technical knowledge were required to interpret the gauges in order to judge the state of the engine and its auxiliary systems. Instruments to aid driving were almost non-existent until the 1920s: even speedometers were non-standard.

The grouping of these instruments was not standardised at first; indeed even today designers have a certain amount of freedom. Whereas the speedometer is commonly placed in a central position, some sports-car manufacturers, such as Porsche, place the revolution counter in this most prominent position, thus highlighting the dominant engine function of their cars.

But the common positioning of gauges on or in the dashboard is a later feature. In very early cars there were often only switches or oil-drip sight glasses directly connected with the innards of the engine,

Figure 6 Until about 1935, gauges were commonly positioned in the middle of the dashboard so they could be read by driver and co-driver alike. Stoewer automobile, late 1920s. Appenzeller, O, Polizeirat Keller, Kraftfahrer und Kraftfahrzeug. Für Studium und Praxis (Stuttgart: 1928)

and pumps for maintaining pressure on the fuel tank. Speedometers found their place on the running boards, whereas temperature gauges were placed directly on top of the radiator, far in front of the driver but close to the mechanical components they were monitoring. This evidently is 'MS-DOS' compared with the 'Windows' of later dashboards, where there is an additional level of 'user-friendly' but indirect instrumentation.

Today there is a significant trend towards abolishing gauges altogether, or substituting them with warning lights. The trend towards digital monitoring which began in the late 1950s – for example in the Citroen DS – can be interpreted only as an interlude. It has been put forward by various designers that digital gauges cannot compete with analogue instruments where ergonomics are concerned. The latter seem to be much more readable at a glance, whereas the driver has to 'convert' digital information. Today, the typical analogue meters, which had to be interpreted by experience and knowledge, have been supplanted by warning lights. These operate with a zero/one logic, i.e. they indicate 'normal status' or 'crisis'. Knowledge of how to interpret changes is no longer essential. If a crisis is shown – for example if the oil warning light shows – the driver is supposed to stop and bring in support systems. In several types of car built in the 1990s this was even taken one step further. The warning lights themselves were hidden in a darkened dashboard, showing only very briefly when the key was turned and the ignition switched on. Such hidden information on the status of the machine is brought to light only in an emergency, in the 'crisis' mode. Often the driver will only become aware of the existence of a warning system in such a situation. Because of the potential invisibility of malfunctions in modern cars, several new types of control and warning lights have been introduced in recent years, such as warning lights for the function of air bags or the lambda function for catalytic converters.

In contrast to the trend towards fewer gauges, new types of information-giving devices that support driving itself have become more common. Examples include trip computers informing the driver about fuel consumption, average speed or the external temperature. This trend began with the clock on the dashboard. Widespread use of electronic devices took on a new significance with the introduction of satellite-based global positioning systems (GPS) providing cars with navigation systems. So far the 'battle of the systems' has not led to a standard for car-based navigation systems; nearly every large manufacturer uses its own version. In general, though, a small screen in the middle of the dashboard has become a common feature in more expensive cars, and communication technology is now firmly established as a driver's support system. Such technology will certainly acquire more importance in the future, helping to combat some of the serious problems of contemporary driving: systemic difficulties which dominate the driving experience, such as congestion, can be detected, warnings issued and traffic rerouted.

In addition to these new guidance networks, private communication devices or cellular phones compete with specific in-car accessories as car mountings and open microphones are becoming more and more common. These communication sets tend to complement the transport function. Increasingly they are used to compensate for problems encountered while driving, for example to communicate that the user is stuck in a traffic jam and will be late. Communication devices have therefore established themselves as an indispensable part and as a necessary element of today's road transport. The consequence for the interior of the car is that it tends to acquire an 'office' character, becoming a new type of mobile workplace. New forms of crossovers between the 'work' of driving and other types of work have been established: truck drivers watch TV on tiny LCD screens, company car drivers receive fax messages, and the use of cellular phones has become ubiquitous.

All this began, of course, with car radios, which were introduced in the United States in 1926.[9] In Europe they have been in use since the 1930s, although here they met resistance because it was claimed that the necessary concentration of the driver would be at risk. This seems to be a general observation: the introduction of nearly every new feature which enhances the 'living-room' character of the car interior is opposed by persons trying to defend 'pure' driving. But the defenders could soon point at the new feature of 'traffic news', introduced in the United States in the 1950s, which broadcast information about traffic jams and other hazards to drivers, thus making the radio an element of improving road safety. This 'utilitarian' aspect of car radios has gradually been supplanted by their entertainment value, allowing drivers to create and enjoy their own artificial and private sound environment. Sound quality was greatly improved by the introduction of the FM band, and today's stereo in-car entertainment systems, integrating cassette and CD players with complex speaker set-ups, have become very elaborate. Yet another car-based subculture has been established.

Back to the aspect of working a machine: there are significant relics of this task left in modern cars. Obviously, there are more traces of it in sports cars than in family cars, and more in European cars than in American cars. Gear shifting is probably the most significant relic of the activity of machine operation, requiring considerable skill when shifting with a non-synchronised gearbox. To avoid the driver being distracted, this had to be done 'automatically', without thinking. From very early times, driving education attempted to teach this by making learners avoid looking at the gear-shift lever and instead shift by hearing. But since the 1930s, technical means to facilitate this task (e.g. synchronisation) have been introduced, even in Europe.

The trend towards automatic activation of all components – not only those of the engine – received a boost in the 1990s.[10] Electrically operated windows, mirrors, door locks and seats have become a feature of even lower-priced cars. This stresses the tendency towards concentration on driving. The shift from working a driving machine to driving proper has often been explained by the fact that cars and their engines and subsystems have become more reliable. But this is only part of the picture.

Slow development of the interior: from open to enclosed car

Early cars were completely open – more or less. Even 'enclosed' bodies were open to the elements, and there were no side glass panels. The windscreen was not commonplace until 1905. From then on it was usually fitted as a standard feature, but it was either foldable or made in such a way that the top part could be tilted so the driver could peep through a slit. These ways of folding or tilting the windscreen were not only a necessary measure against the all-pervading road dust with which the windscreen quickly became coated (Figure 7). They were also a safety feature – there was no safety glass and in case of an accident the windscreen (or any glass) had better be safely out of the way of a passenger impact. Windscreen wipers to keep the glass clean when in place were introduced before the First World War; a patent (DRP 204343) on them had been taken by the Prussian Crown Prince Heinrich in 1908.[11]

Brake levers and gear sticks were outside and had to be operated by moving one's arm out of the interior. This was rather cumbersome

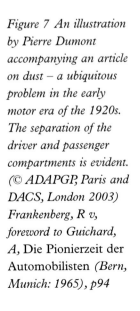

Figure 7 An illustration by Pierre Dumont accompanying an article on dust – a ubiquitous problem in the early motor era of the 1920s. The separation of the driver and passenger compartments is evident. (© ADAPGP, Paris and DACS, London 2003) Frankenberg, R v, foreword to Guichard, A, Die Pionierzeit der Automobilisten *(Bern, Munich: 1965), p94*

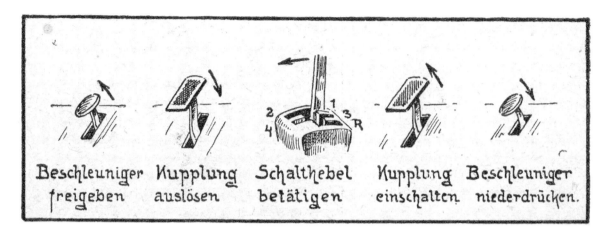

Beschleuniger   Kupplung   Schalthebel   Kupplung   Beschleuniger
   freigeben   auslösen   betätigen   einschalten   niederdrücken.

Figure 8 Serving a machine: shifting gears and using the clutch. The individual steps comprise: 'free accelerator', 'activate clutch', 'operate gear lever', 'release clutch' and 'depress accelerator'. From an Austrian study book for learner drivers, 1922. Schmal, A, Die Kunst des Fahrens (Vienna: 1922), p51

when fixed body sides were present. In consequence, the gear-shift lever and brake moved in from the outside and into the middle of the driver's compartment. This seemed at first to be a reversal of the general trend towards keeping 'machine gear' out of the interior, but on the other hand it was consistent with the tendency to integrate all components in the driver's compartment (Figure 8).

Open touring automobiles gradually became less common after the First World War, and there were several types of design before a proper 'interior' was developed. The last stage was the sedan, named *Innenlenker* (inner steerer) in Germany in the 1920s. Sometimes the driver would sit in the open, whereas his passengers enjoyed an enclosed body, as in the 'city cars' of the period. This idea had its counterpart in contemporary aeroplanes, e.g. the Junkers F13 of 1919. Thus the separation between 'operator' and 'passenger' compartments was actually strengthened. Theories were put forward to justify this arrangement: it was said that in order to fly a plane one has to feel the slipstream, and the pilots had to be in contact with the air. As late as the Second World War some pilots preferred to fly their enclosed planes with hoods pushed back for reasons of 'feeling'. In the case of road driving, similar claims have been made, but passengers, freed from all driving tasks requiring 'road contact', could enjoy an increasingly comfortable enclosed interior.

This process in which the car body became completely closed, which L T C Rolt termed 'probably the most striking phenomenon in the history of the motor trade',[12] initiated a redefinition of the car. The comfort of these types of vehicles (which became a 'delightful living room on wheels', in the words of one 1920s commentator)[13] defied the idea that cars were rugged adventurous playthings. By acquiring the comforts of a mobile home, cars progressed towards being a truly practical means of transport, keeping their passengers warm and dry. The advent of the market for closed cars, an important step on the route from 'adventure machine'[14] to transport vehicle, thus brought to an end the earliest motorcar era.

70

This leads to the question of the agents of change for the trends described. The reasons for the introduction of enclosed bodies – the 'most significant design invention', as Virginia Scharff termed it[15] – are complex. There are certainly technical reasons, caused by the tendency to use pressed steel and monocoque bodies in order to facilitate mass production. Abolishing the use of wood, which was one of the factors limiting production on fast-moving assembly lines, played a part as well.

But more significant were the changing car culture and the changing demands of buyers and drivers. First regarded by contemporary engineers as typically being for women, closed bodies were soon bought by men too. There is a controversy about the gender issue of closed cars.[16] It has been argued that men declared closed cars to be 'women's cars', but nevertheless enjoyed the comfort they provided, while still upholding the older 'sporty' and 'virile' image of open tourers. The result was clear: coupés, saloons and other closed-body styles soon took over the main share of the automobile market. But it has to be pointed out that open cars were and are coded in different ways in different car cultures. The US car culture was pioneering the trend, as it did in other features of car culture, but drivers in countries like Britain did favour open cars for a longer period.

With the introduction of fully-enclosed bodywork, a discussion arose about the dangers and merits of this feature. Similar theories as in the case of aeroplanes were debated: open bodies were obviously regarded as more 'sportsman-like'. In addition, it was assumed that they prevented the driver from becoming tired, gave a better view of the road and were much more safe. This last feature was important, since closed bodies not only cut drivers off from the surrounding traffic but also presented a danger in the case of an accident of splintering. Moreover, they induced 'limousine illness', defined as slow poisoning by carbon monoxide owing to exhaust gases being drawn in. A German textbook for gentlemen drivers of 1922 sums up:

> It would be sad if our weatherproof open air drivers gradually degenerated into limousine people as one only has the true sporty enjoyment of car driving in an open automobile. But the car is not only a sports vehicle, it also serves serious practical needs.... An argument that can be brought forward against [the inner steerer] is that the driver is separated from the outside world in such a vehicle. But this has little meaning. If one drives a little slower with an inner steerer than in an open air car ... then, as I can conclude from my own experience, accidents will be as rare as with an open car.[17]

The 1920s was the most significant period not only for the development of the closed-body car but also in terms of creating its social acceptance. There was no longer any need for specialised travel clothing, hoods or goggles for eye protection, which confirmed the transformation of the car from an item of sports equipment to a practical transport machine. By abolishing the need for specialised travel clothing and headgear, which was regarded by many as cumbersome and even disfiguring (goggled drivers were a staple feature for caricaturists), cars could be integrated into everyday life. The rule was: the more domesticated and bourgeois the user, the more closed the car.

But even the open car had its attractions as a self-contained travel capsule. Eugen Diesel describes the cluttered but comfortable interior of an open NAG (*Neue Automobil Gesellschaft*) during a journey to Italy in 1905: baskets, umbrellas, travel coats and food baskets filled the available space completely, making their car an untidy 'home from home'.

Finally, the tendency of enclosing and creating a 'mobile living room' extended even to two- and three-wheelers. This might seem rather unlikely, but the popularity of sidecars, which in the interwar period in Germany could even be enclosed with folding hoods, is symptomatic. The success of the scooter after the Second World War was partially a result of its 'civilised', partially enclosed character.

A significant trend: towards an artificial environment

The introduction and increasing dominance of the fully enclosed body had several consequences. One was that elements of the car exterior ceased to form any part of the interior (Colour plate 5). On the majority of models the inner fairings of passenger doors are now completely concealed. Visual traces of the enamelled exterior panels of the car body, which were common until the late 1980s, are substituted today by plush interior fairings (Colour plate 6). Carpets are common even in the cheapest models.

In addition, the bonnet and other exterior parts of the car are increasingly no longer visible from the interior. Sloping bonnets dictated by (symbolic) wind-tunnel design are often completely outside the driver's field of view. Drivers of contemporary cars are seldom able to see the corners of their vehicles, a fact often criticised by car sceptics. As a result, all drivers usually see from their own cars is the interior. In some cases they are unable to see a single square centimetre of the body shell, so cannot even see what the exterior colour of the vehicle is. Consequently, the 'surrounding machine' is played down for drivers and the interior becomes their visual world.

The complete enclosure of the passenger compartment was only the first step in the process of separation from the surrounding environment. Gradually, the closed car body came to be complemented by safe and well-controlled heating devices. Until the 1930s such devices were mostly simple 'add-ons': basic charcoal heaters or hot water bottles. Ways of using the waste warmth generated by the engine were later fitted as standard. These had to be incorporated into the design of the car, since the heat exchangers and the air ducts into the interior could hardly be added as an afterthought. Later still, air conditioning and cooling systems became available. But the terminology remained uncertain at first: *Klimaanlage* (air conditioning) in a 1950s German car advertisement meant an 'automatic' heating system where additional fresh air could be led in to be mixed with warm air, and air ducts were integrated.

True compressor-operated cooling systems, which had been standard for decades in American cars, caught on rather late in Europe. Today, more than a third of new cars sold in Germany come factory equipped with an air-conditioning system. To take isolation from the surroundings a step further, many expensive cars are now equipped with a very fine mesh or even activated charcoal filter to effectively remove pollen and dust. The tendency towards seemingly total independence from the environment is obvious.

Glare is also blocked out: tinted glass, originally intended as a means of reflecting sunlight to keep the interior cool, has acquired the additional function of making the compartment invisible to onlookers from the outside. Cheap add-on tinting foils were popular for a time, but suffered from blistering and splitting. Since the 1980s, many manufacturers have supplied factory-fitted tinted glass. Complete tinting of glass panels, as popular in American car culture as it is in India, is illegal in Germany and other EU countries. But the add-on detail of light tinting of side and rear glass proved to be very popular in Europe in the 1990s.

Another step in the long trend of isolating the interior is soundproofing of the car. Insulating carpets, quality cloth covers, padded mats, padded bonnets and better sound-isolating glass panels all contributed to this. Double glazing, though, was a short-lived feature, introduced in the heavy S-class Mercedes of 1992 but omitted again in more recent models. Better sound isolation, and the introduction of more and more elaborate sound systems, has led to the aural environment also becoming increasingly private. Better wiping, cleaning and demisting systems for the windscreen have contributed to the feeling of drivers and passengers that they are not connected to the road, inhabiting an artificial environment with many of the domestic features drivers are used to in their homes. (In fact, his home might be equipped in a much less elaborate way.)

This becomes evident when inclement conditions prevail outside the vehicle. Modern motorists hardly seem to be affected by sleet, snow or fog. They inhabit private 'technoid cells', connected to the outside temperature only by an electronic thermometer. But this is evidently a false proposition: under these conditions the speeding private interior can fail spectacularly. To be cut off from 'natural' phenomena like ice on the road may prove fatal if the technology means they are noticed too late.

Not only is this interior now dominated by artificial temperature and sounds, but even the driver's sensitivity is affected. Better seats, suspension systems and roadholding contribute to a completely different feel: the driver is less influenced by centrifugal and other dynamic forces and by the feel of road surfaces. Every driver of today's cars experiencing a 'classic' car is immediately aware of this: earlier cars seldom have this 'engineered' stability. Physical forces are much more evident, as there are closer connections with the road conditions.

However, one can find relics of the 'old paradigm' in some older car types still in use, such as the Citroen 2CV. In this car, with its anachronistic features, direct contact with the air outside is possible by opening a flap to allow in air directly under the windscreen. But, usually, modern cars also have fresh-air ducts in the dashboard. Folding and sliding roofs, often in addition to air conditioning, have become popular options. Ergonomics, a key word in interior design, is partly responsible for the introduction of electrical and automated elements. The ergonomic aim is to make drivers and passengers more comfortable in their speeding cells and to structure the machine according to the driver's needs.

The consequence is a trend towards a total 'uncoupling' of drivers and passengers from the elements, the surrounding landscape, the driving environment, and from other drivers in their cars. Therefore drivers are isolated in their machines and separated from the systemic transport environment. The development and the special structure of the interior heighten the image of 'lonely and free' driving. I would not go as far as to label the interior of the car as a skull, as Finch did ('In a sense, the shell of the automobile is a steel cranium, a protective enclosure.'),[18] but the isolation of drivers in their speeding cells had consequences for their feelings of protection and autistic isolation, and their attitude towards the task of driving.

Two conflicting functions of the interior: driver's workplace and living room

Tension between the two functions of the interior, which had been latent even in the open car, broke out when enclosed cars became standard. Two different ideas of the role of the interior are reflected in its design and functional elements, which illustrate this conflict clearly up to present times. Passengers enjoy the living-room quality to its full extent. But even the driver himself performs his tasks in an environment that has acquired a living-room quality.

In the 1920s and 1930s there were two firmly established car paradigms: the adventurous sports car, which was basically an open car that could be closed, and the functional sedan (or family car), which was closed but could be opened (*Cabriolimousine* in Germany). These two paradigms tended to merge in the 1960s and 1970s. Even in 'sporty' types of cars, the amenities of closed cars – such as heating or sound systems – were included, whereas the family sedan acquired a more sporty character, not only from increased power output but also from redesigned interiors. Some crossover types set trends, for example the Ford Mustang. Consequently, when cars as driving machines and cars as intimate transport vehicles took on similar shapes and configurations, the functions of the driver's workplace as a machine panel and as a piece of domestic interior converged. It was now possible to control the speeding machine and to enjoy the interior simultaneously, making the driving experience a highlight of everyday life.

A trend to include more and more features previously not found in the standard specifications confirms this. Most significant is the point where optional interior elements become standard, appearing in even the most basic models. Generally, the introduction of features in cars comes in a sequence: first, new features are sold by specialist shops, then they are made available by the manufacturers as optional extras, then these are incorporated in the 'upmarket' models, and finally they become standard equipment in basic models. This sequence can be exemplified with car heating. Until the 1930s there were several manufacturers of mobile heaters, employing different principles of generating heat. From the 1930s onwards, heat exchangers were available as expensive extras for more expensive cars. Only from the early 1960s did cheaper cars have heating systems that blew in heated or fresh air (this was called *Klimaanlagen*, air conditioning, in German car advertising, although it did not supply chilled air) as a standard feature.

One can trace influences from contemporary interior design on car interiors. Fitted carpets became a common feature at roughly the same time in homes and cars. Colour schemes, too, have been developed in close relation to each other. Wood panel inlays were a fashion in British homes and cars of the 1960s, but were not very popular in Germany. The 1970s saw an upsurge of bold colours invading the car interior. Today designers aim for a unity of appearance of all car elements. This striving for a unified appearance and these attempts to integrate every element that characterises car design have probably not yet come to an end.

Is this true in the opposite direction? Does contemporary interior car design influence interior decoration? It seems so. Car interiors are more avant-garde and could set trends. Drivers and passengers generally enjoy a 'better' – in the sense of better engineered, designed and coloured – environment in their cars than at home. Better materials and more convenient electrically operated features are present in their cars. If ergonomics or 'adaptability' of furniture is characteristic of modernism, as Sigfried Giedion argues,[19] these features will probably move from cars into homes in the future.

The split between the two functions presents a problem for interior designers aiming at a unity of appearance. Today the 'machine' elements necessary for driving are functionally separated but stylistically integrated. Since the 1950s, instruments have been concealed deep inside the dashboard. If they are boldly displayed, they are in harmony with the 'living-room' interior. A typical element that could cause functional or stylistic problems is the gear lever. To integrate it, this clearly technical component is given 'living-room design' by the same material being used for the knob as for the fairing or dashboard padding. A sack-like device conceals the lower end, which is the mechanical 'core' of this element, allowing it to move. In cars of the 1950s the gear lever often ended in a slotted frame, allowing a view of the gear-shifting mechanism.

But this stylistic concealment of technical elements seems not to be the end of the development process. The car industry is preparing for the realities of an overloaded road transport system where the act of driving may be played down even further. Development is moving beyond the navigation aids that are now options for buyers of more expensive cars. Automatically guided systems which substitute the act of driving with various means of electronic control are now beyond the experimental stage.[20]

Vehicles themselves are being adapted to the realities of car travel today: designers are increasingly regarding child passengers as important. They restructure the interior to meet the specific needs of children, integrating special seats, window shades, pouches, tables and lockers. The 'jam car' concept produced by Volkswagen specialises as a mobile family living room, complete with refrigerator and front seats that can be turned around to reunite the family circle. This vehicle significantly plays down its role as driving machine. Here the balance is shifted yet again towards the 'living-room' character.

Safety and the interior[21]

Emphasis on the 'living-room' function will probably continue to increase. The history of the introduction of seat belts makes an interesting case study of the conflicting roles of car interiors. Since the 1960s, seat belts have been broadly recognised as a major contribution to car safety. Their technology was transferred from civil aviation. Hugh de Haven, an academic safety researcher at Cornell University, introduced two-point seat belts in the United States in 1955. The patent for the three-point belt common today was granted to Swedish engineer Nils Bohlin of Volvo.

But this safety feature was fiercely rejected by users at first. Early safety belts had a feature that made them uncomfortable to wear: they were fixed, which meant that a person using them was unable to move more than a few centimetres. Obviously this conflicted with the demands of 'sitting-room' comfort and explains the strict opposition to wearing safety belts at the outset. The long struggle to make them compulsory was helped by the introduction of 'automatic' seat belts, activated by inertial blocking of the mechanism, which allowed the wearer much more movement. But still the very fact of being restricted produced – and to a certain extent still produces – opposition. The state's interference had to overcome the insistence of drivers on their 'living-room' comfort, even if their lives were at risk.

The core of the safety discussion thus was the question of the function of the interior of the car. Persons opposing safety devices did not want to have the attractions of their mobile living room spoiled. They insisted on preserving the image of the car interior as a comfortable, seemingly indestructible and invulnerable shell. The very real risk involved in driving should not manifest itself as an object like the seat belt. The industry reacted to this attitude of their customers by attempting to develop other safety devices that did not restrict the enjoyment of the interior. Preferably, they would even be hidden out of sight until the point of crisis, i.e. the crash.

This was one important incentive for the development of the air bag.[22] This device was intended to be used on its own, without having to rely on seat belts, therefore providing 'invisible' protection which did not get in the way of a comfortable interior. It did not fulfil the hopes of its designers, since it works properly only in combination with safety belts and head rests. These continue to be the reminder that the moving living room is driven in a very dangerous and potentially lethal environment.

Safety belts have now been accepted after being made compulsory for drivers and passengers. Since the automatic roll mechanism has made them more comfortable, there has been a tendency to adapt their appearance to their surroundings. Coloured seat belts, matching the colour scheme of the interior, are now quite common. More significant is the complete concealment of their mechanism. In today's passenger cars the roll mounted near the floor is completely invisible: the seat belt disappears into the interior fairings. This serves the purpose of integrating 'technical' elements and keeping the 'living-room' interior visually intact.

Another solution for making the car interior safer actually enhanced its 'living-room' quality: the trend of padding the dashboard and recessing switches and levers in order to 'defuse' hard edges and to soften their 'secondary impact' in case of a collision. Crash tests in the late 1950s had proved this measure to be very efficient. It was slowly introduced by Mercedes Benz and by US manufacturers as an optional extra. A decade later nearly all cars had padded upper and lower dashboard edges and soft knobs, thus transforming the somewhat harsh-looking metal dashboards into integrated parts of an interior dominated by fabrics, plastics, fairings and coverings. 'Naked' enamelled sheet metal later disappeared from the instrument panel, and finally from doors as well.

At the other end of the spectrum, apparently moving away from the integrated 'living-room' image, sports cars seem to display more of their 'technical' interior elements – from a prouder design of their gauges to 'racing' or 'rallye' gear-lever knobs and pedal surfaces. Even four-point or 'garter' belts, as used in racing, are found in sports cars. But even these cars, intended or sold as 'pure driving machines', such as the Porsche 911SC with its reduced interior padding and fairing, kept a minimum of 'living-room' comforts. Moreover, 'rallye' details in contemporary cars are seldom only functional elements. Mostly they are symbolic add-ons, transforming still comfortable interiors only visually into 'sporty' cockpits.

Even the tendency towards reintroduction of open roadsters and 'rag-top' cars, which occupied a growing share of late-twentieth-century car markets, is only superficially contrary to the growing intimacy of the car interior. Motivated by the opposition to and dissatisfaction with the described tendencies towards speeding living rooms, roadsters seem to offer the desired distinction quality by recreating the older image from the 1920s of pure driving machines. But even these open cars today share the amenities of enclosed bodies – for example two-layer tops, efficient heating and sound isolation – and they are driven more and more in enclosed mode. Therefore they could be labelled post-modern roadsters. The trend towards a closed, intimate and isolated interior is unbroken. The driving-machine image is not a substitution of the living-room image, but an addition with only a slight twist.

This has consequences for the attitudes of drivers. They feel detached from the environment and from the surrounding traffic in their private interior. In consequence they feel less part of a system and more a 'lonely-and-free' individual in an isolated vehicle. This goes far beyond the observation that 'the driving experience became easier, and at the same time somewhat passive'.[23] Recent developments in electronic devices aim at interfering with the autonomy of drivers from different directions: there is automatically activated braking when the distance to the vehicle in front decreases, or power-assisted emergency braking. These devices 'help' drivers to avoid a crash, but in fact take over central driving functions and make drivers more passive. Experiments with fully automated driving without active driver participation are much discussed now, but even below this level 'the system' will be able to interfere, for example by limiting the top speed when entering towns. The required technologies already exist – introducing them is the question. The trend towards telematics – 'dialogised' guiding or automated driving devices – fits into the history of automation of automobility: first the burden of 'serving' the machine was taken from the driver, and now driving in the traffic system and navigating is on the verge of being replaced by electronics.

It is remarkable that these modern electronic devices which alter the act of driving are quite unobtrusive in the interior. They hardly make their presence felt, but they influence the 'user surface' of the car indirectly. Even so, passive drivers can be made to enjoy their isolation. A case in point is the traffic jam. This increasingly common event – which could be described as the maximum intrusion of the systemic into the illusion of the private, the denying of the 'freedom of the road' by the dreaded system – does nothing to destroy the myth of 'lonely and free' driving. On the contrary: in the traffic jam drivers, relieved from their driving tasks, are able to enjoy the 'living-room' features of the vehicle's interior to its fullest extent. Comfortable interiors therefore tend to make the demands and systemic restrictions of modern traffic tolerable and even offer ample compensation.

To conclude, this article has pointed out that the negation of the systemic aspect of road transport and the stress on isolated, individualistic driving have been strong factors in the success of the car.[24] Of course the image of isolated driving and the consequent playing down of the system have complex causes. But the situation of modern drivers confined to their speeding living rooms has played its part in keeping alive this objectively obsolete image of antisystemic individual motor vehicles, even in the highly systemic mass transport systems of the late twentieth century.

Summary

The development of the interior of passenger cars has reflected changing attitudes towards the act of driving and shows different concepts of the interaction between driver and vehicle. Therefore, the history of the motor-vehicle interior, its ergonomics and decoration, is significant for the most important man–machine relation that has been established so far. Interpreting the passenger compartment as a crossover between 'cockpit' and fast yet intimate living room helps us to understand the attraction of motor vehicles.

Notes and references

1 Recent texts have included: Gartmann, D, *Auto Opium: A Social History of American Automobile Design* (London, New York: 1994); Kieselbach, R, 'Vom Torpedo-Phaeton zur Ganzstahl-Limousine: Zur Geschichte des Auto-Designs', in Zeller, R (ed.), *Das Automobil in der Kunst 1886–1986*, exhibition catalogue (Munich: 1986), pp287–97; Möser, K, 'Autodesigner und Autonutzer im Konflikt: der Fall des Spoiler', in Schmid, G (ed.), *Technik und Gesellschaft. Jahrbuch 10: Automobil und Automobilismus* (Frankfurt am Main, New York: 1999), pp219–36.

2 See, for example, Ludvigsen, K E, 'A century of automobile comfort and convenience', *Automotive Engineering*, 103 (1995), pp27–34.

3 Möser, K, 'The First World War and the creation of desire for cars in Germany', in Strasser, S, McGovern, C and Judt, M (eds), *Getting and Spending: European and American Consumer Societies in the Twentieth Century* (Washington DC: 1998), pp195–222

4 Dr St, 'Kauf und Behandlung eines Automobils', *Der Stein der Weisen*, 28 (1902), p43

5 Diesel, E, *Autoreise 1905* (Stuttgart: 1941)

6 Schivelbusch, W, *Geschichte der Eisenbahnreise: Zur Industrialisierung von Raum und Zeit* (Frankfurt am Main: 1977)

7 Mom, G, *Geschiedenis van de Auto van Morgen: Cultuur en Techniek van de Elektrische Auto* (Deventer: 1997)

8 Hans Dominik in 1904, quoted by J Wachtel in the preface to *Querschnitt durch frühe Automobilzeitschriften* (Bern, Munich: n.d.), p11

9 Bussien, R (ed), *Automobiltechnisches Handbuch*, 14th edn (Berlin: 1941), p1231

10 Ludvigsen, K E, note 2

11 von Seherr-Thoss, H-C, *Die deutsche Automobilindustrie: Eine Dokumentation von 1886 bis 1979*, 2nd edn (Stuttgart: 1979), p37

12 Rolt, L T C, *Horseless Carriage: The Motor-car in England* (London: 1950), p113

13 Scharff, V, *Taking the Wheel: Women and the Coming of the Motor Age* (New York: 1991), p125

14 Mom, G, 'Das "Scheitern" des frühen Elektromobils (1895–1925): Versuch einer Neubewertung', *Technikgeschichte*, 64 (1997), p271

15 Scharff, V, note 13, p122

16 Scharff, V, note 13; Scharff, V, 'Gender, electricity, and automobility', in Wachs, M and Crawford, M (eds), *The Car and the City: The Automobile, the Built Environment, and Daily Urban Life* (Ann Arbor, MI: 1992), pp75–85

17 Filius (Schmal, A), *Die Kunst des Fahrens. Praktische Winke, ein Automobil oder Motorrad richtig zu lenken* (Vienna: 1922), p176f

18 Finch, C, *Highways to Heaven: The AUTObiography of America* (New York: 1991), p327

19 Giedion, S, *Die Herrschaft der Mechanisierung: Ein Beitrag zur anonymen Geschichte* (Frankfurt am Main: 1982), pp528–51

20 Schuh, H, 'Freie Fahrt in der Kolonne: Intelligente Elektronik koppelt Fahrzeuge aneinander', *Die Zeit* (17 June 1999), p27f. This trend was criticised by Wolfgang Zängl in *Der Telematik-Trick: Elektronische Autobahngebühren, Verkehrsleitsysteme und andere Milliardengeschäfte* (Munich: 1995).

21 See new literature on safety technology: Gnadler, R, 'Sicherheitstechnik heute und morgen', in *Mobilität und Gesellschaft: 150 Jahre Carl Benz* (Stuttgart: Daimler-Benz AG, n.d. [1996]), pp53–66; Niemann, H and Hermann, A (eds), *Geschichte der Straßenverkehrssicherheit im Wechselspiel zwischen Fahrzeug, Fahrbahn und Mensch* (Bielefeld: 1999); Weishaupt, H, *Die Entwicklung der passiven Sicherheit im Automobilbau von den Anfängen bis 1980 unter besonderer Berücksichtigung der Daimler-Benz AG* (Bielefeld: 1999).

22 Möser, K, 'Lebensretter für Insassen: der Airbag', *Schweizerische Technische Zeitschrift*, 7–8 (1998), p128

23 Finch, C, note 18, pp327, 283

24 Möser, K, *Geschichte des Autos* (Frankfurt am Main, New York: 2002), chapter 18.

Peter Lyth

Reverse thrust: American aerospace dominance and the British challenge in jet engines, 1941–58

At the end of the Second World War the United States dominated civil aircraft production and was at least five years ahead of Britain, the only other nation at the time with the capacity to manufacture commercial airliners. The British were aware of their deficiency and were determined to catch up. Government policy aimed to foster a new generation of British civil aircraft in order to provide continued employment in the aircraft industry and save the state-owned airlines (BOAC, BEA and BSAA) from spending precious funds on US types. There was also a view, widely held in government and in the civil service, that Britain needed a major civil-aircraft industry in order to maintain the prestige and technological prowess befitting a great power. The problem was how to go about it. Should Britain simply copy the best airliners coming out of the United States, staying abreast with, but not getting ahead of, proven technology? Or should it attempt to leapfrog the Americans by exploiting its lead in jet engines? It chose the latter path and made the jet engine 'the basis for a bold but flawed challenge' to American postwar domination.[1] Thus turbo-prop and pure jet engines were fitted to conventionally-designed aircraft such as the Vickers Viscount and the de Havilland Comet 1, the world's first jet-propelled passenger aircraft. Then, in 1954, the Comets began crashing and the risks of the leapfrog strategy became painfully clear.

This paper considers the background to the Comet's development in the 1940s and the policies which led Britain to seek economic revival on the basis of the narrow technological advantage represented by leadership in jet engines. It also spotlights the Comet itself, both as a symbol of the new Elizabethan age of the 1950s and as a key artefact of Britain's much-vaunted jet engine programme.

The European jet, 1935–45

The jet engine, as one of the leading researchers in the field has pointed out, is a striking example of the commercialisation of military technology.[2] Like a number of other innovations which changed the lives of ordinary people in the twentieth century, it was born out of the Second World War.[3] However, it was in the 1930s that the principles of its operation were first studied and understood. Until that time no-one conceived of an aircraft power plant as being anything other than a sophisticated internal combustion engine, a technology borrowed from automobile engineering. The two figures credited with first seeing the potential of jets are the Englishman Frank Whittle and the German Hans von Ohain.[4] Whittle's patent for a turbojet engine was registered in 1930, so there is some basis for seeing him as the father of the jet. However, because there was a six-year delay before Whittle's ideas gained acceptance, the Englishman was overtaken by Ohain, who had begun a fruitful collaboration with the Heinkel aircraft company and who ran a static test of his first engine in 1935. From this time onwards, the endeavours of Whittle and Ohain proceeded neck-and-neck, although they worked independently in Britain and Germany and were unaware of the other's progress. In 1937 Whittle ran the first test of his engine, the W1, but two years later Ohain's He-S8B engine powered the world's first jet-propelled flight in the Heinkel He-178 aircraft. Whittle had to wait until 1941 until his W1 engine powered the first British jet aircraft, the Gloster E28/39 (Figure 1), by which stage another Heinkel, the He-280, was flying with two Ohain He-S8A jet engines.[5] By 1944 both the British and the Germans had jet-propelled fighters in operational use: the Gloster Meteor, with a developed version of the Whittle jet, known as the Rolls-Royce Derwent, and the Messerschmitt Me-262, with Junkers Jumo 004 jets.

Figure 1 Gloster E28/39, the first British jet aircraft. (Deutsches Museum)

By the end of the war the Germans had at least three separate full-scale company-based jet engine programmes in progress, as American and British interrogators discovered to their astonishment in the summer of 1945. Ohain's original test engine, the He-S3B, had been built for simplicity with a centrifugal compressor like Whittle's, but Heinkel had then proceeded to more advanced designs like the He-S30 with axial-flow compressors. Meanwhile at Junkers, Germany's leading engine maker, Anselm Franz had led the development of the Jumo 004, a simpler axial-flow turbojet, which went into mass production and powered the Me-262 fighter. A third programme at BMW produced the Bramo 003 engine, which featured a counter-rotating compressor, different from both the Jumo 004 and the Heinkel He-S30. Ultimately it was this Heinkel design, incorporating both rotors *and* stators, which became the standard configuration for commercial jet engines.[6]

On this evidence it is clear that the Germans were decisively ahead in the field by the spring of 1945. And this feat is all the more extraordinary when one considers that they lacked vital raw materials with which to make heat-resistant turbine blades, such as nickel, cobalt and manganese, and that their work was continually disrupted by the Allied bombing campaign.[7] By contrast the British were proceeding on a narrower front, with Whittle's relatively primitive design remaining the main empirical reference point for British engine manufacturers. As in Germany, all the main manufacturers had begun jet programmes, but without the same conceptual range and variety as their opponents. De Havilland, for example, announced the successful trial of its Vampire jet fighter in 1945, powered by the company's own Goblin engine, which used a centrifugal compressor, like the Rolls-Royce Derwent. Frank Whittle himself was to leave the industry, a somewhat disillusioned man, in 1948, while his company, Power Jets Ltd, was nationalised and reduced to the status of a research establishment. The business of mass-producing his creation shifted to the private engine firms, who by the end of the war were beginning to consider peace-time applications for the new technology. Rolls-Royce, the leading company, decided that it would switch entirely from piston engines to turbine-driven power plants and had initiated its own research programme, advancing somewhat beyond the hitherto sacrosanct Whittle design as early as 1944 with the Nene engine.[8]

There is not much doubt that had Germany not been defeated it would have led the world in jet engine development in both the military and civil sectors. As it was, the Allies not only enjoyed a windfall at the end of the war, with both German engines and German engineers falling into their hands, but they also had the satisfaction of seeing the race leader stopped dead in its tracks: German aero-engine production was halted and did not resume to any significant degree before the 1960s. The British were now in front, but for how long? And where had the Americans been?

The American aero-engine industry, 1930–45

The American aircraft industry in the 1930s had been innovative and successful. Civil airframe builders like Douglas, Lockheed and Boeing had produced a new generation of transport aircraft with all-metal, stressed-skin construction and retractable undercarriages. These aircraft were powered by air-cooled, radial piston engines manufactured either by the Wright Aeronautical Company or its rival Pratt & Whitney. Neither company had any inkling of the work being carried out in Europe on the jet engine, or of its potential. Radial piston engines were the bedrock of their commercial success: they were strong and dependable, gave good economic performance to the new airlines springing up in America and were the principal source of the companies' profits.[9]

The fact that American engine manufacturers carried out no work on jet engines before the war is not surprising: British and German companies (with the notable exception of Heinkel) did not do so either. What is more striking is that there was no activity among the scientific communities in universities and government-sponsored research establishments. Why, for instance, did America produce no Ohain or Whittle? The answer may lie with the fact that those American research establishments that did work on aeronautical science tended to confine their activities to solving problems already encountered by the engine companies with *existing* technology.[10] And as for the companies themselves, the high degree of competition between them meant that *fundamental* research was not carried out or was carried out by each company separately, entailing a great duplication of effort.[11]

While jets may have been ignored by the Americans in the 1930s, there was important work being done in the United States on turbines and turbine-driven power plants, for example by Eastman Jacobs at the National Advisory Committee on Aeronautics (NACA). More significantly, knowledge on turbines was acquired from work on piston engine superchargers. Superchargers had been around since the First World War and were especially applicable to aircraft engines because they substantially increased the intake of air at high altitudes. Their power was drawn from a turbine driven by the engine's exhaust gas and applied through gearing to the crankshaft. The technology of supercharger turbines progressed steadily during the interwar years in the United States and a whole range of new nickel alloys were created to build temperature-resistant fan blades: the same technology, with similar theoretical problems, which was required to build jet engine turbines on the other side of the Atlantic. Moreover, the technology was pushed forward not only by the aero-engine builders – Wright and

Pratt & Whitney – but also by companies that previously had been associated with large stationary turbines for power generation. It was Sanford Moss's work with General Electric (GE) which produced the Moss turbocharger, a device that turned the B-17 bomber from an aircraft approaching obsolescence at the time of Pearl Harbor into one of the most effective offensive weapons of the Second World War.

Thus the intellectual climate in the United States at the beginning of the Second World War can be summarised as being *scientifically* conducive towards jet engine development, but *commercially* very much less so. The traditional engine makers were complacent, although they possessed crucial technical know-how from their work with super-chargers, and official opinion was doubtful. In 1940, for example, the American Committee of the National Academy of Sciences stated in a report that: 'In its present state, and even considering the improvements possible in adopting the higher temperatures proposed for the immediate future, the gas turbine could hardly be considered a feasible application to airplanes, mainly because of the difficulty in complying with the stringent weight requirements imposed by aeronautics.'[12]

Into this environment was introduced the catalyst of war, which, as so often happens with major technological breakthroughs, accelerated the pace of research and converted sceptical minds. In 1940 news of Whittle's jet was brought to the United States by Sir Henry Tizard, the head of the British Air Ministry's Aeronautical Research Department.[13] Then in March 1941 General 'Hap' Arnold of the US Army Air Corps visited England and learnt of the Whittle engine's forthcoming test in the Gloster E28/39. Arnold was an immediate convert and saw the British engine as the seed corn for a whole new field in the American aeronautical industry. Within months a disassembled Whittle engine was crossing the Atlantic, under a veil of military secrecy, and heading not for Wright or Pratt & Whitney, but for GE. Arnold chose GE partly because of the work the company had done for the Air Force on the Moss turbocharger, partly because of its experience with new heat-resistant alloys like Timkin and Vitallium, and partly, it seems, because it was *not* Wright or Pratt & Whitney and therefore had more to gain from pioneering a new technology.[14]

It is easy to see the British government's decision to hand the Americans the jet engine as an act of extraordinary and misguided generosity, and this is certainly the way some commentators have seen it.[15] The explanation, of course, lies in the war. In the autumn of 1941, when the Whittle engine was sent to America, the news from the Soviet Union was not encouraging and the United States was still neutral. Britain remained vulnerable to Nazi invasion and many people still considered that such an invasion was likely. For the British, sharing the jet engine with its best potential ally made political as well as strategic sense against the background of the war and the hard bargaining which was going on over the Lend-Lease Agreement.[16]

Having obtained the British engine, however, the Americans worked with customary speed. Indeed, the speed with which General Electric, Westinghouse and airframe makers like Bell and Lockheed converted Whittle's invention into prototype engines, and very soon thereafter into jet fighters, should have given the British a lesson, if they needed one, on competition with American industry. The US was able, by virtue of its size, resources and advanced production techniques, to adopt the inventions of others long after the initial research process had been completed and still deliver production models *before* the inventors did.

By the end of 1942 the Bell Airacomet XP59 was flying with the GE I-14 engine, a copy of the Whittle design, and in 1943 de Havilland's Whittle-type engine, the Goblin, was being reproduced by Westinghouse for installation in the Lockheed Shooting Star jet fighter.

Britain's lead, 1945–54

The initial transfer of jet engine technology from Britain to America can be seen as a direct consequence of the Second World War. After 1945, however, the transfer continued in the same direction against the backdrop of the Cold War. American research was catching up, and its progress received a major boost from the assistance of German scientists after the end of the war in Europe. But Britain still retained a clear lead in jet engines, one of the few remaining areas in high technology where she could make this claim.

With the exception of Napier, all the British engine manufacturers had made a somewhat dramatic switch to turbine technology. Indeed, the amount of turbine activity in Britain in 1946 was remarkable: de Havilland was working on turbines, Bristol on heat exchangers, Armstrong-Siddeley on the design of their Sapphire jet engine, and Rolls-Royce on a whole range of engines including the Derwent, the Nene and the highly advanced Avon.[17] British plans included turboprop as well as pure jet engines, but piston engines were definitely seen as obsolete. This is surprising, not only because the manufacturers still had successful piston engines in production – for example Rolls-Royce with its liquid-cooled, in-line units (Merlin, Griffon) and Bristol with its sleeve-valve radial engines (Centaurus) – but also because jet engines were by no means a fully-developed aircraft propulsion system and many important commercial as well as technical questions remained to be answered.

Jet engines consist of compressors, combustion chambers and turbines, and nobody at this stage was entirely sure of the best way to design and build any of them.[18] The choice of compressor, for example, remained a major locus of contention. Should it be of the simpler centrifugal type adopted by Whittle, or should it be of the axial-flow design favoured in the later German engines? In Britain this debate divided the Whittle supporters from the followers of the scientist A A Griffith. Griffith had done important work on axial-flow technology in the 1930s for the Royal Aircraft Establishment, but had preferred the turboprop solution to the pure jet engine and as a result had not garnered the laurels of fame as Whittle had.[19] The axial-flow compressor, which offered a much higher thrust per frontal area, eventually prevailed, but in the late 1940s it was still uncertain which design would become the standard, particularly as the axial-flow compressor required far-reaching scientific skills at the foremost edge of thermodynamic theory.[20] Other problems related to whether jet engines could be mass-produced and how the very high temperatures in the turbine were to be dealt with: by using the new heat-resistant alloys which the Americans had in abundant supply, or with the turbine blade cooling pioneered by the Germans?[21]

Although mechanically far simpler than the reciprocating engine, the jet required a level of engineering sophistication beyond that which was found in the majority of British engine companies in the prewar era. So why did Rolls-Royce, Bristol, Armstrong-Siddeley and de Havilland throw themselves with such abandon into jet and turboprop manufacturing? An explanation lies in the greater degree of cooperation that had been built up between the British companies during the war, manifest in the Gas Turbine Collaboration Committee (GTCC). This committee, which was set up by the government in 1941 and to which all the companies sent experts, met on a regular basis until well into the 1950s. It functioned with a high degree of openness, initially to make Whittle's findings available to all the British manufacturers, later as a general forum for the exchange of information on jet engine development. It represented a degree of collaboration between private companies which would have been quite impossible in the United States, with its strong antitrust tradition. Moreover, in addition to cooperation between the companies, the jet engine received a boost in Britain from active government involvement. We tend to think of Frank Whittle as an inventive genius from humble origins who fought single-handedly against a hostile scientific establishment to gain acceptance for his ideas.[22] In fact he seems to have been a catalyst in a wider government-coordinated programme of technological research. As early as 1943, the premier British engine builder, Rolls-Royce, received a letter from Sir Stafford Cripps, Minister of Aircraft Production, in which he had written that 'nothing, repeat, nothing is to stand in the way of the development of the jet engine'.[23] The historian David Edgerton has written of Britain's technological culture at this time in terms of a contrast between the Americans, who 'were felt to be unimaginative and unsubtle', and the English, who 'had daring and unconventional boffins'.[24] Whether or not this is true, the government, in the shape of the Air Ministry and the Ministry of Supply, seized on their 'boffin' (Whittle) and his invention (the jet engine) to spearhead the advance of an important industrial sector. And as the end of the war approached, British officials saw a new window of opportunity in American 'backwardness', namely the early application of jet engines to *civil* aircraft.

The Comet

'There is no reason whatever', wrote a senior civil servant in a letter to Cripps in early 1946, 'why Britain should not design and produce civil aircraft as good as, if not better than America.'[25] Whether or not this was realistic, there were many senior figures in the postwar Labour government who thought this was true, although the same cannot be said of Britain's newly nationalised international airlines. The United States led the world in transport aircraft at the end of the war with new four-engined types such as the Douglas DC-4 and the Lockheed Constellation. Could Britain catch up? A start had been made with the Brabazon Committee and its list of five new civil types which were to be developed for British airlines. From its beginnings in 1943, this committee had stressed the need to capitalise on Britain's jet engine know-how in the construction of transport aircraft. Not all the Brabazon types succeeded, of course, and at least one was an unmitigated disaster (the Bristol Brabazon). But two path-breaking airliners did emerge from the programme in the early 1950s: the Vickers Viscount and the de Havilland Comet (Figure 2), and both were distinguished by their turbine-driven power plants.

There is no question, however, that the early application of jet engines to commercial aircraft by the British was a risk and a gamble. At the end of the war there was concern on both sides of the Atlantic that jets, while fine for fighters and bombers, would prove too unreliable for commercial aircraft and have too high a fuel consumption for airline operation. Moreover, the airlines themselves could hardly imagine passengers flying at speeds of 500 mph and there were even doubts (reminiscent of the early railways in the nineteenth century!) that the human body could withstand it. The fact that jet engines and cabin pressurisation would actually make flying *more* comfortable at high speeds and altitudes seems to have been little understood.

Of the five Brabazon types, the de Havilland Comet was by far the biggest gamble. The chronology of the Comet's history is well known. Conceived as a four-engined jet mail plane, it quickly evolved into a passenger aircraft and made its first flight in 1949. It entered service with the flag-carrier BOAC to great acclaim in 1952 and in 1953 it enjoyed a year of enormous popularity with passengers and considerable commercial success. Then, eighteen months after their introduction, Comets began breaking up in midair, and in the summer of 1954 they had to be withdrawn. There followed a prolonged period during which a Comet was tested to destruction in a pressure tank

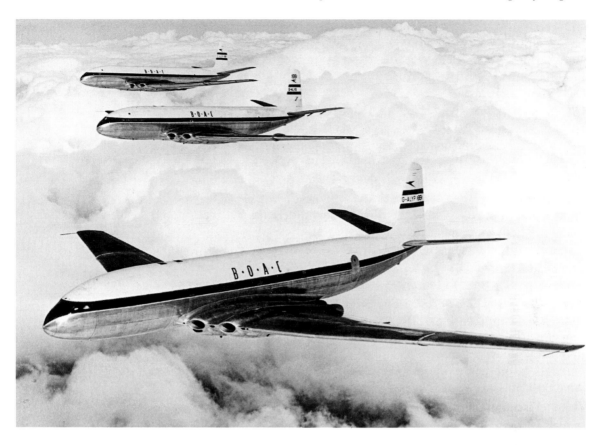

Figure 2 De Havilland Comet 1, the world's first jet airliner. (Deutsches Museum)

before the cause of the crashes was finally revealed as metal fatigue of the pressurised fuselage. Only in 1958 did the aircraft reappear, with a much smaller fanfare, as the Comet 4.

Behind these bare facts is a more subtle picture which focuses on the idea of the Comet as a symbol of Britain's postwar industrial recovery. The aircraft itself was conventional in design, without the swept wings that were being adopted on military jets in the United States and even in the Soviet Union by this stage.[26] It was also quite small, carrying a maximum of 44 first-class passengers at a time when its main piston-engined rivals (the DC-6, the Super Constellation) could carry at least 70. It was very fast, of course, cruising at nearly 500 mph at 35,000 feet. But despite its popularity in the year of Queen Elizabeth II's coronation, it was very much a prestige vehicle in terms of the air transport industry, indeed a throwback to the prewar era of elitist air travel. An instructive way of seeing the Comet is as a showcase for its jet engines, which were, initially at least, the Ghost jets manufactured by de Havilland's own engine company. The Ghost was a development of the wartime Goblin, built during the war by de Havilland to the Whittle formula with a centrifugal compressor. It was a good engine in itself, but it was not the best engine for the Comet, either in terms of thrust or fuel economy. The best engine, and the engine which was planned for the Comet, was the Rolls-Royce Avon – one of Britain's first two commercial jet engines with an axial-flow compressor (the other one was the Armstrong Siddeley Sapphire).[27] The Avon was more powerful and inherently superior to engines with centrifugal compressors such as the Derwent, Nene (Figure 3) and Ghost.[28] Unfortunately, it also took almost seven years to develop and was simply not ready in time to power the first Comets in 1952. De Havilland therefore installed their own Ghost engines in the aircraft until the Avon was available.

It has never been suggested that the de Havilland Ghost engines were in any way responsible for the Comet crashes, or that their replacement with Avons would have made any difference. The cause of the crashes was simply lack of knowledge on the part of the de Havilland airframe company of the dynamics of metal fatigue in pressurised aircraft cabins – an ignorance which it shared with every aircraft manufacturer in the world. The deeper lesson of the Comet story, however, is the penalty which is paid by pioneers and first users: in other words, being first is not always the most economical way of getting into business. While the Americans patiently built up experience with military types like the Boeing B-47 and B-52 bombers before finally launching the Boeing 707 in 1958, the British adopted a policy of jets-at-all-cost and accepted an undistinguished airframe in the Comet to win 'the race' with the Americans. That the British government saw jet engine competition with the Americans in terms of 'a race' is apparent from government records. Indeed, the jet seems to have become as much an obsession for the British as the atom bomb had been for the Americans: it was seen as a key to the maintenance of Britain's economic and strategic power, however narrow a technological basis it represented. It was argued that Britain needed to concentrate on manufacturing products which its economic rivals could not match in engineering sophistication and which yielded a high unit gain. Aircraft were such products and the only way aircraft could be sold in the face of the entrenched power of the American manufacturers was to put jet engines in them. The idea that Britain was engaged in a race with the Americans is evident in the tone and phrasing of an important statement of policy by the Minister of Supply, Duncan Sandys, in 1952 (the year of the Comet's launch):

> During the next few years the UK has an opportunity, which may not recur, of developing aircraft manufacture as one of our major export industries. On whether we grasp this opportunity and so establish firmly an industry of the utmost strategic and economic importance, our future as a great nation may depend. [...] If our aircraft industry is not sustained by export orders, it will not be able, qualitatively, to meet all our own needs, and we shall have to resign ourselves indefinitely to dependence on America.

Figure 3   Rolls-Royce Nene engine, 1955. (Deutsches Museum)

Sandys reckoned that Britain's competitive position was strong because British costs were lower than American costs and aircraft did not lend themselves 'to the mass production technique in which the Americans excel, to the same extent as other products such as motor cars. [...] In this particular industry (aircraft and aircraft engines) we are less exposed to the competition to which we are so vulnerable elsewhere.'[29]

Even assuming that Sandys' analysis was correct, which is doubtful given that aircraft production eventually proved itself to be as amenable to 'mass production' as any other technologically advanced product, the idea of the 'race' was misplaced in dealing with the Americans. This is partly because the Americans themselves did not conceive of civil aircraft production in such terms, but more importantly because such a contest could not be won, at least in the long term, against a nation with far greater human and material resources. The best indication of this is in the field of testing. The key to the whole lengthy and complicated process of aero-engine development – indeed aerodynamic progress generally – is the wind tunnel. This piece of equipment is vital in testing the limits in performance of new engines and aircraft shapes, yet Britain was desperately short of them. A senior British scientific advisor to government wrote in 1953:

> The USA now have 5 times as much equipment for the collection of basic information and 3 times as much for the testing of complete aircraft models as we have in the UK. We lost the initiative in aerodynamics soon after the 1939–45 war. At least one high Mach-number tunnel of reasonable size will be required even when the present building programme at National Gas Turbine Establishment has been completed.[30]

The shortage of wind tunnels and altitude chambers for testing engines was symptomatic of the threadbare infrastructure involved in the British approach to jet aircraft and engine development. The British, to use Edgerton's formulation, relied on brilliant individuals – 'boffins' – to make up for the lack of scientific hardware that the Americans possessed in comparative abundance. They were short of resources, both money and raw materials, so they used their brains. Unfortunately this was no longer enough: making aircraft and engines was far more complicated and expensive in the 1950s than it had been in the 1930s. To ensure a decent return on the investment in research and development required to make a jet engine, an even larger investment had to be made in trials and permanent testing equipment. And this is where the more thorough approach of the Americans ('unimaginative and unsubtle' in Edgerton's phrase) paid its eventual dividend: they may have lost the 'race' to get the first passenger jet aircraft into the air in 1952, but they won the competition to dominate the jet age after 1958.

The responsibility for what one might call the 'Comet syndrome' (but which refers equally to other British hi-tech projects which were attempted on a shoestring, for example the high-speed Advanced Passenger Train in the 1970s) lies with the government, the only institution that had the power and resources to provide the basic testing infrastructure needed by the British engine companies. In 1955 engineers from Rolls-Royce visited the American engine testing facilities at NACA in Cleveland, Ohio. They were shocked and delighted at the lavish extent of the installation in comparison with what they had to work with in Britain. As the aviation historian Virginia Dawson has put it, 'they lamented that their company had been "led up the garden path" by the Labour and Conservative governments, that had promised "to provide full-scale test facilities for the British gas turbine industry since 1945"'. The politicians had failed the scientists and 'although in 1955 the British made plans to build a large altitude test facility to test full-scale engines at the National Gas Turbine Establishment at Pyestock, with a second at Bedford, these facilities came too late to recoup the British lead'.[31] The race was lost.

Reverse thrust – the American response

The Comet jet airliner is a perfect example of the characteristic British approach to high technology and a prime artefact of Britain in the 1950s. The crashes of 1954, however, shook the confidence of the whole industry. The fantasy-inducing enthusiasm of 1949, when it was expected that everyone would be flying in jet aircraft by 1954, was replaced by traumatised inaction, so that plans to produce other British jet airliners like the Vickers V-1000 were shelved. The V-1000 was to have been based on the Vickers Valiant bomber, which was already flying with Avon engines. Had this project gone ahead it would have reflected American practice, which allowed for the protracted trial of new designs in military versions before they were adopted for passenger-carrying roles. The best example of this approach was the Boeing 707 airliner, which went through earlier incarnations as the Boeing B-47 and B-52 bombers, and the Boeing KC-135 jet tanker.

After the Comet crashes, the American engine companies moved inexorably to the fore in jet engines. In the late 1940s the two senior companies, Wright and Pratt & Whitney, had pursued research and development into jet engines for *military* aircraft, while continuing with the still-profitable manufacture of radial piston engines for the civil market. Wright engines, which had begun with the famous 575 hp Cyclone in 1931, were raised in power output to around 3850 hp by 1955 – ironically by using the same turbine technology, known as 'compounding', which was used to build pure jet engines.[32] But Wright was to be the major casualty of the shift to jet engines: after collaborating with Armstrong-Siddeley to build the Sapphire engine under licence (the J-65 in US designation), it got into severe difficulties with its successor, the J-67, and was forced to abandon aero-engine production altogether.[33] Pratt & Whitney began its experience with jets by acquiring a licence to the Rolls-Royce Nene (the J-42) and followed this with a further Rolls-Royce design, the Tay, during the Korean war. The latter engine, known as the J-48, was the last and the most powerful American jet based on the original Whittle concept with a centrifugal compressor. In the early 1950s, Pratt & Whitney moved out of the shadow of the British manufacturers with its own axial-flow engine – the famous J-57 – incorporating an innovative twin-spool compressor.[34] This engine enabled the company to shift production entirely to jet engines; the J-57 not only powered numerous American combat aircraft, but it also, in its civil version, powered the Boeing 707 and Douglas DC-8 airliners (Figure 4). Meanwhile, GE, which had begun its jet engine history by assembling the Whittle engine for General Arnold, had since developed its own expertise and in 1947 had brought out the 12-stage axial-flow J-47. This was immensely successful in military application, powering the F-86 Sabre jet and, more significantly for civil transport, the early swept-wing Boeing B-47 bombers.[35] GE followed this in 1954 with

Figure 4 Douglas DC-8 jet airliner in flight. (Deutsches Museum)

the J-79, an engine built in response to Pratt & Whitney's J-57, and incorporating for the first time the innovation of variable stators in its six-stage compressor. By the mid-1950s the two companies were on their own, innovating for themselves, and the only remaining American companies producing jet engines.

It is interesting that while British civil airframe design did not keep pace with British aero-engine development, in the United States the situation was reversed, and more easily corrected. The Americans were cautious and undecided about civil jet aircraft when the Comet was launched, and because of this caution the world's airlines were not easily persuaded that jets could be operated on an economical basis, despite BOAC's single triumphant year with the Comet in 1953. This caution made it more difficult for de Havilland to achieve sales before the crashes, and seemed justified to the airlines afterwards. However, when Boeing and Douglas began building their own jet airliners in the mid-1950s, the airlines (including BOAC) rushed to order them straight from the drawing board. As the economic historian Nathan Rosenberg commented on Anglo-American jet airliner rivalry: 'In retrospect it is apparent that the American delay was salutary rather than costly to them, and that Boeing and Douglas chose the moment to proceed better than did de Havilland.' Because the Americans were slower, more powerful engines (like the Pratt & Whitney J-57) were available to them and they could build their aircraft bigger.[36] Moreover, the Boeing 707 and the Douglas DC-8 were both technically and from an operational viewpoint superior to the Comet, largely thanks to basic research done in wind-tunnel testing. In particular they embodied two features borrowed from American jet bombers, which were to prove paradigmatic in the long-term history of jet airliner development, namely thin swept wings and podded engines.

In the year after the Comet crashes, de Havilland comforted itself with the thought that it had been its pioneering role that had convinced a sceptical industry in America.

> The Americans were taken aback by the success of the *Comet* and the fact that it could be operated in exactly the same way as a conventional piston-engined aircraft; they had nothing of comparable performance even on the drawing board and needed at least 6 years to bring a new turbine-engined aircraft into passenger service.[37]

On this last point, however, the firm was in error. The fact that a major British aircraft manufacturer could seriously underestimate the productive capacity of the American aircraft companies suggests that there was an element of self-delusion about Britain's entire civil aircraft effort in the 1950s. The Americans produced their jet airliners with remarkable speed once the decision had been taken to go ahead: a result of their much larger capacity, and in particular, their higher rates of manufacturing productivity.

By way of a postscript to the story of the Comet it is worth considering the last jet engine which demonstrated a British lead over the Americans – the Rolls-Royce Conway. The Conway began life in the late 1940s at the same time as the Avon, but was a more radical departure from the prevailing design philosophy of the time because it was a *bypass* engine. Bypass jet engines use a front fan to duct colder, slower-moving air past the compressor and turbine, to the exhaust gas jet, thus increasing the mass of the jet and its thrust. Bypass engines have the advantage for airline operations of being both quieter and more economical with fuel. The more air that they divert past the hot compressor and turbine, i.e. the higher their bypass ratio, the more thrust and the greater potential economy that will be achieved. In fact the Conway had a low bypass ratio because it was intended, like the Avon, for a bomber (the Handley Page Victor) and British bombers at this time, like the Comet, had engines 'buried' in the wing roots – a design which did not allow for a wide front fan. Nonetheless, the principle of the Conway represented a significant breakthrough, on a par with the shift from centrifugal to axial-flow compressors.

The Conway's superiority over American civil engines was recognised by Boeing, who recommended the replacement of the launch engine on the Boeing 707 (the Pratt & Whitney JT3C, the civil version of the J-57) with a bypass unit. Thus the large-scale use of bypass engines in commercial aviation began in the 1960s with the Conway's adoption for the Boeing 707 and Douglas DC8. The improvement in fuel consumption and the lower takeoff noise which it offered appealed to the airlines, although it did not significantly outperform the JT3C, and Pratt & Whitney were initially reluctant to follow Rolls-Royce and adopt the bypass system.[38] Eventually, however, the Americans caught up and overtook the British. The Conway stimulated US manufacturers to produce much larger engines with much higher bypass ratios, culminating in the Pratt & Whitney JT9D, the GE CF6 and finally the British response to the American challenge, Rolls-Royce's own RB-211. As with the Whittle engine in the 1940s and the jet airliner in the 1950s, the Americans copied the idea of the bypass engine and improved on it.

Aircraft and aero-engine design and development, as does any other field of advanced technological research, reveals strong national characteristics that can determine the manner and speed at which the work is done. There are different national cultural approaches at play here. In the United States there has been a distinct preference in aerospace for broad-based progress at a steady, but unspectacular tempo, drawing to the maximum extent possible on national resources at the research and development stage before moving into an efficient and commercially-orientated production phase. In Britain high-technology enterprises like the Comet have tended to assume an iconographic value in terms of national culture; they have advanced at a more frenetic pace, on a narrower front, with less clearly identified commercial goals, and more than once have given the impression that winning the race to be first is more important than being the best competitor.

Notes and references

1 Hayward, K, *The British Aircraft Industry* (Manchester: 1989), p29

2 Dawson, V P, 'The American turbojet industry and British competition', in Leary, W M (ed.), *From Airships to Airbus: The History of Civil and Commercial Aviation*, Vol. 1 (Washington DC: Smithsonian Institution Press, 1995), p127

3 Radar is another obvious example.

4 Two more Germans, Herbert Wagner and Helmut Schelp, were responsible for crucial work on turbines and compressors. For the race to get the jet engine operational, see Constant, E W, II, *The Origins of the Turbojet Revolution* (Baltimore, MD: 1980), pp178–207.

5 Golley, J, *Whittle: The True Story* (Shrewsbury: 1987)

6 The progress made by the Germans up to 1945 is outlined in Schlaifer, R, *Development of Aircraft Engines* (Boston, MA: 1950), pp377–428. American gains enabled by interviews with captured German scientists are described in Lasby, C, *Project Paperclip: Germans Scientists and the Cold War* (New York: 1971).

7 Constant, E W, II, note 4, p208

8 Work on the Rolls-Royce Nene began in May 1944 and the engine was ready for testing in October 1944. In the words of its designer, Sir Stanley Hooker, 'In five months the company had built the most powerful aircraft engine in the world.' Although the British never found a use for the Nene, many other countries did, including the United States, where Pratt & Whitney turned it into the excellent J-42. In 1946 the Nene was innocently sold to the Soviet Union, where it was copied and used to power the MiG-15 and MiG-17 fighters. See Hooker, S, *Not Much of an Engineer: An Autobiography* (Shrewsbury: 1984), pp90–8.

9 For the history of American air-cooled engines, see Schlaifer, R, note 6, pp156–98. Also useful is Sherry, M S, *The Rise of American Air Power: The Creation of Armageddon* (Newhaven: 1987).

10 Dawson, V P, *Engines and Innovation: Lewis Laboratory and American Propulsion Technology* (Washington DC: 1991)

11 Dawson, V P, note 10, p14

12 Quoted in Golley, J, note 5, p114.

13 Kevles, D J, *The Physicists* (New York: 1979), p302

14 Schlaifer, R, note 6, pp328–9

15 According to one rueful authority, 'the entire turbojet engine industry of the United States grew directly from the acquisition of two British engines' (the Whittle W.1/GE I-14 and the de Havilland/Westinghouse Goblin). Gibbs-Smith, C H, *Aviation: An Historical Survey from its Origins to the End of World War II* (London: HMSO, 1970), p213.

16 Dawson, V P, note 10, p41

17 Points from the Gas Turbine Collaboration Committee Proceedings, 21 June 1946, Public Record Office, Ref. AIR 62/963

18 In understanding technical matters, the author has found it helpful to consult Smith, G G, *Gas Turbines and Jet Propulsion* (London, New York: 1955). For a more challenging introduction, see Meyer, C A, 'The turbojet engine', in Lancaster, O E (ed.), *Jet Propulsion Engines* (Princeton, NJ: 1959), pp82–198.

19 For Griffith's work on axial-flow turbines in the 1930s, see Constant, E W, II, note 4, pp110–14.

20 Dawson, V P, note 2, pp133, 138

21 The Americans were ahead in high-temperature materials in 1941, and even in the early 1950s had better supplies than the British of vital metals like titanium. See Whittle, F, 'General impressions', development work by GEC, July 1941, liaison with the USA, AIR 62/1009; 'Titanium for engines', 1952–55, Public Record Office Ref. AVIA 65/57.

22 See, for example, his own story: Whittle, F, *Jet – The Story of a Pioneer* (London: 1954).

23 Quoted in Hooker, S, note 8.

24 Edgerton, D, *England and the Aeroplane: An Essay on a Militant and Technological Nation* (Basingstoke: 1991), p90

25 Cribbet, G, letter to Sir Stafford Cripps, 7 February 1946, aircraft production, 1946, Public Record Office Ref. AVIA 9/89

26 De Havilland did consider a swept-wing version of the Comet at an early stage, but did not proceed with it.

27 Sharp, C M, *DH. A History of de Havilland* (Shrewsbury: 1982, first published 1962), p315

28 The Rolls-Royce Avon became a highly successful engine in the 1950s, powering military aircraft such as the Hunter fighter and the Canberra and Valiant bombers, as well the Comet and French Caravelle airliners. The adoption of axial-flow compressors on engines like the Avon and the Sapphire raised the critically important compression ratio before combustion from about 4:1 (for centrifugal engines) to about 7:1.

29 Memorandum by the Minister of Supply (Duncan Sandys) and the Secretary of State for Air, Cabinet Economic Policy Committee, 23 May 1952; 'The aircraft industry as a major exporter – policy', Public Record Office Ref. AVIA 63/25

30 Banks, F R, Ministry of Supply paper, 22 April 1953, Public Record Office Ref. AVIA 65/14

31 Dawson, V P, note 2, pp144–5

32 The Wright turbo-compound engine which used the radial's exhaust gases to drive as many as three separate turbochargers may have been an immensely impressive piece of machinery, but it was the last hurrah of an obsolete technology. See Smith, G G, note 18, pp283–5.

33 Fansel, R W, *What ever happened to Curtiss-Wright?* (Manhattan, KS: 1991)

34 The twin-spool compressor had two axial compressors rotating at different speeds. See Smith, G G, note 18, p252.

35 Smith, G G, note 18, pp248f

36 Rosenberg, N, 'On technological expectations', *The Economic Journal*, 86 (1976), p527

37 'The future of the Comet', De Havilland Public Relations, 11 March 1955, Public Record Office Ref. AVIA 63/26

38 The early engine most used on the Boeing 707 was the P&W JT3C, a civil version of the J-57. Later Pratts introduced the bypass JT3D turbofan version. See Newhouse, J, *The Sporty Game* (New York: 1982) p112.

Andrew Nahum

'I believe the Americans have not yet taken them all!': the exploitation of German aeronautical science in postwar Britain

Introduction

The exploitation of Germany's scientific research and its scientists by the USA, and particularly the transfer of Wernher von Braun and the other rocket experts from the V2 programme, has received considerable attention, both at a scholarly and a popular level.

There have also been broader studies of the well-known American programmes 'Overcast' and 'Paperclip', which brought many German scientists to the USA. Of these studies the most comprehensive and analytical must be that by the American historian John Gimbel which puts 'Paperclip' into the context of the whole intelligence-gathering operation mounted in Germany at the end of the war and its translation into a kind of undeclared programme to extract 'intellectual reparations'.[1]

By contrast, the substantial British efforts after the war to utilise German science and technology have received surprisingly little study, although Tom Bower has characterised UK efforts as amateurish and piecemeal.[2] Similarly, Bill Gunston, a writer well regarded by the aircraft industry and the former Technical Editor of *Flight* magazine has asserted, quite misleadingly, that in postwar Britain designers struggled to create advanced aircraft without proper equipment because 'all the transonic windtunnels found in Germany were pinched by our allies'.[3]

Even a 1996 work on technology transfer out of Germany after 1945 largely neglects Britain. This neglect of the British efforts to exploit German science is a major gap in the study of the postwar period in Europe and the section here will focus, in particular, on the use made in Britain of German aerodynamics and aeronautical science.[4] However, there is a movement to re-evaluate these events, of which this work is a part, and Matthew Uttley has recently discussed 'Operation Surgeon' and has questioned why the achievements of German specialists who came to Britain are so much less celebrated than, for example, those in the USA.[5] It will be argued here that this resulted from the specific character of the postwar organisation of British defence research and industry and the culture of the government establishments to which the specialists largely went.

The paper suggests that the British initiatives for the utilisation of German science were actually carefully targeted, ambitious and probably at the limit of what was practical in the immediate postwar environment. The effect of this influx of German technique should certainly be analysed in the context of British postwar aviation, since it appears to have had a significant influence on both defence research in the government establishments and on the aircraft projects that were undertaken.

First impressions

As the Allied forces entered Germany, a variety of intelligence-gathering operations and missions were put in hand to investigate German technique and the apparent lead in many areas of weaponry. The initial British attitude to much of the German research that was uncovered was equivocal. The proliferation of surprising secret weapons and new kinds of aircraft had done little to slow the Allied advance and some of the projects, produced in response to the pressure for wonder weapons, would under normal conditions, 'have been considered technological charlatanism'.[6]

Sir Roy Fedden, leading one mission, contrasted this profusion of projects with 'the simple, but sound, British aeronautical programme [...] pursued with very little interruption throughout the war, but accompanied all the time by intelligent improvisation until there was really very little in the way of development to come'.[7] But if the policy directing the German effort seemed diffuse, the actual technique of production was of excellent quality in most centres, although not, in the opinion of the investigators, superior to British methods.[8]

On 7 June 1945, a month after the German surrender, Air Marshal Sir Alec Coryton at the Ministry of Aircraft Production (MAP) invited members of the aircraft industry to survey a cross-section of the corresponding German industries under the leadership of W S Farren, Director of the Royal Aircraft Establishment, Farnborough (RAE). The Farren Mission included eight industry designers and managers, the Director of Technical Development (DTD) at MAP and the economist A K Cairncross, representing the Director-General of Programmes, Planning and Statistics at MAP. It left on 9 July, returning just over two weeks later. The Mission observed that there had been no central direction of the industry in Germany and no operational research 'as we know it'. There was also no organised resident German air ministry representative at the firms equivalent to the British post of Resident Technical Officer. It also noted that 'the firms were forbidden to make contact with the Service [and] considered that the inability of the designers to obtain first-hand knowledge of [...] performance of aircraft under operational conditions was a serious hindrance. [...] This lack of direct contact with the Service may well have been one of the contributory causes of the violent changes in Air Staff requirements.' Thus the Farren Mission was able to take comfort from failures which Britain had avoided, and claimed that 'when U.K. personnel reached Germany after the war, the surveys supported a view that the MAP had been successful'.[9]

What certainly was different, in the German case, was the sophisticated level of the aeronautical research effort and the quality of the associated equipment in the firms, where – it was noted – corporate research and development departments were well organised and staffed with 'relatively young men of experience, energy, and enthusiasm'. Farren observed that although the German methods did not differ greatly from the British 'their resources were greater'.[10]

It also began to be appreciated increasingly by British investigators that jet aircraft like the Messerschmitt Me 262, which were entering service by the end of the war, would have proved a grave embarrassment if they had been made available only a little earlier and in sufficient numbers.[11] In addition there were other innovations such as rocket interceptor fighters, anti-aircraft rockets, the V1 and V2 missiles, and radio-controlled anti-shipping glider-bombs. Although, in most cases, these could scarcely be regarded as mature and practical weapons systems, they nevertheless pointed to a huge German lead in the technology of high-speed flight, propulsion, guidance and control, as well as the research facilities for the mechanical and aerodynamic analysis of aero structures in a new high-speed aerodynamic regime. As the British missions moved through the parts of Germany to which they had access, the scale and quality of the advanced research being done began to astonish them.[12] In a rider to his defence of the pragmatic British production programme, Sir Roy Fedden observed that the Allied victory had been won by 'obsolete types, from which every ounce of development had been wrung'. American commentators reached a similar conclusion, suggesting that the air war had been won with brawn, not brain: 'we choked them with the weight of our planes'.[13]

Perhaps this advanced work should not have been so surprising for, before the war, Germany had hosted many visits by British aeronautical engineers, including Roy Fedden (who went several times), Sir Harry Ricardo, the noted engine research engineer, and a delegation from Rolls-Royce which toured a range of companies and research establishments. These tours always impressed with the scale and quality of the facilities and, no doubt, were offered to persuade British opinion that to challenge Germany in the air would be fruitless.[14] Nevertheless, when revisited in 1945, the scale on which Germany's government defence research establishments had moved ahead was startling. The first challenge to British investigators appeared to be the exploitation of the plant and physical resources found in the British area of control in Germany.

The Hermann Göring Research Institute in Völkenrode

A very wide-ranging list of intelligence targets had been developed in concert by British and US investigators prior to the invasion under the Combined Intelligence Objectives Subcommittee (CIOS) programme covering almost all industries and techniques. However, it is argued here that it was in the field of aviation, and aerodynamics in particular, that Britain targeted its efforts.

Six important research facilities fell inside the British Zone of Occupation. They were:

• Luftfahrtforschungsanstalt (LFA) Völkenrode

• Aerodynamische Versuchsanstalt (AVA), Göttingen

• Kaiser Wilhelm Institut für Strömungsforschung, Göttingen

• Dispersal wind tunnels from AVA, Reyershausen

• Rocket Research Station and liquid oxygen plant, Trauen

• Focke-Wulf structural testing laboratory, Detmold.

Many of these facilities, such as the AVA at Göttingen (partly equivalent to the RAE at Farnborough), were well known before the war. However, the greatest surprise, as well as the greatest prize, was found in the LFA – the immense Deutsche Forschungsanstalt für Luftfahrt at Völkenrode, near Braunschweig (Brunswick), which had been named after Air Marshal Hermann Göring just before the war.[15] The institute had been conceived on a vast scale by British standards and was equipped particularly to deal with the new problems of high-speed flight. It was hidden in a forest and extraordinary care had been taken to conceal it from Allied photoreconnaissance flights. No large roads led there, the power lines had been buried underground, and the whole site was elaborately camouflaged.[16]

Ben Lockspeiser, as Director of Scientific Research in the MAP (DSR), went to appraise the site in May 1945 when the British army advised that there were 'some wind tunnels in a large forest' and was amazed to find 'the finest aeronautical establishment he had ever seen'.[17] His report to the Minister for Aircraft Production revealed the contemporary excitement at the discovery.

'It is concealed and dispersed in a large forest. [...] Its aero-dynamic, supersonic and high speed equipment is far ahead of anything in this country, and as far as my knowledge goes, ahead of American equipment also. [...] in several directions the equipment is unsurpassed anywhere.' W S Farren, thinking clearly of his own facilities at Farnborough, observed independently that Völkenrode had 'a magnificence [...] that beggars the imagination of anyone who has seen similar institutions in the UK'.[18]

Initially the site was under the control of Colonel Donald Putt of the US Army which had discovered it shortly before, but it fell inside the British Zone and was shortly to be handed over to the British Army. Putt, in fact, was the officer in charge of the American intelligence operation 'Lusty' ('Luftwaffe secret technology') and a major proponent of the American 'Paperclip' programme to bring German scientists to the USA.[19] Lockspeiser considered that Britain ought, without delay, to put the site back into use or, in view of the possible political difficulties of allowing the installation to remain intact in Germany, transfer the most valuable equipment to the ambitious new research establishment – the National Aeronautical Establishment – which had been planned during the war and was already taking shape at Bedford. The scale and sophistication of the equipment made such an impression on Lockspeiser that he judged exploiting the Völkenrode facility meant that:

> we should bridge over the gap of some five to ten years which I see no means of doing by any other method. [...] The equipment [...] is such that we cannot expect to be able to build its parallel within a number of years and the knowledge possessed by its scientists is such that it will fill in gaps which otherwise would take us similarly many years to fill in from our own resources and researches. It would, in our view, be difficult to exaggerate the importance to this country of exploiting these facilities to the full.[20]

Lockspeiser's reports from Germany also reflected the difference in approach between the USA and Britain in acquiring this intellectual booty. The British model was that the material would be acquired by government agencies, such as that at Bedford, the RAE or other research establishments, and then be put at the disposal of firms for assistance with specific Ministry research contracts under security conditions. The American approach seemed looser and at odds with this British 'government rationing' attitude. Lockspeiser observed that 'a large part of the scientific service provided by America for this kind of investigation is in the hands of industrial representatives who have been placed in uniform and there is no doubt a great temptation in the way of individuals to profit their employers'.[21]

Lockspeiser was correct about the attitude of the Americans, although it is not clear whether the American 'industrial representatives' regarded this as a temptation or simply a normal duty. In fact, he visited Völkenrode at the same time as the noted aerodynamicist Theodore von Karman, who had arrived from CalTech as part of the 'Lusty' operation.[22] George Schairer, the head of the Boeing aerodynamics department and a member of this group, wrote home from Völkenrode to his deputy at the Boeing company within a day of Lockspeiser's own note to the MAP, giving his colleagues important details of the German research into the use of swept-back wings for high-speed flight.[23] This information was incorporated into Boeing engineering policy so quickly that the XB-47 bomber project, then under development, was delayed while this new aerodynamic theory could be incorporated. Boeing's readiness to incorporate this new thinking led, within a few years, to a generation of transport aircraft with a significant speed advantage over British (and other American) rivals.[24]

Lockspeiser also asked for a ruling to stop the records of scientific establishments being moved and for them to be microfilmed 'for the benefit of all'. In fact, some 1500 tons of documents, many of them from Völkenrode, were taken by US agencies.[25] Roy Fedden (Figure 1) told his biographer some years later that he had two loaded trucks with equipment collected for the new College of Aeronautics taken away from him by American forces at gunpoint. He also alleged that American investigators with whom he had examined wind-tunnel models of swept-wing aircraft at Völkenrode went back secretly by night and took them away.[26]

The initial report from Völkenrode by Lockspeiser was among the first to air 'the problem of the German scientists'. He mused 'what is to be done with them? They are, in my opinion, primarily scientists with an almost pathetic eagerness to continue as scientists working for us or anybody else. If they are deprived of their equipment they would inevitably drift to other countries. [...] I suggest that those who are really first class [...] should be brought over here to work under supervision.'[27]

In July 1945 Sir Frank Tribe at the MAP proposed a scheme to dismantle and remove the plant and equipment to Britain, suggesting that 'this would eventually constitute once-for-all delivery to us on reparation account'. He also noted that the plan could have the incidental result of collecting together at Völkenrode a few of the best German aeronautical scientists and technicians, observing that 'I believe the Americans have not yet taken them all!'. The most suitable could then, he suggested, be transferred to the RAE or UK aircraft design firms, 'if and when Government policy here permits'.[28]

This proposal had interesting links with earlier discussions in Britain as to how a resurgence of German air power might be prevented. Tribe observed that

> our feeling is that the UK government will eventually be driven to the conclusion that no effective plan for preventing the export of German scientists to foreign countries, or, in the long run, controlling their activities in Germany beyond a certain point, will be successfully evolved, and that therefore it would be desirable to have the best of those who might be particularly dangerous from the point of view of war potential (e.g. aeronautical scientists) under American or British control while at the same time gaining substantial advantage to our own war potential.[29]

Figure 1 The Fedden Mission to Germany, 1945, one of the earliest expert intelligence-gathering missions to visit Germany, in June 1945. Roy Fedden, the Bristol aero-engine designer (and adviser to the Minister of Aircraft Production) is supervising the unloading of a jeep from the Mission's Dakota aircraft. (Science Museum archives)

For a time the MAP considered an alternative strategy of operating and administrating the Völkenrode establishment on its existing site. R V Jones, Deputy Controller of Research and Development (DCRD) at the MAP, listed 17 aircraft projects of interest, including rocket-powered and swept-wing types and suggested that the aircraft should be completed by their designers and staff 'to the point at which the Germans fly them and prove them to be airworthy' before taking them to England for further study.[30] He also proposed that 'the maximum concentration of MAP will be in Volkenrode and we hope that we shall be able to consider that station as our MAP headquarters in Germany'.[31]

One school of thought held that allowing German scientists to continue working in advanced defence fields (whether in Germany under supervision or in the Allied nations) carried the penalty of enabling them to keep up to date with advanced technique. Set against this was the argument for a policy of 'denial' which held that the Allies should use the best scientists, both for their own benefit and to stop them gravitating to some other potentially hostile nation where they might still keep up their skills but with less chance of supervision.

However, the idea of running a defence research establishment in Germany was ultimately rejected because it was considered both politically too sensitive to utilise the site and because this would also have had the effect of preserving an element of German war potential. The problems of managing work there must also have seemed insuperable. The decision was taken, therefore, to remove the research papers and records to Britain and to dismantle the research plant and equipment for use in Britain.

Operation 'Surgeon'

The resources assembled to dismantle Völkenrode were impressive. At a meeting at the Air Ministry on 12 July 1945, Sir Charles Ellington, as Assistant Chief of Air Staff (ACAS) observed that under the government's policy for war reparations only six months were available 'in which to satisfy our requirements from places of scientific value in Germany such as Volkenrode'. The task was to be a special operation and would be run largely by the RAF as the MAP did not have the administrative or command organisation to undertake the task.[32]

This operation, code-named 'Surgeon', was assigned a commanding officer from the British Air Forces of Occupation and senior MAP officials including Major George Bulman, DCRF, Director of Construction of Research Facilities, MAP, (formerly director of aero-engine development), the aerodynamicist W J Duncan, scientific and technical officers from the MAP, a librarian and representatives from the aircraft and engine companies.

The operation consisted of two phases. Firstly, detailed information was to be collected from German scientists in the form of monographs on their research work, followed by the removal to the UK of the equipment that would be of value. Initially, some 35 British scientists came out to Germany to recommission and supervise the cleaning-up of the facility (it had become occupied by displaced persons and by troops), to run the wind tunnels and become familiar with the apparatus. This group also identified and located the former German scientific staff and brought suitable individuals back to write technical monographs summarising the wartime research in their various fields. For example, Johanna Weber of the AVA recalled that after the surrender 'we were [working] in the fields with the farmers' until the British investigators came to find them. By October 1946, 180 scientists and technicians from Völkenrode and the Göttingen institutes had been located and employed to write these reports. From the Völkenrode staff alone some 250 monographs were commissioned, translated and reproduced by a press and printing department specially established there.[33]

The work was scheduled to begin on 5 January 1946 under the supervision of Major Bulman, who had been tasked with responsibility for building the National Aeronautical Establishment at Bedford by Stafford Cripps (as Minister for Aircraft Production). This underlines the complementarity between the 'Surgeon' operation and British plans for the construction of research facilities, with the MAP noting that 'the Treasury have given approval to the special arrangements necessary for removing this valuable equipment, and they will look

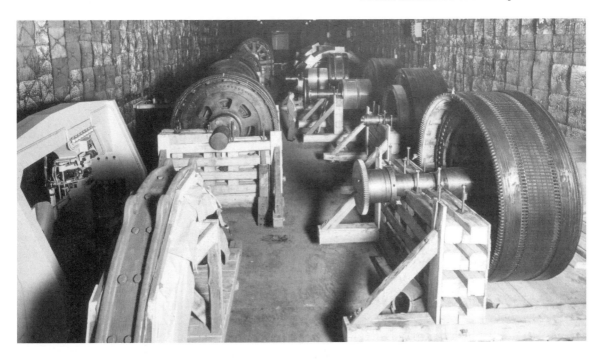

Figure 2 German heavy wind-tunnel motors from Operation 'Surgeon' in storage at Thurleigh airfield near Bedford, awaiting possible use in the new Bedford aeronautical establishment or elsewhere. (Science Museum archives)

to the use of it to save some of the very large expenditure which is planned for Bedford'.[34]

The intention to reuse the material was facilitated by the fact that the specialised dismantling team from the Ministry of Works largely consisted of the same individuals who were responsible for the erection of heavy capital plant for Bedford and other government research facilities such as the RAE, Farnborough and the National Physical Laboratory (NPL).[35]

The bulk of the structure of the large Völkenrode wind tunnels formed substantial civil engineering structures which were relatively 'low tech' and not worth transporting. However, the 6000-hp Siemens electric motors and their control gear were precious and many were shipped to England with their associated mercury arc rectifiers and compressors and were used in the construction of the '8-foot' and the '3-foot' supersonic tunnels that were built at Bedford (Figure 2). However one complete smaller supersonic tunnel was disassembled and transported to be rebuilt for projectile studies at the Armament Research Department at Fort Halstead near Sevenoaks. Also invaluable in Britain was the advanced ancillary optical equipment used for flow visualisation in the tunnels.[36]

Much of the lighter and more delicate freight was flown back to Farnborough. A Douglas DC-3 and a Junkers Ju 52 aircraft were dedicated to this, with approximately two flights per week in each direction scheduled.[37] In addition three or four Hudson aircraft brought a constant stream of personnel back and forth from England for study. These included both government and industry scientists, a considerable number of RAF and service personnel and politicians such as Arthur Woodburn (Parliamentary Secretary for the MAP), who went to see the progress of Operation 'Surgeon' in January 1946.[38]

Some idea of the scale of the operation can be gained from the provision of six road tractor units and low-loader trailers of 100-tons capacity which were used to take loads up to Hamburg for shipping. The total quantity of material identified for removal to the UK amounted to some 14,000 tons.[39] The curious emotions that must have existed in the German civilians at the time can be judged by the fact that the British team had the willing assistance of the Siemens company's chief export packer for the electrical equipment.[40] This equipment was delivered to several hangars at Great Storton airfield which marked one end of the proposed 5-mile runway at Bedford and from there delivered to the various research establishments controlled by the Ministry of Supply.[41]

Emigration from Bizonia – the employment of German scientists

In July 1946 the decision was made by the British and American governments to fuse their respective zones of occupation in Germany into a single administrative area termed the 'Bizone'. (British officials, more playfully, tended to refer to the area as 'Bizonia'). This fusion implied, or perhaps made more overt, a direct competition between the Anglo-American allies and the Soviet Union for the scientific and economic spoils of Germany; there was substantial, and exclusive, Anglo-American cooperation.[42]

However, there was inevitably rivalry between Britain and the USA, although this should not be overstated compared to that which existed in relation to the USSR and also France. Thus it is interesting to recall the claim by Bower, alluded to above, that British efforts were poorly focused and inconclusive, since the study by Lasby, written from American sources, shows that American officials considered British plans to be very effective.[43] Colonel Putt wrote in November 1946 that 'the Board of Trade handles all scientists coming here and has little interference from anyone. Once it is decided they want a man he is brought over and put to work. [...] Whether he is lily-white [does] not worry them too much. If any man can be of assistance in realigning a segment of their economy which is out of adjustment, they try to get him.'[44]

Putt had a strong personal commitment to the utilisation of German scientists for the United States and perhaps overemphasised British efforts. In fact, British policy, like that in America, was initially ambivalent over the employment of 'ex-enemy aliens'. There was less concern about the acceptability of this where pure defence research was involved and scientists could be brought to establishments like the RAE; but the question of using a wider range of personnel to assist industry at large in Britain was the subject of some debate.

However, Board of Trade officials were generally keen to utilise German developments, as were British defence personnel actually serving in Germany. Similarly American military personnel in Germany were initially more enthusiastic than State Department officials at home. Indeed, it was the value put on German science by the military of both allies that led to mutual suspicion and competition between British and American officials actually on the ground in Germany, as glimpsed from Putt's remarks above. Both groups were excited by the new technologies they had found and both considered their own governments to be irresolute in forming plans to utilise German personnel. Both groups reported to their home administrations that the other ally was being less scrupulous than themselves about former Nazi affiliations among the candidates in order to request greater urgency.[45]

In Britain the arguments for an expedient approach came quite quickly to dominate policy, while some moral doubt still was felt in American government circles over the question and it was said that German scientists often migrated back to the British zone after tiring of waiting for US employment.[46]

Thus a cipher telegram from the Cabinet Offices to the British Embassy in Washington on 14 February 1946 observed that:

> 750 Germans evacuated from the Russian zone and frozen in the American zone may be released to Russian zone if not designated. [...] We have deferred from submitting a list of Germans solely because American policy is not yet determined. It would therefore be manifestly inequitable if our scrupulous regard for the proprieties should prejudice our chance of exploiting the Germans now detained.[47]

A further telegram advised the embassy that the British list would be ready for exchange by 1 February and that 'we consider it not unreasonable to request crystallisation of American policy'. It suggested that if this were not forthcoming in a month 'we shall consider ourselves free to go ahead on a unilateral basis'.[48]

There was now growing pressure from many areas of government and particularly the Board of Trade and the firms themselves to extend the exploitation of German technique beyond the purely military sphere. This was a contentious issue and conflicted with what has been called the 'rigidly moral approach' of the postwar Labour government and the feeling that private industry and individual firms should not profit from the wartime sacrifice of Allied lives by gaining special access to the German work.

Thus Stafford Cripps (now President of the Board of Trade in the postwar Labour government) is said, initially, to have suggested that employment for the Germans in non-military industries in the UK was only tolerable if they were 'sucked dry of their knowledge in a short time'.[49] However, Arthur Woodburn argued that 'there is no possibility of getting these men to put all they have into our research if the arrangement is merely to suck them dry and throw them back into Germany'.[50] Therefore, it was proposed, scientists and technicians brought to the UK would normally work for trade associations or research establishments, since the work done there might be expected to augment the capability of a whole industrial sector, rather than enriching particular companies or groups of individuals.

These concerns were addressed by a scheme for civil industry administered by a panel chaired by Sir Horace Darwin, Director of NPL. This was announced by Stafford Cripps in parliament in December 1945, when he declared that 'it is the Government's policy to secure from Germany a knowledge of scientific and technical developments that will be of benefit to this country'. He remarked, perhaps disingenuously, that 'although we were generally ahead there are certain fields in which the Germans held a temporary lead'. The panel was to examine the requirements of British industry and to scrutinise the credentials of those whose names were put forward. Another role of the Darwin panel was 'to see fair play between the firms'.[51]

Alongside the announcement of the scheme, measures were devised to pre-empt objections from labour organisations. A brief drafted by the Board of Trade for issue by the Ministry of Labour offered arguments for employers to deploy. It suggested that 'it is evident that there must be some industrial technique in which [...] Germany has surpassed us. It is intended to bring certain German scientists, specialists and technicians [...] into civil industry [...] in order to gain the most up-to-date knowledge and perhaps save ourselves many years of research. The Americans and the Russians are exploiting the Germans in the same way'. It also stressed that the inventions and discoveries would be available to industry as a whole and that 'they will have no authority over British workpeople'.[52]

An elaborate system was set up to prepare the ground in the firms and local areas, with the Board of Trade acting as go-between for the employers and the Trades Union Council (TUC).[53] In addition, Sir Walter Citrine, as General Secretary of the TUC, was extensively briefed by the Board of Trade, which stated that 'Germans would normally work in Government Establishments and Research Associations'. Although 'exceptionally they might find their way into individual firms Germans are, however, under a contract with the British government'. It added that:

> the number of Germans who will serve in this country will not exceed one or two hundred [...] no known pro-Nazis will be admitted [...] only those Germans who have a real contribution to the national interest [...] the results of their discoveries and inventions will be available to industry as a whole.[54]

Inevitably there was some negative publicity and officials noted that 'the Beaverbrook press were running the story in a big way' with 'uninformed press criticism' and that a story in the *Daily Mail* for 5 January 1946 reported that 'a rumour-monger [sic] is sweeping Barrow [...] the shipyard workers resent the arrival of former Nazis who are still pro-Nazi'.[55]

However the British public displayed a remarkably sanguine view about the utilisation of German science and the superiority in many areas which this implied over UK technique. In December 1945 Stafford Cripps opened an exhibition of German industrial products at Millbank which showed parts of Germany's wartime advances in science and industrial technique. It also sought to promote the British Intelligence Objectives Sub-Committee (BIOS) reports on German developments for British industrial use. These amounted to 1400 reports on a great range of industries and techniques compiled by some 10,000 investigators. Cripps urged British industry 'to make the fullest and speediest use of the knowledge gathered [...] there was no time to waste'. Among the wonders promised were 'powdered white of egg which whips better than the real thing, a bath enamel you can hit with a hammer without chipping, the perfect baby food [...] and, for women of all ages "lizard" shoes and handbags, flexible, durable, dyed in rich shades and made out of haddock skin'.[56]

The *Daily Graphic* reported that 'we so often have occasion to criticise the obstructiveness of the Board of Trade that it is a considerable satisfaction to be able to compliment its President, Sir Stafford Cripps, on the apparent thoroughness of his investigations into German trade methods'. The exhibition was intended to tour Cardiff, Birmingham, Manchester, Leeds, Nottingham, Newcastle, Glasgow, Belfast and Bristol.[57]

In October and November 1945, the RAE put on a display of captured German aircraft and equipment which included not only service types like the piston-engined Focke-Wulf Fw 190 and Messerschmitt Me 109, but also the Messerschmitt Me 262 jet fighter and secret types such as the twin jet-engined Arado Ar 234 B-2 bomber which had not been used operationally before the fall of Germany. Jet engines, bombsights, communications gear, as well as V1 and V2 missiles, were also on display. A few months later three aircraft with most of the engines and other small equipment were moved to the Science Museum to form a popular exhibition entitled 'German aeronautical developments' and it is interesting to note, in the era before the Cold War, how openly this advanced German defence technology was displayed in Britain (Figure 3).

German high-speed aerodynamics and British defence science

The greatest concentration of British efforts was certainly in aeronautics. In November 1946 Arthur Woodburn, for the Ministry

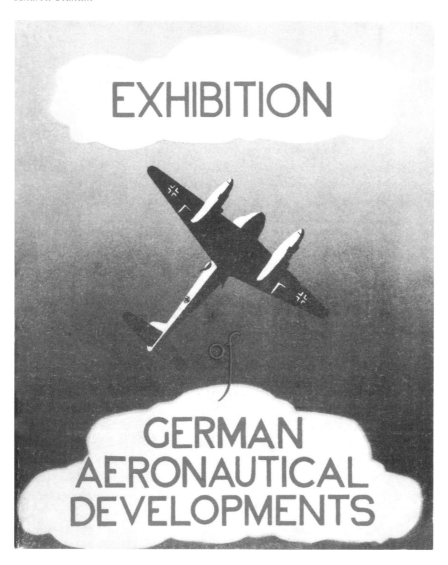

Figure 3 Cover of the catalogue for the exhibition of captured German aircraft at the Science Museum in 1946. This featured jet and rocket engines, a V1 flying bomb, V2 rocket and a wide range of equipment. These displays were remarkably open, in the light of the security climate of the Cold War which was shortly to dawn. (Science Museum archives)

of Supply (MoS), had announced that German scientists were to be employed at the RAE and at the recently created Guided Projectiles Establishment at Westcott, near Aylesbury in Buckinghamshire. The press statement was careful to emphasise that the pay 'will be comparable to that of British technicians [...] but at a slightly lower figure'. Any suggestion of featherbedding former enemies was countered by the announcement that 'the men will be accommodated in Army huts'.[58] Some 124 individuals were eventually selected by the Deputy Chiefs of Staff (DCOS) committee for the DCOS or 'defence scheme' to bring in German scientists for employment. They included guided-missile experts, rocket engineers, aerodynamicists, flutter analysts, instrumentation engineers, an archivist, experts in servomechanisms, control guidance, gas turbines and, most curiously, two naval historians.[59] Of these scientists some had already been

Figure 4 Letter regarding salary scale for German scientists, 10 March 1948. (Public Record Office CAB 122/352)

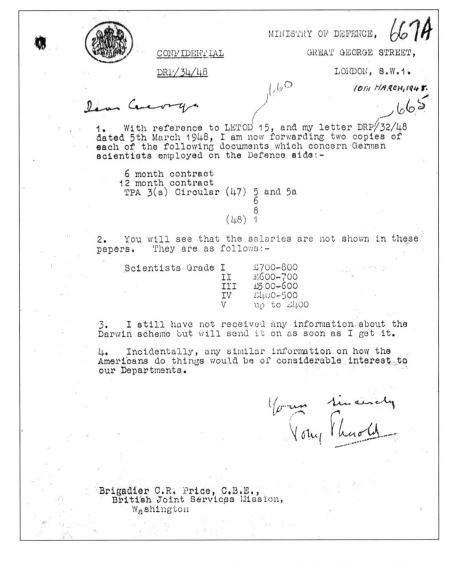

brought to Britain for interrogation, in effect as VIP prisoners of war. The aeronautical scientists were taken to the Beltane School at Wimbledon, which had been requisitioned for the purpose as part of a separate operation known as 'Inkpot'. By late 1945 about 250 of the best German scientists and engineers had been brought there for interrogation and a number of these were subsequently offered employment on a special pay scale within Civil Service terms, graded as 'German Scientist I to V' (Figure 4).[60] For example, Adolf Busemann, one of the foremost experts in the world on swept wings and supersonic flow, was retained in Britain and worked at Farnborough and at NPL, but soon left to work in the USA.[61]

However, others such as the Göttingen aerodynamicist Dietrich Küchemann were offered employment freely while they were still in Germany, writing the reports for the British investigation of their wartime work. Initially these contracts were for six months, and Küchemann's associate, Johanna Weber, who took up a similar offer to follow some months later, recalled that the short period of these initial contracts was a major factor in inducing German scientists to accept.[62]

Apart from the lucky find of Völkenrode the British search had not been hit or miss – CIOS targets even specified minor Messerschmitt dispersal factories. There was also a specific search for personnel with particular skills, such as those involved in work on flight control and stability on the new high-speed aircraft. This brought Morien Morgan of the RAE to Germany to seek out Karl Doetsch, who had been working on the directional instability of the Messerschmitt Me 262, since Britain's new jet fighter, the Gloster Meteor, was similarly afflicted with this 'snaking' problem.[63] Doetsch had unique skills, being both a highly trained research engineer and also a test pilot who had been working particularly on control and stability problems at the Deutsche Versuchsanstalt für Luftfahrt at Berlin-Adlershof, which fell inside the Russian zone, and he had, by then, taken refuge in Bavaria until other aeronautical scientists directed Morien Morgan to him.[64]

The two schemes were the official channels for the employment of German specialists and they show that 124 German scientists and technicians were formally brought into the UK under the Defence Scheme while another 257 Darwin Panel nominees were listed in 1946, although it is not clear how many of this latter group came.[65]

It also appears that other Germans did come under less formal conditions. One example, which may not have been exceptional, is that of the engineer August Stepan who had worked on the Doblhoff tip-jet-driven helicopter system in Austria. In 1947 he was given a contract by the Ministry of Supply and worked at the Fairey company on the Rotodyne passenger helicopter project until 1962. However, he does not appear on the lists of Darwin Panel scientists so far found by this author or in the separate DCOS scheme for defence scientists, and his case raises the question of how many others there may have been like him.[66]

The integration of German and British high-speed aerodynamics at the Royal Aircraft Establishment, Farnborough

The expansion of British aircraft production during rearmament and war relied largely on government finance and had produced a highly directed industry with centralised state control through the Ministry of Aircraft Production. This merged to form the new Ministry of Supply from 1945, with control over all Britain's aeronautical R&D and the responsibility for procurement and administration of all contracts for aircraft, missiles, engines and weapons on behalf of the RAF. It also had equivalent responsibility in the period for civil aircraft.[67] Thus the British pattern for the utilisation of German science was to concentrate these assets in government research establishments under

MoS control. The reports, personnel and equipment thus were located principally at Farnborough while the actual hardware initially went to the new Bedford research centre which stayed under Farnborough control.

The presence of German personnel at Farnborough, in addition to the captured documents and reports, ensured that British transonic research made striking speed in the immediate postwar period. This absorption took place partly with the assistance of intermediaries who were at home in the German language, such as the aerodynamicist T R F Nonweiler, who was the son of German-Jewish immigrants and acted as a security vetting officer for some of the German aerodynamics reports.[68] Since many British aerodynamicists were competent in scientific German, it would be tempting to cast the analysis of these events in terms of technology transfer, as it is generally understood by historians of technology, but more particularly, in terms of the transfer of 'tacit knowledge', as analysed by Collins.[69] The essential elements in such a case, it might be argued, include a body of advanced technical and theoretical knowledge, complemented by subtle practical and experimental 'know-how' (in this case wind-tunnel and modelling technique) mediated by key personnel.

However, an analysis along either of these lines would fail to capture the complexity of these events. It would also undervalue the state of British aerodynamics at the end of the Second World War and could also imply that it had developed in isolation from Continental work. In fact, RAE aerodynamicists were well informed about German research during the 1920s and early 1930s. For example, Hermann Glauert, the outstanding theoretician at the RAE in the interwar period, was at the forefront in spreading an appreciation of the work of Ludwig Prandtl and the 'Göttingen school' of aerodynamics in Britain.

These contacts disappeared as German aerodynamics became incorporated into German war planning. Probably the last open international exchange took place in Italy at the Volta High Speed Conference in 1935, and there British, American, French, Italian and German aerodynamicists gave papers on current thinking about future high-speed developments (Figure 5).[70]

Ed Constant has concluded, from a study of the papers given at the conference and the citations in them, that Germany was pre-eminent in theoretical aerodynamics in 1935, with Britain only slightly behind. By contrast, the USA (excepting the special case of Theodore von Karman who, from 1930, in essence imported German aerodynamics to CalTech) was rather backward in theoretical high-speed aerodynamics, although the National Advisory Committee on Aeronautics was 'widely recognised for the excellence of its empirical data and for little else'.[71]

At this conference the aerodynamicist Adolf Busemann presented a paper on supersonic flight which mentioned the possibility of using swept wings in the transonic region.[72] This was almost the last opportunity for international exchange, and following the Volta conference the German work became increasingly secret, while in Britain the expansion of the RAF and the introduction of new types of aircraft absorbed a great proportion of the time and energy of government scientists at the RAE.

During the war the RAE did nevertheless manage to do some advanced work in high-speed flight and in a notable investigation began flight trials with a Spitfire which was dived at an angle of 45 degrees from a height of 40,000 feet, increasing the speed attempted in each flight, until over Mach 0.9 was attained. At the same time a scale wind-tunnel model was tested in parallel in the new high-speed Farnborough tunnel. In this way an unusually good understanding for the time was developed into the interaction between the effects of compressible airflow at speeds approaching that of sound and the effects on the control and stability of the aircraft.

There was also some advanced theoretical work undertaken at the RAE during the war, including a study on a hypothetical supersonic biplane. This derived from an ingenious proposal also aired by Busemann at the 1935 Volta conference and relied on the interference between the shock waves reflected between the superimposed wings

Figure 5 The Volta High Speed Conference at Rome in 1935, the last major occasion on which German aerodynamicists met with British and American colleagues before the war. Ludwig Prandtl (with beard) is in the front row on the right, while the figure with spectacles in the second row is David Pye, soon to become Director of Scientific Research at the Air Ministry. To his left is Adolf Busemann. (By kind permission of the Royal Aeronautical Society)

to cancel each other out and thus avoid the high drag (and power requirement) associated with supersonic flight.[73]

Thus although Busemann's swept-wing proposals were not explored in Britain during the war and the extent to which German research on swept wings in the transonic regime had progressed came as a surprise in 1945, these studies were not received by a naive or theoretically unsophisticated audience. British aerodynamicists realised the point of all this work as soon as they saw the reports. They had the theoretical and mathematical equipment to be able to extend it and rapidly began to incorporate the thinking into proposals for operational aircraft.

The case of the reception of German high-speed aerodynamics in Britain does not therefore fall into the generally understood categories of technology transfer or the communication of tacit knowledge that have been discussed by historians of technology. Rather, it represents a reintegration of a particular branch of theoretical aerodynamics which had been undergoing separate evolution since German science had 'gone off the air', as it were, in the late 1930s. The character of Farnborough itself was essential to the utilisation of this German expertise and, in spite of sporadic objections and newspaper reports, the absorption of German specialists into British government defence research establishments and into firms was remarkably harmonious. Karl Doetsch, as we have seen, was recruited, along with other aeronautical specialists, to come to Farnborough, initially on a six-month contract. He recalled that his Home Office immigration papers were marked 'ex-enemy alien – for exploitation only', but 'the welcome at RAE was quite different', and Morien Morgan begged him 'not to take the "ex-enemy" business too seriously'.[74]

Doetsch's view was that the RAE wished only to retain scientists who could be integrated into the existing British government research establishment system. He also had the strong impression that there was a wish at the RAE to avoid 'German language islands' which it was then believed had happened in the USA. After about two years 'it was obvious which scientists would be fully integrated' and the number reduced to a highly integrated residuum. However, in response to this desire for integration, coupled with the government policy that, in the early years, Germans not could have authority over British workers, a particular paired working structure emerged in which leading Germans were allowed a German collaborator and assistant. Thus Dietrich Küchemann worked with Johanna Weber, with whom he had previously cooperated at the AVA, Hans Multhopp with Martin Winter and Doetsch with Werner Pinsker (Figure 6).

By 1953 the whole pattern of collaboration within the RAE had become looser. Küchemann and Doetsch were promoted to Senior Principal Scientific Officers and were in the process of becoming naturalised as British subjects, while the civil service category of 'German scientist' was dropped. However, naturally enough, some

Figure 6 German scientists in Farnborough Court in 1947. In the front row, Adolf Busemann is third from the left (with cat – symbolising, to the author, a remarkable domesticity in these arrangements). To his right is Gerald Klein, Head of the Siemens autopilot group, and the penultimate figure to the right is Professor H Schlichting (Göttingen and Braunschweig). In the second row, from the left, Karl Doetsch is no. 2, Martin Winter is no. 6 with Hans Multhopp (no. 7) to his left. Dietrich Küchemann is in the rear row between Winter and Multhopp. (By kind permission of Flugbaumeister Prof. Dr.-Ing. Karl Doetsch Hon. DSc)

of the specialists did not really settle down. Kurt Tank said of Hans Multhopp (formerly his leading aerodynamicist and theoretician in the Focke-Wulf design office) that he 'had not found really satisfying work'.[75] Within RAE circles Multhopp came to be considered by some as arrogant, and eventually went as chief scientist to the Martin-Marietta aircraft company in the USA.[76] Doetsch attributes this alienation to Multhopp's outspokenness in a period when Morien Morgan and RAE aerodynamicists were impressed by the tailless German high-speed aircraft such as the Messerschmitt Me 163 rocket fighter (which appears to have inspired the ill-fated de Havilland DH 108 Swallow in which Geoffrey de Havilland was killed). He sought an opinion on a scheme from Multhopp, who replied simply 'Oh, this awful fashion'.[77]

However, in his period at RAE Multhopp had a powerful effect on the direction of advanced British aircraft work. In 1948, he and Martin Winter proposed an experimental swept-wing transonic research aircraft (Figure 7) which rested heavily on his earlier work at Focke-

Figure 7 Swept-wing transonic research aircraft proposed at the RAE in 1948 by Hans Multhopp and Martin Winter. The concept drew on Multhopp's experience with the Focke-Wulf Ta 183 project, but also drew inspiration from the new Rolls-Royce Avon jet engine. This 'paper aeroplane' (particularly with the parallel chord alternative wing) can be viewed as the conceptual antecedent of the English Electric Lightning fighter. (Science Museum archives)

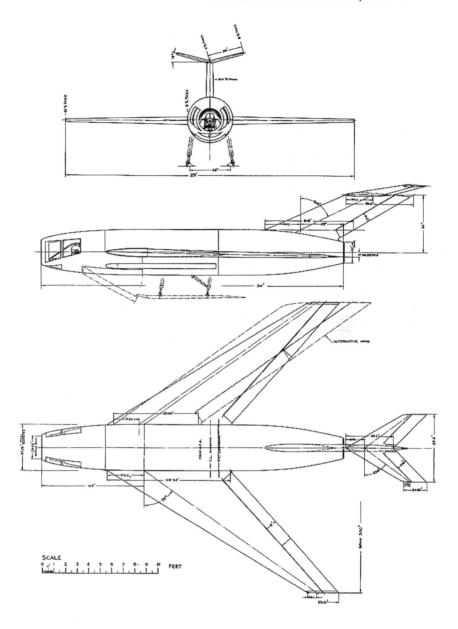

Wulf, where he was notably engaged in developing the Focke-Wulf 183 jet fighter, now considered to be an important influence on the MiG 15 and the North American Sabre.

They calculated that the new Rolls-Royce Avon engine was just sufficient to give the aircraft a supersonic performance of Mach 1.24 at 36,000 feet 'if equipment and instrumentation are restricted to only the most essential items'. The other restriction was to keep the diameter of fuselage to the absolute minimum dictated by the Avon engine and to this end the pilot was to be located in a prone position in a compartment placed, in effect, within the inlet duct. The prone

pilot idea was also derived from German work and had been
developed in an experimental aircraft in part by Martin Winter as a
member of the Berlin Technical University *Akaflieg* group. Interestingly
Doetsch had also flown this aircraft at Adlershof and encouraged the
incorporation of the prone pilot feature in the RAE project. The wing
was to be swept back at an angle of 55 degrees to delay compressibility
effects, while the tailplane was to be mounted high on the fin to
keep it clear of the transonic shock waves generated by the wings or
fuselage and to avoid the loss or alteration of pitch control which had
been encountered approaching transonic flight – 'a scheme which was
developed some years ago for the Focke Wulf 183 fighter'.[78]

This aircraft was not built, but later, in 1948, another RAE paper
by Owen, Nonweiler and Warren proposed a larger supersonic
fighter which derived from it.[79] In general, layout and wing plan for
the proposed fighter followed closely the Winter–Multhopp design,
including a version with a prone pilot position, although an alternative
layout was sketched with a conventional pilot position above the
intake and a radar scanner dish faired into the centre of the intake
duct. However, the Winter–Multhopp aircraft was only supersonic
by dint of scrupulous streamlining and avoidance of all unnecessary
structure. A practical fighter would need much more power to attain
this performance, and the new feature of this June 1948 proposal
was the use of multiple engines staggered so that the thickest part
of one lay over the thinner part of the other – the so-called 'hip and
waist' arrangement. It is significant that, in this period, Winter and
Multhopp, as German scientists, were able to work on the research
aircraft but not on the fighter proposal, which passed to British
colleagues. However, this policy soon changed and Multhopp was to
have considerable input into the English Electric P.1 Lightning which
derived from this project.[80]

By November 1948 the Advanced Fighter Project Group, which
had been set up at the RAE, reported on work to date, stressing the
difficulty in predicting the nature of the threat (in terms of speed and
altitude) for which 'the fighter which must stop the bomber' should be
designed. The task, they proposed, was that of defending 'this island
against the attacks of enemy bombers similar to the long-range high
altitude bombers we ourselves are developing' – high-speed aircraft
capable of delivering atomic bombs at 500 knots and from 50,000
feet.[81]

The group considered that, although the state of knowledge
on aerodynamics, stability and control was still developing, the
main uncertainty centred around the structure. The operational
supersonic fighter was required to be a large and complex aircraft
weighing perhaps 30,000 lbs (at a time when the relatively simple
'first generation' jet fighters such as the de Havilland Vampire and
Supermarine Swift weighed only 8000 to 10,000 lbs). The gamble of

estimating strength and weights closely in the absence of 'real guiding experience' or established design principles is shown by the structural challenge of providing enough stiffness to wings and tail surfaces to prevent flutter and aileron control reversal. The catch here was that the forces would be higher than those met hitherto, although the surfaces were required to be much thinner and, for geometric reasons, the high degree of sweepback also would tend to compound the problems of twist and aero-elastic distortion. However, the price of a slightly 'safer' and more conservative design, increasing the structure weight by a factor of only 3 per cent, would reduce flight endurance from 55 minutes to 29 minutes – scarcely a useful fighter.[82] German aerodynamic work had been highly influential in suggesting supersonic shapes, but it had not provided design and structural data for this new high-speed regime.[83]

But even in the light of these technical reservations the RAE took a bold and even propagandist role in weapons development policy, arguing that 'a fully operational supersonic fighter would be an immeasurably valuable asset to the defences of this country' and actively promoting work on it in spite of the many uncertainties, noting that 'the unknown factors are many and frightening but the prize may be immense'. It would be 'an appalling gamble' and 'the obvious way to achieve this prize would be to tackle the problem slowly'. But in view, implicitly, of the dawning atomic threat, the RAE proposed the 'short-cut' approach, going straight to the design of a fully operational supersonic fighter and suggesting that 'a first class design team from the Industry' be asked to proceed with the design on the lines sketched out by its scientists.[84]

In August 1948 the MoS issued Operational Requirement F.23/49 based on this RAE thinking which asked for 'a minimum top speed of Mach = 1.2 or higher' and a fantastic climb performance allowing six minutes from the moment the pilot presses 'the first button' to reaching 50,000 feet. The MoS then began to pursue discussions with English Electric as the most likely company to build the aircraft and, by March 1949, confirmed to the company that it was to develop the concept as the English Electric P.1 – the prototype that was to lead to the Lightning fighter.[85] Thus the project, it should be noted, was set in train at virtually the same time as the transonic Hawker Hunter (and long before the Hunter flew), with the intention of leapfrogging a generation of fighters.

The initial development of the Lightning took place in the context of a range of suggestions for fast-climbing manned rocket or hybrid rocket and gas turbine-powered fighters. Sir Charles Gardner (as Director of Guided Weapons Development) also gave a glimpse of a certain optimism for defence when he noted that 'the Million-fold increase in striking power of a single aircraft has transformed the defence problem from one in which an attrition of 5 or 10 percent

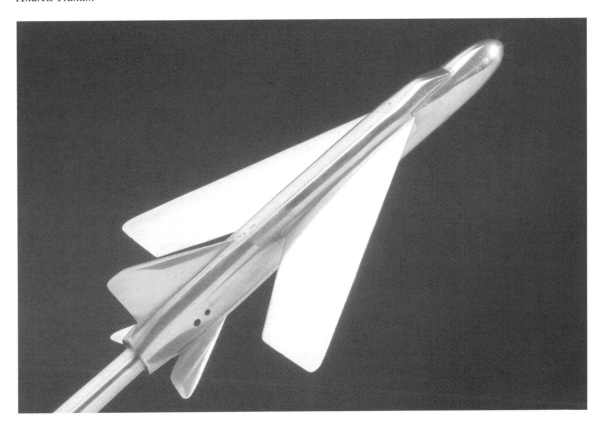

could be worthwhile [...] to one in which it is necessary to achieve an annihilation defence in which virtually every aircraft must be destroyed'.[86]

The initial English Electric 1948 project drawings mirrored closely the planform of the RAE study, including an ingenious staggered 'hip and waist' engine arrangement. This became a distinctive and successful feature of the production aircraft, although in the case of the T-tail English Electric became convinced that RAE advice was wrong. In this they proved to be correct and the low tail position eventually adopted proved far more effective in the nose-high landing attitude (Figure 8). The Lightning, when it entered service in 1960, certainly vindicated the early RAE advocacy of the supersonic interceptor, but – although, like so many British aircraft, it arrived awfully late – the performance substantially exceeded the initial RAE predictions. It was, however, an aircraft that was predicated on the special air defence and quick reaction needs of Britain. In this role it was probably the most potent interceptor at the time in the world, but this specificity of role denied it really substantial export sales, although 40 were sold to Saudi Arabia and a further 14 to Kuwait.

Among the very many British aircraft development projects, a considerable number can be regarded as relating to, though not actually derived from, German work. For example, in the case of

Figure 7 The English Electric company's 1/84th scale model built in 1951 for research and development of the P.1 Lightning fighter. For this programme the company acquired the first supersonic wind tunnel outside government establishments like the RAE. (Science Museum Inv. No. 1963-160) (Science & Society Picture Library)

the V-bombers, Britain's main Cold War deterrent force, the basic aerodynamic designs were strongly influenced by German work, although the initial concepts were developed more in the firms than at the RAE. In the case of the Handley Page Victor, German aerodynamic influence was imported directly into the company, since one of its designers, G H Lee, was a member of one of the Allied technical missions in Germany.

The Avro Vulcan represents another fusion of German theoretical work with British pragmatic technique. The Avro designers accepted the need for a swept wing for the high-speed bomber requirement, but were not confident that long swept wings, as on the Victor, could be built stiff enough and conceptually reinvented the 'delta' wing planform by 'filling in the gap'. However, in this period, no major defence aircraft project could proceed without a major commitment of continuing RAE research throughout development. The RAE contributed an enormous amount of aerodynamic work to refine the Vulcan wing, with Dietrich Küchemann also providing a solution for blending the tailfin and stabiliser in the Victor.[87]

The pattern of these projects illustrates the connection between German wartime aeronautics and postwar British programmes and the process of integration of this German science and technique into UK defence research. However, the structural solutions for designing these advanced supersonic aircraft had not been imported from Germany, although they were to prove critical to success. In fact the problem of airframe distortion and oscillation in high-speed airflow became an RAE specialism. Much of the theoretical work needed to analyse these complex interactions was done at the RAE, by and under the direction of Ted Broadbent.

Thus German swept-wing work, at the end of the war, was suggestive, but it was not a complete recipe, and it was only in a place like the RAE with deep resources for theoretical and wind-tunnel aerodynamics research, combined with resources for advanced structural analysis, that it could have prospered. It is certainly suggestive that in Argentina the work on the Pulqui II fighter under a team led by Kurt Tank, the former Focke-Wulf chief designer, did eventually founder. The work was conducted by an imported German team which, though highly able, could not match the truly enormous resources then deployed at the RAE for structural testing, aero-elasticity and 'flutter' calculations, and accident or failure analysis. One Pulqui broke up in flight – a failure attributed to 'faulty welding'.[88]

Conclusions: the utility of German science

The range of aerodynamic work studied and the number of specialists brought to Britain does not support the assertion, referred to at the outset, that Britain was backward in exploiting German work in comparison to the USA. The official British total so far discovered of 381 German scientists should be compared with the declared initial total of 210 who were taken initially to America under the auspices of Project 'Paperclip'.[89] A more reasonable judgement is that the number of German scientists actually brought to Britain was probably in line with what the government and industrial research establishments could absorb. The quality and the experience of the individuals recruited also shows that Britain sought out individuals in the top rank of German aerodynamics and aeronautical science and, as we noted with the case of Karl Doetsch, the intelligence evaluation and preparation was already in place to enable British investigators to locate them.

However, it is unlikely that a quantitative judgement can ever be reached on the contribution to the British aeronautical industry of the various programmes to exploit German science. The value of the physical equipment as well as the intellectual contribution made by the personnel and the research documents brought to the UK is literally incalculable for various reasons. One could, for example, put a notional value on the R&D work from which the Winter–Multhopp transonic aircraft design sprang, but this might not represent the cost which the RAE would have had to expend to get to the same point without them. In such cases it may often be sufficient for other workers to learn of a new possibility in broad detail in order to jump to it quite rapidly by their own efforts.

In some areas of British aviation technology, postwar development was practically untouched by a knowledge of German work. This was certainly true of the gas-turbine development carried on at Rolls-Royce, de Havilland, Bristol and Armstrong-Siddeley, which built exclusively on what had been done during the war in these firms. The German jet engines were analysed at Farnborough by RAE scientists and by Power Jets (R&D) who concluded that there was little to learn from them. It is also noteworthy that only two German turbojet engineers were brought to Britain in the DCOS scheme and one of them, Max Bentele, with high-level experience of turbine blade design at Heinkel-Hirth, was not used in the British jet aero-engine programme but was despatched to a fairly low-priority project for a gas-turbine tank engine at C A Parsons, in Newcastle upon Tyne.[90] This sparing use of German turbojet personnel argues again for a purposeful and highly selective British approach to German engineering and scientific personnel.

In contrast to the UK, France, which had missed out on turbojet development during the war, considered the BMW design team to be a great prize. BMW was located in Munich, in the American zone, but the team and the chief engineer H Oestrich appear to have been 'spirited away' by French agents while awaiting travel to the USA. The team reappeared in Switzerland in a new organisation, the Atelier Technique Aéronautique Rickenbach, and the first French jet engines put into production by the nationalised SNECMA aero-engine company bore the designation ATAR.

However, the British jet-engine teams were quick to appreciate the superior quality of German test facilities and instrumentation. The de Havilland team spent several weeks at the BMW high-altitude test cell in Munich, completing over 70 hours of testing on the Goblin engine, providing information which could not then have been obtained anywhere else. The cell could be depressurised to simulate altitudes of up to 50,000 feet, while the inlet air speed could be regulated up to 550 mph and refrigerated to –70 °C.[91] The team noted that the speed at which results were obtained was much better than if flight tests only were used and the information far more complete. The BMW test facility was removed to the USA, but the practical experience of the utility of the installation certainly helped establish the need for test cells working on the same principle at the National Gas Turbine Establishment near Farnborough.

Germany was, of course, closely identified with advances in rocketry, and British liquid-fuel rocket motors certainly owed much to the V2 engine concept. Much work was done on these, for rocket-assisted takeoff applications, for the abortive rocket fighter programmes and particularly for the Blue Steel and cancelled Blue Streak nuclear weapons. The idea of the fast-climbing rocket fighter, for which prototypes were commissioned in the mid-1950s from three separate manufacturers, was clearly derived conceptually from the Messerschmitt Me 163B.

Within the British zone, at Kiel, was Helmuth Walter's Walterwerke concern which produced rocket engines for various weapons. The firm had also developed a hydrogen peroxide steam turbine for submarines which promised very high underwater speeds. The Walterwerke scientists were captured in a commando raid planned by Ian Fleming as Kiel fell to the Allies. Thus followed the adoption of concentrated ('high-test') hydrogen peroxide as the oxidiser in a wide range of British rocket engine projects, following wartime practice at Walterwerke and elsewhere and the presence of a considerable number of German specialists at the newly-formed Guided Projectiles Establishment at Westcott in Buckinghamshire. Douglas Millard, at the Science Museum, has pointed out that the 1946 British Beta rocket developed there was derived from the Walter 509 motor and has found on it a fuel valve stamped 'T-stoff – inlet'. The use of this Anglo-German hybrid term certainly seems eloquent.[92] Andrew Jeffs, a long-term Westcott scientist, has confirmed that 'thousands of captured German solenoid valves' for rocket fuel control came to Westcott without which 'we'd have been flummoxed' and that 'we were using them into the 1980s'. In the immediate postwar period, terms like T-stoff and C-stoff were routinely in use at Westcott and even some of the fuel stocks came out of Germany.[93]

Interestingly, Jeffs recalls that Westcott did not reflect the RAE working pattern of paired German scientists who were not allowed to direct British colleagues initially and that 'Dr Walder, who did the Gamma motor was very definitely the head of the team'. To Jeffs, who worked at the time with Willi Kretschmer, an engineer on the Walter 109 rocket motor for the Messerschmitt Me 163, this was probably because Westcott was new – 'we hadn't got any history at all – we were not so hidebound'.[94] The Beta and Gamma motors at Westcott demonstrated a technology which passed from there into the engine firms de Havilland, Napier and Bristol-Siddeley. Indeed the Gamma was quite closely followed by Bristol-Siddeley for the Stentor motor for the aircraft-launched nuclear standoff Blue Steel missile – the principal British nuclear weapon between 1963 and 1968.

In contrast to the liquid-fuelled motors, the solid-fuel rocket technology which was used in many anti-aircraft and air-to-air weapons was a largely home-grown and successful British technology. Thus the Bristol Bloodhound missile, which emerged as an effective ground-to-air defence system against high-altitude hostile bombers, relied largely on British technology for its solid-fuel core motor and radar guidance, and not, for example, on the German Wasserfall liquid-fuel anti-aircraft missile which had been studied with interest by Allied investigators.[95] In cases such as these the fact that Germany had done a thing, or had begun a project, was perhaps sufficient stimulus for British research engineers to accept that it could be done and to successfully attempt it, but in their own way.

Perhaps most significant, in the long term, for British aeronautics was the employment at Farnborough of the Göttingen aerodynamicist Dietrich Küchemann and his collaborator Johanna Weber. Küchemann took British nationality in 1952, becoming head of the Supersonics Division of the Aerodynamics Department in 1957 and overall head of RAE aerodynamics in 1966.[96] Both Weber and Küchemann had a major impact on the Concorde programme, but if any single person can be considered as the 'father' of the aerodynamic design of Concorde it is, in the opinion of this writer, Küchemann.

In this context Concorde is certainly an interesting case, since it represented such an enormous technological and scientific effort. It might therefore be tempting to regard the heritage of German scientific influence in both America and Britain as a kind of technological supremacism, for in some respects Concorde can be regarded as the British equivalent of the American Apollo space programme.

In this connection, one German commentator has suggested that engineers and scientists under National Socialism contributed to this through 'an aggressive cult of feasibility'.[97] While Britain had made notable use of scientific research in many areas, the new technologies and weapons systems demanded quite a new scale of expenditure and effort. Germany had been among the first to realise the returns that might be available from this intense application of science and research. Thus the effect on the Allies of their analysis of German science was as much moral as direct. Although in many cases the postwar programmes of the former allies did not build directly on the weapons and solutions that had been attempted in Germany, the scale and extent of research and the degree to which engineering science was applied to German war projects was eloquent. Nevertheless, it must be borne in mind that the Second World War had marked a step change in the application of science to weapons systems among all the combatant nations.

In conclusion, the study of Cold War aero science in the UK leads to the view that this episode really concerns the integration of German and British aeronautical science and the resurgence of the RAE as a uniquely capable research establishment with its own particular character.[98] Thus it would be unhelpful to try and consider whether Küchemann and Weber's narrow supersonic delta work should be considered as 'German' when it was conceived and nurtured within the RAE long after both had left Germany. It is simplest and most satisfactory, perhaps, to regard it simply as RAE work.

This 'integrationist analysis' also goes some way to answering the question touched on at the beginning – why was the work of the German specialists in the UK so little known? The interplay of Farnborough expertise with a firm such as English Electric in the development of the Lightning, touched on above, reveals something of the culture of government research establishments and the RAE in the period. RAE involvement was unknown in the wider community at the time – government scientists were virtually anonymous and the names even of senior figures such as the director of the RAE were unknown to the public; indeed they would have counted any kind of celebrity a grave embarrassment. In this sense, the German specialists who stayed on were completely integrated into the ethos of British defence science and behaved and were treated in exactly the same in this respect as British-born research workers.

In the rapid pace of Cold War aeronautics it quickly became meaningless to attempt to unravel what work was notionally 'German' and the term would certainly have seemed irrelevant to the participants. We should also recall that this study traverses a trajectory of 'mind-sets' about nationalism and identity, taking us from the still-fresh sensibilities of the war, in 1946, through the perceptions of the Cold War and on to the approaching entry of Britain into the European community with new and still emerging perceptions of nationalism and identity.

Appendix: a conundrum – the financial value of German defence science

In the immediate aftermath of the Allied exploitation programmes there were efforts made to assess the value of what had been taken, both from the German side and on behalf of the British and American governments of occupation. The main motivation behind this was for German trade associations, but also Allied occupation bodies such as the Bizonal Economics Administration, to estimate the value of intellectual and other properties removed from Germany in order to establish a credit figure towards the reparations account.

Of course, a major component of this material was concerned with military R&D, which could be taken as having no realisable value in a defeated and disarmed Germany, although a huge quantity of information and actual products and prototypes for civil technologies were taken, which clearly had important potential for the reviving economy of Germany. To some historians, indeed, the whole exploitation programme should be comprehended in terms of undeclared intellectual reparations.[99] Arriving at the value of this material proved extraordinarily difficult and the final assessment reached by the commission established by the administration for this purpose came up with an estimate of between $4.8 billion and $12 billion.[100]

Estimating the share of this which fell to Britain would be extraordinarily problematical and, moreover, would not represent its utility. Firstly, there is the possibility, quite strong in many cases, that British manufacturers would have in time adopted types of plant, processes and designs that were in use in Germany anyway, and that there was a process of modernisation which had been deferred by the war. Another reason to suggest that the value to the recipient is lower than the value estimated by the loser is suggested by a 'housebreaker' analogy where the burglar never obtains the full value of items taken away. In the case of German science, the utility that patents, processes, scientific knowledge and so on would have had when stripped out of the milieu in which they developed must have been vastly reduced. It seems likely that the only environments where this special knowledge could have been absorbed and transferred without high dilution could have been in defence establishments such as the RAE.

Another factor which also makes a proper assessment difficult, if not impossible, is the problem of valuing 'false starts' and dead ends in technology. Germany had been found to be so extraordinarily fertile in new technologies applicable to aviation that the Allies tended to assume that almost all these leads might prove valuable, and the German estimators certainly have echoed a high estimation of value. Thus General Electric considered that expertise with helicopters powered by tip jets at the ends of the rotor blades, acquired from the inventor, Dr Doblhoff, was worth $1 million.[101] One of Doblhoff's engineers, August Stepan (mentioned above) also brought experience of the system to Britain, where it was used for the experimental Fairey Rotodyne. The Rotodyne was intended to be a short-haul helicopter airliner linking both cities to cities and cities to international airports, but proved to be an expensive diversion. By 1957 it had consumed some £7.6 million in development money and was cancelled shortly afterwards.[102] Neither Britain nor the USA developed useful machines with jet-powered rotors and the whole concept could be viewed as an expensive 'negative dowry'.[103]

Another example where the value is highly contentious is provided by the case of BMW aero engines. The firm's report on the removal of 50 crates of reports and drawings to Wright Field by American personnel valued the material at more than 325 million Reichsmarks (about £32 million in contemporary sterling value) – the sum spent in research and development since 1937.[104] The problem with such a figure, for the purposes of economic analysis, is that it does not reflect the value of the intellectual property to either party. In the case of BMW, the special knowledge which it had acquired in aero engines was effectively made useless by the defeat of Germany, since even if there had been no Allied exploitation it no longer had a customer for military goods and was prevented from making warlike material for any other state. The value to the USA would also be grossly overstated by this figure. Much of BMW's special expertise related to air-cooled radial piston engines (such as that in the Focke-Wulf 190), but although Allied experimenters were naturally intrigued by the competing solutions developed in Germany, the USA in 1945 had two producers, Wright and Pratt & Witney, making highly developed air-cooled radials. There is no suggestion that either firm altered their designs after the war in the light of knowledge from BMW. In fact, developed versions of American Second World War service types powered the first postwar civil airliners, while for military use the piston engine was being rapidly replaced by the jet and little new development engineering on piston engines was done.[105]

Notes and references

1 Gimbel, J, *Science, Technology and Reparations; Exploitation and Plunder in Postwar Germany* (Stanford: 1990). For a critical reassessment of Gimbel's book see Judt, M and Ciesla, B (eds), *Technology Transfer out of Germany after 1945* (Amsterdam: 1996).

2 Bower, T, *The Paperclip Conspiracy* (London: 1988). Bower makes the curious judgement that the British programme was characterised by excessive scrupulousness with respect to scientists with Nazi associations, vagueness about objectives and 'lost opportunities', while at the same time he castigates the Americans for being too greedy and too ready to whitewash the record of

'desirable aliens'. See also Lasby, C G, *Project Paperclip* (New York: 1971).

3 Gunston, B, *Bombers of the West* (Hersham: 1973). This comment ignores not only the massive haul of German equipment, which this paper sets out to study, but also the substantial UK investment in government research which made the Royal Aircraft Establishment (RAE) at Farnborough the biggest research establishment in Europe in the Cold War era.

4 There is also a need for a far wider study of these events, which is beyond the scope of this study, taking in the use made of the whole range of scientific and technical material brought to Britain including German industrial chemistry, plastics and synthetic materials, textile handling, photography, film developments and much more.

5 Uttley, M, 'Operation Surgeon and Britain's post-war exploitation of Nazi German aeronautics', *Intelligence and National Security*, 17/2 (summer 2002), pp1–26

6 Heinemann-Grüder, A, 'Keinerlei Untergang: German armaments engineers during the Second World War and in the service of the victorious powers', in Renneberg, M and Walker, M (eds), *Science Technology and National Socialism* (Cambridge: 1994), pp30–50

7 Fedden, R, 'Final report – The Fedden Mission to Germany', Ministry of Aircraft Production, June 1945 (Science Museum archives). Fedden had been chief designer for Bristol aero engines but after his rift with the company board became special adviser to the Minister for Aircraft Production. In Germany his principal brief was to select equipment for the new College of Aeronautics at Cranfield.

8 Both Britain and Germany suffered, in terms of economy of scale, from generally smaller plants and shorter production runs relative to the USA, although Britain had probably gone further in training and incorporating new labour into the aircraft plants, whereas in Germany the power of the master craftsman or *Meister* in engineering shops seemed little diminished. Although in Germany much airframe manufacture was improvised and dispersed, Hans-Joachim Braun has argued that engine manufacture tended to rely on established German high-skill craft technique and multipurpose tooling. The introduction of single-purpose ('mass-production') tooling was relatively slow and where engine manufacture was dispersed, productivity was generally poor. See Braun, H-J, 'Aero-engine production in the Third Reich', *History and Technology*, 14 (1992), pp1–15.

9 Public Record Office Ref. AVIA 10/411, 'Farren Mission to Germany'. Helmuth Trischler has discussed the frustration of aerodynamicists at the lack of access to the experience gained by the fighting services – in direct contrast to the First World War – in 'Self-mobilisation or resistance? Aeronautical research and national socialism', in Renneberg, M and Walker, M (eds), note 6, pp72–87.

10 *Ibid.* Sir Alec Cairncross has also left his recollections of the mission recalling that 'the Farren Mission was greatly impressed by the lavish scale on which the German government had supported research and development, employing in 1945 5,000 workers (in a private firm) in five separate establishments, and

stressed the contrast with the parsimony of the British government in financing research and development in aviation'. Cairncross, A K, *Planning in Wartime* (Oxford: 1991), pp137–40.

11 Public Record Office Ref. AIR 8/784, minute of 24 January 1945. The threat of the new Messerschmitt jet fighters was serious enough for Lord Portal to predict that 'if Germany has not been beaten before July 1945 she will have dominance in the air over Germany and above the armies during good flying weather'.

12 Gunston, B, *By Jupiter: The Life of Sir Roy Fedden* (London: 1978), p130

13 Gunston, B, note 12; Senator Albert D Thomas, quoted in Judt, M and Ciesla, B (eds), note 1, p101.

14 The subject of these various high-level missions into Germany before the war and German intentions in facilitating them is a curious one which has not been explored. It is interesting to note that Tizard wrote to Lord Swinton, Secretary of State for Air, in 1936 about one such: 'H R Ricardo, of whom I expect you have heard, has just returned from Germany where he has been shown German engine developments. I think that it would be helpful to you if you had a talk with him. His news is very reassuring in some ways.' (Public Record Office Ref. AIR 2/1866, 'Committee for the Scientific Survey of Air Offence'). The facilities given to the Rolls-Royce mission in 1937 are particularly intriguing, since these were top-level engineers who could see the significance of what they were shown. The three Rolls-Royce men were A G Elliot, Chief Designer, H J Swift, General Manager, Production, and J Ellor, the firm's supercharger expert. They saw, among other things, the Daimler-Benz, Junkers and BMW aero-engine works and were provided with a Junkers Ju 52 aircraft. They were deeply impressed with the scale of organisation and the provision of enclosed 'silent' test-beds with instrumentation grouped outside, noting that the facilities of plant, buildings, equipment and personnel for research and development 'was superior to anything we have seen in this country'. They also noted the open layout of factory sites with buildings widely spaced 'evidently planned [to make] air attack extremely difficult'. Report reproduced in *The Archive* (journal of the Rolls-Royce Heritage Trust), 2/2 (1984) and subsequent issues.

15 Public Record Office Ref. AVIA 9/88, 'Visits to Volkenrode'. Paper on file: 'MAP interest in German research establishments', 3 January 1946. This notes 'of these, by far the most important is Volkenrode'.

16 Some authors have seemed to imply that the development of aeronautical research facilities and advanced weapons was a response to the Allied bombing campaign. The development of the LFA was part of a long-planned dispersal of aeronautical facilities which was well advanced in the mid-1930s. Thus Helmuth Trischler, note 9, pp74–6, has described the preparatory prewar work for aerodynamic facilities. In January 1946, Arthur Woodburn, Parliamentary Secretary for the MAP, visited Völkenrode and observed that 'the Herman Goering wind tunnel was covered by a special cement platform covered with tons of earth in which shrubs, grass and even trees were planted. [...] the fact that all this [...] was planned and prepared long before the war and so

carefully hidden [is] itself a silent indictment of the Nazi preparations for war'
(Public Record Office Ref. AVIA 9/88).

17 Lockspeiser, B, introductory remarks as Chairman on 9 October 1946, to
Smelt, R, 'A critical review of German research on high-speed air flow',
Journal of the Royal Aeronautical Society, 50 (1946), p900

18 Public Record Office Ref. AVIA 10/113, quoted in Bower, T, note 2

19 Lasby, C G, note 2, pp28–9. According to Lasby, Putt was one of the most
vocal and influential advocates for the transfer of German scientists to the
USA. 'Lusty' was just one of a large number of the intelligence missions
intended to investigate and exploit German science after the surrender. These
also included ALSOS (the mission to investigate the state of German atomic
research), CIOS (Combined Allied Intelligence Sub-Committee) and BIOS
(British Intelligence Objectives Sub-Committee).

20 Public Record Office Ref. AVIA 15/2216, Hermann Goering Research
Institute at Volkenrode (Luftfahrtforschungsanstalt Hermann Goering, LFA),
Ben Lockspeiser, DSR to Minister (through CRD and DTD), 11 May 1945.

21 *Ibid.*

22 Irving, C, *Wide-Body, the Making of the 747*, (London: 1993), pp75–94

23 Schairer wrote 'the Germans have been doing extensive work on high speed
aerodynamics. This has led to one *very* important discovery. Sweepback or
sweepforward has a large effect on critical Mach No.' and he gave sample
calculations to illustrate the theory. Letter, G S Schairer to Benedict Cohn,
10 May 1945, reproduced in facsimile in *50 Jahre Turbostrahlflug*, DGLR-
Symposium proceedings, Munich, 26–27 October 1989. The fact that Schairer
wrote 'Censored' on the cover of his letter and signed this statement himself
could indicate a desire to avoid US government control, although one account
attributes his action to a desire to 'avoid delay'. Schairer and Cohn would
have immediately realised that the swept-back wing allows a subsonic aircraft
to approach the speed of sound without suffering the effects of buffeting and
trim change (pitching up or down) – the so-called compressibility phenomena
which had been encountered by the increasingly powerful Allied service aircraft
used in the war.

24 Irving, C, note 22.

25 Gorn, M, *The Universal Man, Theodore von Karman's Life in Aeronautics*
(Washington DC: 1992), pp105–6. Much of this haul, amounting, it has been
said, to 3 million documents, was air-freighted back to the USA, to form the
nucleus of the Armed Services Technical Information Center.

26 Gunston, B, personal communication, 1997 (also see note 12). Gunston
recalled Fedden saying 'it was the law of the jungle out there'. It is possible
that Fedden had encountered in this case an American unit of the Allied army
'T-Forces' which had armoured infantry and antitank weaponry in order to
gather material in target areas immediately resistance ceased. In general Anglo-
American cooperation was good and apart from these intelligence-related
issues, Fedden specifically noted the generosity and helpfulness to the Mission
of the US Army (Fedden, R, note 7).

27 Public Record Office Ref. AVIA 15/2216. Lockspeiser to Minister, 11 May 1945.

28 *Ibid.*

29 Public Record Office Ref. AVIA 15/2216. Tribe's paper also noted 'I am sending a copy of this letter to Barlow at the Treasury because of the reparation issues involved.'

30 Public Record Office Ref. AVIA 15/2216, Jones, R V, MAP statement on Völkenrode to ACAS, Air Ministry, 6 July 1945. Jones ascribed the highest priority to a supersonic swept-wing jet-powered project, the DFS (Deutsches Forschungsintitut für Segelflug) 346. This was intended for reconnaissance and to achieve the startling performance of 1250 mph (Mach 1.9) at 60,000 feet.

31 Public Record Office Ref. AVIA 15/2216, Jones, R V, MAP statement on Völkenrode to ACAS, 6 July 1947.

32 *Ibid.*

33 Weber, J, interview with author, 1 June 1998; Public Record Office Ref. AVIA 12/82, 'Operation Surgeon – memorandum no. 2'.

34 Public Record Office Ref. AVIA 9/88, 'MAP interest in German research establishments'. It was noted to Sir Alec Coryton, Controller of Research and Development (CRD) that 'Mr Gorrell Barnes of the Treasury is therefore accompanying you [to visit Völkenrode] to obtain a general picture of the equipment involved and the scale of the operation'.

35 Fletcher, P, conversation with the author, March 1996. As 'Superintending Engineer – Heavy Research Plant' for the Ministry of Works, Fletcher was concerned with the engineering of all the large government research installations in the UK and was in overall charge of the engineering side of the dismantling of Völkenrode and the transport of its equipment. He was also involved in the planning and layout of the Bedford site and the building of the wind tunnels, spinning tunnels and engine test facilities at Bedford so that there was a close integration between these programmes. The Ministry of Works engineers in the 'Surgeon' team referred to themselves ironically as 'Operation Spanner-hammer'.

36 For example, Schlieren interferometry equipment. The superb quality of the German optical and mechanical instrumentation can be seen in the case of kinetheodolites – calibrated camera devices used on ranges for tracking the trajectory, height and speed of projectiles and aircraft. In 1965 the RAE were still using and maintaining what effectively were German Askania instruments of prewar manufacture. ('Kinetheodolite planned maintenance manual', Workshops Department in conjunction with Instrumentation and Ranges Department, July 1966, Science Museum Technical File for Inv. No. 1993-2547).

37 Public Record Office Ref. AVIA 15/2216. It was also noted that 'at Göttingen there is [...] equipment deposited by Sir Roy Fedden [for the College of Aeronautics]. This should be included in general plans.'

38 Public Record Office Ref. AVIA 9/99

39 Public Record Office Ref. AVIA 12/82, 'Operation Surgeon, memorandum no. 2'. The scale of this removal is all the more remarkable when it is recalled that this 'take' consisted of 'high-tech' research equipment rather than general industrial plant. By 1 October 1946 approximately half the identified material

had been shipped (7620 tons by sea and 144 tons of more delicate equipment by air) and it was reported that shipments were going out at a rate of 1800 tons per month. For the new College of Aeronautics at Cranfield alone, which was the junior partner in allocations, 400 tons of research equipment and machine tools were packed in Germany during October 1945 by Wing Commander Hereford. (Harrington, J, Librarian, Cranfield University, personal communication, 1996). Some equipment did still remain *in situ* at the end of the agreed period and was destroyed punitively.

40 Fletcher (note 35) recalls the attitude among the Siemens men as 'We have a good name and we want to see that it comes out tidily.'

41 Public Record Office Ref. AVIA 9/88, MAP, Ashworth, E C, 'Interest in German research establishments', note for CRD, PS 15, 3 January 1946 and paper 'Organisation of Operation Surgeon'. The Ministry of Aircraft Production was amalgamated with the Ministry of Supply during the course of this programme.

42 Public Record Office Ref. BT 211/46, 'Employment of German technicians and German reparation labour generally', March 1946. The secret and contentious nature of these arrangements is illustrated by the instruction on a telegram in the file from the British administration in Vienna to the Board of Trade: 'This message will not be distributed outside British or US government departments or HQs or re-transmitted, even in code, without being paraphrased.'

43 Bower, T, note 2; Lasby, C G, note 2

44 Note from Colonel Putt to 'Hap' Arnold, Commanding General, AAF (Army Air Force), 4 November 1946, quoted in Lasby, C G, note 2, p170.

45 Public Record Office Ref. BT 211/46, Preston, G E, minute of 27 September 1945

46 Lasby, C G, note 2

47 Public Record Office Ref. AVIA 15/3846, 'Panel to consider employment of German scientists, specialists and technicians for civil industry in the United Kingdom'.

48 Public Record Office Ref. AVIA 15/3846, telegram of 19 January 1946 to British Embassy, Washington. In fact the MAP had noted that in early January 1946 'Air Vice Marshall Jones paid a special visit a few weeks ago to Volkenrode and Göttingen to disclose the broad policy in connection with the German scientists in the UK [...] at Headquarters in London arrangements are now in hand for the preparation of the contracts and for the accommodation, programmes of work etc. for those Germans who elect to come to this country.' (Note from PRO AVIA 9/88, PS15).

49 Public Record Office Ref. BT 64/2879, quoted in Bower, T, note 2

50 Public Record Office Ref. AVIA 9/88, Woodburn, A, 15 January 1946

51 Public Record Office Ref. AVIA 15/3846, 'Panel to consider employment of German scientists, specialists and technicians for civil industry in the United Kingdom'. The Darwin Panel nominees handled by the 'German Division' at the Board of Trade formed an extremely diverse list including specialists in cameras, lenses and optics, photographic film, fuel injection, but also oddities

like the chief engineer for a fully-fashioned hosiery machine company and a designer of sugar and chocolate machinery.

52 Public Record Office Ref. BT 211/47. The press release on the Darwin scheme, released in December 1945, also made these points and added that 'during their stay the Germans will not be in any position of authority, and will, in no case, serve in any vacancy which could be filled by a British employee'.

53 *Ibid.*, minute of 25 February 1946.

54 *Ibid.*, paper of 9 January 1946.

55 The Germans referred to at Barrow-in-Furness were Helmuth Walter and his team which had produced a hydrogen peroxide submarine power plant to allow sustained high-speed underwater running. The Admiralty had managed to install the Walter team at Vickers in advance of any general resolution of the policy doubts over placing the Germans in specific companies.

56 'To brighten your life', in *Sunday Pictorial*, 24 November 1946

57 Public Record Office Ref. BT 211/47

58 *Ibid.*, cuttings in file from *The Times*, *Daily Mirror* and *Daily Telegraph*, 1 November 1946, *Daily Worker*, 8 November 1946.

59 Public Record Office Ref. CAB 122/352

60 *Ibid.*

61 Karl Doetsch attributed his desire to leave to the fact that, intellectually, Busemann felt isolated at NPL and that 'there was no one of his calibre' there. Doetsch, K, conversation with the author, 5 October 1998.

62 Weber, J, note 33

63 Doetsch, K, note 61. Doetsch was one of the German scientists offered employment at Farnborough. He and Dietrich Küchemann were the only ones offered 'German Scientist I' grade salary.

64 *Ibid.* Doetsch recalled that 'Lindner and Multhopp pointed me out'. Interestingly, Morgan has also provided an account of his encounter in Morgan, M M, Morris, D E, and Truran, W C, 'Notes on a visit to Southern Germany, July 8th–18th, 1945, to interrogate German technical staff on stability and control matters, with special reference to flight testing'. RAE Tech. Note No. Aero 1673 (Flight), August 1945.

65 Although the intention to recruit under this scheme was announced early in 1946 and many individuals appear to have come to the UK in 1946 and 1947, the details of procedure, contract terms and so on were not formally defined until March 1948, and are detailed in PRO CAB 122/352. The Ministry of Supply paid for removal expenses of Germans and their families.

66 Stepan, A, personal communication, 1990

67 Edgerton, D, 'Whatever happened to the British warfare state? The Ministry of Supply, 1945–1951', in Mercer, H, Rollings, N, and Tomlinson, J D (eds), *Labour Governments and Private Industry, The Experience of 1945–1951* (Edinburgh: 1992), pp91–116

68 Conversation with Steve Thornton, Librarian at RAE Bedford, December 1996. Nonweiler also wrote a comprehensive overview of German work for the RAE, Nonweiler, T, 'German high speed aircraft and guided missiles', Royal Aircraft Establishment Aero Reports 2070, 2071, 2072, August 1945.

The study covers aircraft, guided missiles, and engines and fuels in three parts.

69 Collins, H M, *Changing Order* (Chicago: 1992), p55. Collins argues for the importance of the human mediation of tacit knowledge in the case of the TEA carbon dioxide laser in one of his case studies by noting that 'no scientist succeeded in building a TEA-laser where their informant was a "middle man" who had not built a device himself'.

70 The Volta High Speed Conference, held under the auspices of the Italian Academy of Science, was held in Rome from 30 September to 6 October 1936. Proceedings were published as: Fondazione Alessandro Volta (ed.), *Convegno di Scienze Fisiche, Matematiche e Naturali*, 'Theme: High Speeds in Aviation' (Rome: 1935, 2nd ed. 1940).

71 Constant, E W, II, *The Origins of the Turbojet Revolution* (Baltimore, MD: 1980), p156

72 Busemann, A, 'Aerodynamischer Auftrieb bei Überschallgeschwindigkeit', in Fondazione Allessandro Volta (ed.), note 70, pp328–60

73 Lighthill, M J, 'A note on supersonic biplanes', Aeronautical Research Committee Reports and Memoranda No. 2002, 27 October 1944. W F Hilton, at NPL, also published a paper 'Further tests on a faired double wedge aerofoil' on 11 May 1944, ARC Fluid Motion Panel 693, which noted interestingly 'centre of pressure calculated by Busemann's method'.

74 Doetsch, K, personal communication, March 1997; Doetsch, K, 'Deutsche Luftfahrtforscher nach 1945 in England', in *Die Tätigkeit deutscher Luftfahrtingenieure und -wissenschaftler im Ausland nach 1945* (Bonn–Bad Godesberg: Deutsche Gesellschaft für Luft- und Raumfahrt eV, 1992). A translation of this paper has recently been deposited in the library of the Royal Aeronautical Society.

75 Conradis, H, *Design for Flight: the Kurt Tank Story* (London: 1960), p154

76 Kervell, B, formerly Curator of the RAE Museum, personal communication, November 1995

77 We can perhaps see in Multhopp's response the view of a 'classical' aerodynamicist (his background was Göttingen and Focke-Wulf) to the 'maverick aerodynamics' of Alexander Lippisch, creator of the Me 163, and the continuation of a disagreement which was already in existence in wartime Germany. Doetsch recalls 'people thought he was arrogant which was untrue – but he was so outspoken in giving an answer. He was actually a very nice person.' Doetsch, K, personal communication, note 74.

78 Winter, M, and Multhopp, H, 'Transonic research aircraft with "Avon" turbine jet engine (A.J.65)', RAE Technical Note Aero 1928, February 1948; Doetsch, K, 'Deutsche Luftfahrtforscher nach 1945 in England', note 74

79 Owen, P R, Nonweiler, T R F, and Warren, C H E, 'Preliminary note on the design and performance of a possible supersonic fighter aircraft', RAE Technical Note Aero 1960, June 1948

80 Doetsch recalled that 'English Electric worked hard to keep Multhopp' when he was in the process of deciding to leave for the USA. Doetsch, K, personal communication, note 74.

81 'Report of R.A.E. Advanced Fighter Project Group', RAE Report Aero 2300,

November 1948

82 *Ibid.*, p11

83 It is possible that the problems of aero-elasticity and structural integrity were beginning to be addressed in Germany during the war but, if so, this work or appropriate specialists do not seem to have reached England.

84 Note 81

85 An 'experimental requirement', ER 103, issued in late 1947, preceded this. The advantages of English Electric were an industrial management that was more solid than that usually found in the aircraft companies and a design team led by Teddy Petter that had, largely through its own initiative, launched the Canberra jet bomber.

86 Gardner, C, 'The future of military aviation', lecture to the Imperial Defence College, 19 June 1957 (Science Museum archives). The hybrid rocket/gas turbine interceptors developed to prototype stage as the Saunders-Roe SR.53 and Avro 177 were cancelled in the aftermath of the Sandys 1957 Defence White Paper. However it was by then becoming clear that the gas turbine engine, with reheat, as in the Lightning, could give impressive climb performance without the complication of mixed power plants and dangerous chemical fuels.

87 Nahum, A, 'The Royal Aircraft Establishment from 1945 to Concorde', in Bud, R, and Gummett, P (eds), *Cold War, Hot Science* (London: 1999), pp29–58. This chapter analyses the relationship between the RAE and the firms in this period, and also teases out something of the internal culture of the RAE.

88 Conradis, H, note 75, pp185–8

89 Bower, T, note 2

90 Bentele, M, *Engine Revolutions* (Warrendale, PA: 1991), pp16–103

91 Moult, E S, 'The development of the Goblin engine', *Journal of the Royal Aeronautical Society*, 51 (1947), pp655–85

92 Millard, D, *The Black Arrow Rocket: a history of a satellite launch vehicle and its engines* (London: 2001)

93 Jeffs, A, former Westcott engineering scientist, conversation with the author, 19 February 2003. Westcott was one of the unloading fields for Operation 'Surgeon' and Jeffs remembers a huge haul of parts, including V2 parts, accumulating there for cannibalisation in experiments. Also 'the odd VW [Beetle] came through – and disappeared'. He recalled that there were British attempts to make solenoid (electrically commanded) valves but alongside the German version 'they were like a donkey compared to a racehorse'.

94 *Ibid.* Heinz Walder was one of the rocket experts brought over under the 'defence scheme'.

95 The AVIA 40 class at the Public Record Office contains more than 5000 drawings on the Wasserfall missile and the V2 which were collected in Germany for the Westcott rocket research establishment.

96 Owen, P R, and Maskell, E C, 'Dietrich Küchemann', *Biographical Memoirs of Fellows of the Royal Society*, Vol. 26, December 1980, pp305–26

97 Heinemann-Grüder, A, note 6, p42. Although Apollo and Concorde were not weapons systems they can certainly be regarded as first cousins to them and

could not have been remotely possible, at the time they were created, without
defence expenditure.

98   Nahum, A, note 87

99   Gimbel, J, note 1. Gimbel is particularly concerned to analyse the tensions
between exploitation and German reconstruction between the various
agencies of the occupying American authority. See also Farquarson, J,
'Governed or exploited? The British acquisition of German technology,
1945–48', *Journal of Contemporary History*, 32/1 (1997), pp23–42.

100   Gimbel, J, note 1, pp153–66

101   Bolling Airforce Base Historical Office, Microfilm A2056, Scientists Program,
frame 0117, quoted in Gimbel, J, note 1, p51

102   Public Record Office Ref. AVIA 65/738, Aircraft Research and Development
Programme 1956–57

103   The tip-jet concept was made possible by the power of the new gas turbine
engine which was used in this application as a gas generator to pump
its high-pressure exhaust air through hollow rotor blades where it exited
rearwards at the tip. The attraction of the system was that it powered the
rotor without the torque reaction resulting from shaft drive. This made
piloting simpler and removed the need for a powered and adjustable tail
rotor.

104   Gimbel, J, note 1, p164

105   The case of the design for the BMW car, taken up in Britain by the Bristol
company, is certainly in a different category, for in that case there was clearly
a sizeable commercial gain for the British company as well as a commercial
opportunity for the German manufacturer, although the home market
for fast cars of the type made by BMW prewar had disappeared and the
company re-entered the market with small economy types.

Colour plate 1
Rocket *as displayed at the*
National Railway Museum in
York during 1999.
(Michael R Bailey)

Colour plate 2
Rocket *drawn in c. 1840*
showing its form when with-
drawn from service. (National
Railway Museum, York)

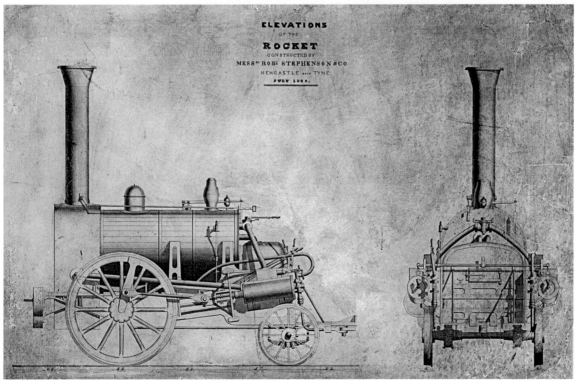

Colour plate 3
Example of a dismantled
component: the left-hand
eccentric rod.
(Michael R Bailey)

Colour plate 4
Left-side driving wheel
showing component,
fitting and maintenance
detail (Michael R
Bailey)

Colour plate 5
The transition period of the dashboard: sheet metal is still visible in the interior, but is beginning to disappear underneath padding and fabrics. From a German textbook of 1960, reproduced in a leaflet, from the archive of the Landesmuseum für Technik und Arbeit in Mannheim.

Colour plate 6
The fully integrated cockpit: padding and soft curves dominate. The driver's view takes in the interior, instruments and the manufacturer's badge – but not the outer shell of the vehicle, a 1995 Volkswagen. (Volkswagen AG)

Colour plate 9
Trams run through a
street scene at The (sic)
National Tramway
Museum, Crich,
Derbyshire, UK.
(Colin Divall)

Colour plates

*Colour plate 11
Early aviation exhibits
at the Musée de l'Air et
de l'Espace near Paris.
(Musée de l'Air et de
l'Espace, Le Bourget)*

*Colour plate 12
Re-creating the village
garage at the National
Motor Museum,
Beaulieu, UK.
(Colin Divall)*

*Colour plate 10
The Vasamuseet in Stockholm. (Stefan Evensen)*

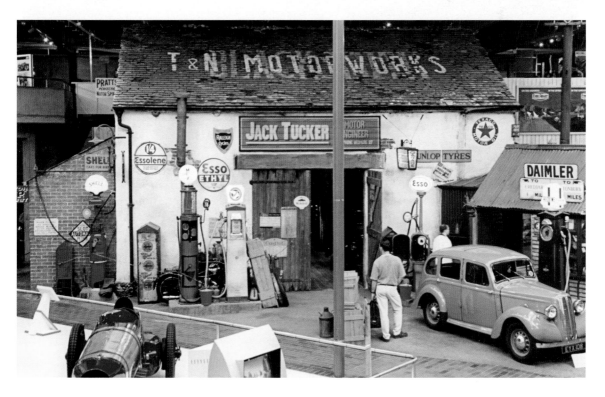

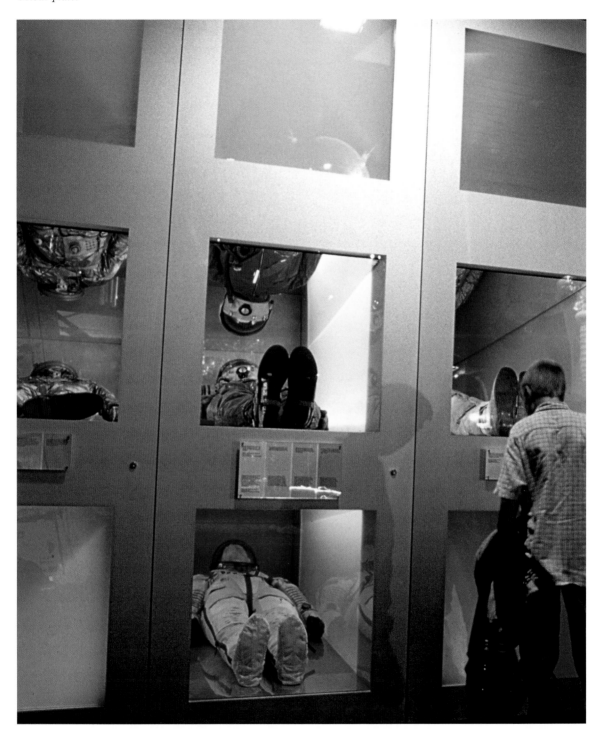

Colour plate 13 In the mausoleum, heroes of the space race (actually their spacesuits) are peacefully united. Enemies in the Cold War, astronauts today are members of a professional elite providing a good example of international cooperation. (Swiss Museum of Transport and Communication)

Colin Divall

The origins of transport museums in Western Europe

Transport museums are among the most numerous and popular of museums in Europe, but they are also widely misunderstood. Frequently they are dismissed as the products of narrow-minded enthusiasts obsessed with technology, full of unimaginative displays of over-restored vehicles reflecting at best a nostalgic view of the past. But the sector's historical roots are both deeper and more complex than is usually thought, and while exhibitions past and present are rarely beyond criticism, these diverse origins are reflected in a rich spectrum of interpretation. In their recent efforts to attract new and wider audiences, museums have concentrated on telling stories about the social effects of transport and travel. These displays have the potential to encourage visitors to reflect critically on the opportunities and challenges presented by transport in the past, present and future.

This article sketches the origins of public displays of transport in Western Europe. It was only after the Second World War that museums dedicated to one or more modes of transport became common. But transport collections date back at least as far as the early nineteenth century, and many of these became publicly accessible, either permanently or on a temporary basis, in industrial museums and at international and national exhibitions. The state often bore the major responsibility for these displays, which consequently tended to tell celebratory stories about industrial progress and nationhood. This was particularly true of mainland Europe, since governments here usually planned and directed the construction of transport systems. In the next century and at a more local level, municipal authorities often commemorated the tramways and other modes of transport which had enabled the dramatic growth of towns and cities. But commercial transport providers also had a part to play in marking transport's past. So too did private collectors, particularly when it came to celebrating non-mechanical forms of transport, such as horse-drawn carriages, as they became obsolete. The relative importance of these groups has varied considerably over time, from country to country and between modes of transport, making it very difficult to generalise. Voluntarism has always been important in Britain, for instance, and in recent decades the voluntary sector in the rest of Western Europe has taken more and more responsibility for saving and exhibiting transport artefacts.

Early origins – the great industrial museums

The great national museums have always told stories about a nation's sense of itself. From their founding in the late eighteenth century, these institutions displayed prized objects symbolising the dominance of humanity over nature, or that of one people over another. Sometimes museums marked the power of one part of society over another. Thus from the middle of the nineteenth century displays of royal carriages in certain European cities, such as Madrid, symbolised the monarchy's long and continuing reign.[1]

With the gathering pace of industrialisation, European countries adopted the machine as a measure of national achievement and a symbol of national identity, displaying key artefacts in technical or industrial museums. Such institutions, usually run by or in some other way closely associated with the state, often displayed vehicles and other transport artefacts as markers of progress and cultural superiority.[2] The oldest and one of the greatest of these museums, the Musée des Arts et Métiers in Paris, acquired as early as 1801 Cugnot's steam wagon of 1771, the first – albeit unsuccessful – example of locomotion. It is still there today, at the start of a recently refurbished transport gallery which – with occasional asides marking crucial technological contributions by other nations – traces French achievements right up to the collaborative European space launcher of 1997. The sight that now greets people at the culmination of their visit vividly expresses the reverential attitude towards transport that has evolved in France over the last two centuries. In the beautiful former chapel of the priory that is now the museum towers a huge steel structure. On this modern altar and on the chapel floor are arranged 20 or more vehicles, while several aeroplanes hang from the high ceiling above: icons at a shrine.[3]

The British state was slower off the mark, leaving private interests to mount the very first permanent celebrations of mechanised transport by displaying a few pioneering railway locomotives, starting in the 1850s. These machines had survived by chance or through the efforts of far-sighted individuals. Some very significant engines passed in the 1860s to the Patent Museum and thus came to be associated with the South Kensington Museum, a product of the Great Exhibition of 1851 and forerunner of the Science Museum, founded as such in 1909. These machines included Robert Stephenson's *Rocket*, winner of the Rainhill Trials of 1829, which sealed the future of steam locomotion; William Hedley's *Puffing Billy* of about 1813–14, an example of the cruder engineering of the railways serving the coal mines of northeast England (a replica is in the Deutsches Museum) (Figure 1); and Timothy Hackworth's *Sans Pareil*, another of the Rainhill competitors. The South Kensington Museum also started collecting ship models in the 1860s, and in time the Science Museum built up good, and in some cases excellent, collections of most forms of land, maritime and air transport. The aeronautical collection was refurbished some

Figure 1 Replica of William Hedley's Puffing Billy locomotive. (Deutsches Museum)

years ago, but unfortunately the Land Transport gallery, opened in the 1960s, was closed some three decades later, although parts of the collection are still on display elsewhere in the Museum. The third of the triumvirate of great European industrial museums, the Deutsches Museum, built up a comprehensive transport collection from its founding in the first decade of the twentieth century. In both Britain and Germany these collections primarily reflected national achievements, although in varying degrees they also marked some of the most significant technological aspects of the international development of transport.[4]

These museums were all, in their rather different ways, initiatives of the state. But even so they could not have built up their collections without the foresight and assistance of private individuals or businesses. *Rocket*, for example, had been sold into colliery service in the 1830s and was presented to the state by the industrialist who had extracted another 20 or so years' service from the engine.[5] Indeed it seems likely that private gifts and voluntary initiatives were responsible for many of the transport artefacts collected by the state museums of Western Europe before 1939. In terms of the sheer volume – if not always the significance – of what is saved, such methods of collecting have almost certainly become even more important since 1945. Transport companies, engineers, antiquarians and enthusiasts all had, and still have, a part to play. Nowhere was this clearer than in the field of railways, from the 1830s until the 1920s the pre-eminent form of inland transport over any distance.

The railway legacy

The distinction of founding the very first transport museum open permanently to the public fell to Norway, where a small railway museum was established in Hamar during 1897. But Britain remains the natural starting point for any history of railway museums, since it was there that mechanically worked railways were pioneered and, arguably, the richest collections in Europe were built up.

Britain's railways brought huge social and economic benefits, as well as not a few drawbacks. The system was largely the responsibility of commercial interests, for until nationalisation in 1948 and with the brief exceptions of the two world wars, the state's involvement in railway administration was, by the standards of the rest of Europe, very modest. These private companies, sometimes cajoled by private individuals and societies of what would now be termed enthusiasts, saved some of the most significant transport artefacts of the nineteenth century and early twentieth century. I have already noted that railway relics were put aside from around the middle of the nineteenth century, if only in penny numbers. Apart from those engines that went into museums, a few of these now worn-out machines were displayed in places associated with their working lives. The most famous was Timothy Hackworth's *Locomotion*, built for the pioneering Stockton & Darlington Railway in 1825, which was put on a plinth in Darlington in 1857.[6]

The timing of these first efforts is notable. The 1850s marked the publication of some of the earliest railway histories, as well as the first of Samuel Smiles' famous if tendentious biographies of British engineers.[7] All of this signalled the popular elevation of railways and their technical specialists to something approaching heroic status. Railways, in short, were becoming part of Britons' sense of themselves as industrial pioneers and worldwide leaders in some of the most important technologies of the industrial age – a feeling of easy superiority that nearly a century later allowed the English historian G M Trevelyan to proclaim that 'Railways were England's gift to the world'.[8] It seems likely that the railway companies were mindful of the benefits, in terms of what would now be called public relations and corporate image, of associating themselves with the industry's pioneering years. A particularly clear example was the North Eastern Railway (NER), which had absorbed the Stockton & Darlington Railway in 1863. In 1875 – a time when the railways generally were coming under increasing criticism – the NER, along with the local authority and other bodies, organised a Railway Jubilee to mark the fiftieth anniversary of the Stockton & Darlington. The festivities included a temporary exhibition of 27 locomotives, including *Locomotion*. Half a century later the NER's successor, the London and North Eastern Railway (LNER), would repeat the exercise on an even grander scale by including a cavalcade, and 50 years after that the nationalised British Rail's Eastern Region mounted yet another cavalcade.[9]

The international exhibitions of the latter half of the nineteenth and the first half of the twentieth centuries – and their more numerous but less-well-known equivalents organised on a purely national basis – were all important sites where technological patriotism intermingled with promotion of corporate image. Right from the start, with the Great Exhibition of 1851, these spectacles celebrated national achievements, tempering their partisanship but a little with professions of the universal benefits to be had from technology. As one of the engineering wonders of the age, the railways were almost always present, exhibiting their most modern achievements. But historical relics also had a part to play, demonstrating the native ingenuity of earlier generations and the progress that had been made since then. The railways continued to exhibit in this way well into the twentieth century. At the 1924–25 British Empire Exhibition, for instance, the LNER's display, 'The First and the Last', juxtaposed *Locomotion* with the then ultramodern *Flying Scotsman*. Such conjunctions were judged appropriate as late as 1951, when ancient and modern locomotives were displayed at the Festival of Britain, a national celebration signalling the beginning of the end of postwar austerity.[10]

The British railway companies were not persuaded of the advantages of a permanent museum until the mid-1920s, although the idea had been floated in the 1890s by antiquarians and enthusiasts. By the First World War such people had become more organised – the pioneering Railway Club was founded in 1899, followed in 1909 by the more narrowly focused Stephenson Locomotive Society (SLS). In the 1920s the SLS bought and restored the first locomotive to be privately preserved in Britain, inspiring similar action in other European countries. The engine was soon to find a place in the York

Railway Museum, opened in 1927.[11] But the founding of the museum was the product of more than enthusiasts' desires, important though these were.

Since the 1890s the railway companies had become a lot more sophisticated about corporate image. This was partly because they were subject to an increasingly strict regime of financial regulation by the state, forcing them to compete with each other in terms of quality of service and image rather than on price. Regulation also gave them a reason to band together in an effort to win over public opinion. The York museum had a small part to play in the process, which became particularly pressing after 1918 as road competition increased. The collection was started in the early 1920s by a middle-ranking official of the NER. But in 1923 the number of important railway companies was reduced by statute to just four, and this simplification of the industry made it easier to draw together material from across the country. By 1939 the museum had become the home of a modest collection of locomotives, rolling stock and small artefacts from across Britain. Some of these had been saved by senior engineers and other railway officials acting in a private or semiprivate capacity, suggesting they were motivated by professional pride or a strong sense of identification with their company. But once senior managers became involved the exhibition of these items inevitably took on a corporate dimension: the machines also functioned simultaneously as symbols of professional, industrial, regional and national identity, and perhaps more besides.[12]

The state took over the York museum and became more widely involved with the exhibition of transport in 1948, when the railways were nationalised along with the docks, inland waterways and certain road and urban transport operations. The newly formed British Transport Commission (BTC) quickly acknowledged that 'a well-placed, attractive, and properly managed British Transport Museum would be of material assistance in projecting the idea of an efficient national transport service', and that in addition to collecting engineering artefacts it had a responsibility towards 'the wider social and cultural heritage' of the transport under its control.[13] Eventually a Museum of British Transport was opened in stages from 1961, in a London suburb, although despite its name the museum covered only certain modes of inland transport. It closed in the early 1970s, along with the York site. The railway collections were transferred to the present National Railway Museum (NRM), which opened in 1975 as part of the Science Museum. This and subsequent changes to the NRM's administrative arrangements means that British Rail had, and its privatised successors have, no direct responsibility for the museum or its contents.

The exhibitions there now embrace elements of the railways' social history, and moves are afoot to include one or two of the most important of foreign vehicles (a Japanese Shinkansen, or 'bullet train', was the first). Nevertheless, many of the artefacts are displayed in ways that help to sustain a patriotic view of technology. Perhaps the best example of this is *Mallard*, an extremely popular icon exhibited as officially the world's fastest steam locomotive. This achievement – which is challenged by some in Germany and was almost certainly bettered by the Americans – reinforces the sense of national pride in the country's railways that, as I have shown, dates back at least a century and a half.

In mainland Europe the most important museums were founded by national administrations, reflecting the closer involvement between state and railway. Industrialisation lagged behind that in Britain, and so, generally speaking, did the commemoration of railways. The pioneering Norwegian museum at Hamar was quickly eclipsed by something altogether more important in Germany, where the railways had played a crucial role in uniting the nation in the latter half of the nineteenth century. The Bavarian state government pioneered railway construction during the 1830s, and some half century later, in 1882, an exhibition of Bavarian railway equipment at the Nuremberg international exhibition excited so much public interest that the collection was kept intact and housed in Munich, although it was open only to transport workers, ostensibly for their education. A permanent home was then found in Nuremberg, and this time the public was admitted, from 1899.[14]

Something similar happened in Prussia. Although initially operated as commercial concerns, by 1882 all the main lines serving Berlin had been nationalised. These were prosperous routes and the railways enjoyed a high social prestige, deriving chiefly from the part they had played in national unification. All this helped the Prussian State Railways justify the establishment in 1906 of the Verkehrs- und Baumuseum (Museum for Transport and Construction) in a disused station in Berlin. Like that in Nuremberg, this exhibition was intended primarily for the technical education of railway workers, although the public was admitted from the start. In 1935, however, the artefacts were rearranged to tell more clearly a story of 'progress' culminating in the Third Reich. The museum closed during the Second World War, and although some of the historic collection remained in the building the museum did not reopen after 1945 because of the political difficulties of operating in the divided city. In the 1960s a group of enthusiasts started to lobby for a new transport museum that would embrace more than just railways and, eventually, in 1980, Berlin's municipal government agreed to establish this. The Berlin Museum für Verkehr und Technik (Museum of Transport and Technology) opened in 1983. Most recently it has been renamed Deutsches Technikmuseum (German Museum of Technology), and has also significantly expanded its transport galleries. The present exhibitions do not shy away from addressing the railways' role in the darker side of twentieth-century German history.[15]

In most of the rest of Europe state and railway officials did little or nothing to commemorate railways until well into the twentieth century. Even Norway's modest memorial to the railways' unifying role closed in 1912 and was not reopened, on a new and grander site, until 1926. The first museum at Hamar had been the initiative of a group of railway officials, and in 1927 a similar arrangement encouraged the Netherlands State Railway to found a museum in Utrecht, where the railway had its headquarters. Other countries did little or nothing until after the Second World War, when modernisation threatened the destruction of much that had survived the hostilities. The completion of a new Nord station in Brussels in the early 1950s provided the location for a small museum; it is still there, the displays almost exactly as described in the late 1960s. In Italy the railways' contribution to national unification was arguably as great as that in Germany, but the Museo Nazionale Ferroviario (National Railway Museum) was not opened, in Naples, until well after 1945. Before this there was a much smaller display at the main terminus in Rome, the objects from which joined other land transport artefacts in Milan's Leonardo da Vinci Museum from the early 1950s.[16]

France serves as a more detailed example of the evolving relationship between public and private initiatives that has so often shaped national collections and their museums. Here the state was less closely involved with railways during the nineteenth century than in Germany, and, as in Britain, it was not greatly concerned about the preservation of material until after 1945. The private companies largely responsible for railway construction and operation showed little interest in a museum until after 1918, probably because their lines were themselves *un véritable musée vivant*. At around this time several locomotives dating back to the 1840s were put aside. None of this amounted to systematic collecting, though; as in Britain, much was left to local initiative at railway workshops or depots. Engineers' sense of professional pride inclined them to save items here and there in the face of managerial indifference.[17]

Private enthusiasts had a part to play as well, although it was not until 1929 that a newly founded group, inspired by the SLS in Britain and similar bodies elsewhere in Europe, started to lobby for a systematic programme of preservation with a museum as an eventual goal. The twin threat of growing competition from other modes of transport and modernisation of the railways – and particularly of the steam locomotive – spurred this action. Some significant artefacts were put aside, but much was lost before 1939. Although the French railways were nationalised in 1938, as SNCF, the Second World War and then a lack of finance in the war-torn country prevented any significant moves towards a national museum for a long time.

In the 1950s local initiatives by railway workers and engineering managers, encouraged in some cases by private societies, helped save more locomotives as wholesale modernisation proceeded. Gradually a preservation policy focusing chiefly on locomotives evolved within the engineering side of SNCF, but it was not until the mid-1960s that such moves were sanctioned at the highest level of the railway's management. Thereafter, the tide turned in favour of establishing a national museum. In 1969 the Ministry of Transport and SNCF agreed with the city of Mulhouse to place the collection in a museum provided by the local and regional governments. The latter saw the initiative as an important contribution to the economic regeneration of a region devastated by industrial decline, a motive which has characterised many proposals for transport museums in the last two or more decades. Opened on a temporary site in 1971, the Musée Français du Chemin de Fer moved to a permanent building in 1976. Recently, however, the museum has experienced difficult times, largely because it has not attracted enough visitors to satisfy the financial imperatives of the municipal authorities.[18]

So far I have dealt with just a handful of the most important railway museums in Western Europe. Railway employees or private individuals were often responsible for starting the collections that lay at the heart of these institutions, but the involvement of state railway administrations, private companies or governments at national or regional level was needed before permanent museums were founded. However, since 1945 and particularly since the 1960s, there has been a tremendous upsurge in interest across Europe in what private citizens, either individually or in groups, can do to preserve and display railway material – particularly, although by no means exclusively, in operating condition. In this brief essay I can do no more than note the phenomenon, and remark that it seems to be associated with a desire to commemorate the passing of a once-common form of everyday transport.[19] In this regard railway enthusiasts are no different in their motivation than an earlier generation of private collectors interested in preserving other, nonmechanical forms of transport.

The legacy of other inland transport

I do not know of any museum dedicated to the commonest and most egalitarian form of transport – walking. But there are some splendid collections of animal- and human-powered vehicles, many of which originated in an impulse to save reminders of folk and aristocratic customs threatened by industrialisation – or, more strictly, mechanisation, for animals remained a common source of motive power for some purposes well into the twentieth century. The folk dimension to this movement found its greatest success first in Scandinavia, in the last quarter of the nineteenth century, before spreading elsewhere in Europe (and North America); the preservation of aristocratic and monarchical material had even deeper roots, as I have already indicated. Dedicated carriage and wagon museums often originated in the collections of wealthy philanthropists, for this mode of transport has rarely been the domain of the sort of large company that might have thought a museum a worthwhile investment. (An exception is the Studebaker Brothers Manufacturing Company, in 1900 the largest wagon manufacturer in the world; but the company's fine collection is located in the United States.) A good example is one of the best collections in Europe, the Tyrwhitt-Drake Museum of Carriages in the south of England, built up after the First World War by the wealthy individual whose name it bears. The material gathered here covers almost the whole range of vehicles that are not mechanically propelled, although there is a tendency, regrettably common among transport collections of almost every kind, to downplay the mundane and everyday.[20]

Navigable waterways predated industrialisation and then evolved in tandem with the industrialising economy. Many, particularly the narrow-beam canals of Britain, remained animal-worked until well into the twentieth century. There are few museums dedicated to them, however, and most of these are comparatively new. Some of the reasons for this are not hard to fathom. Although of great importance in the late eighteenth and early nineteenth centuries, canals and navigable rivers were eclipsed by railways in Britain and mainland Europe, except in those few areas such as the Netherlands, Belgium, north-east France and the Ruhr where circumstances favoured ships or large barges. Thus corporate interests of the kind that helped to underpin early railway preservation in Britain were virtually absent. And since inland waterways did not unify nations in the same way as the railways, they did not attract the same levels of public interest or state support for their commemoration. Folklorists were not interested in canals and river navigation until the 1930s or 1940s, perhaps because waterways were still associated with the grimmer side of industrialisation, and perhaps too because it was only then that the real threat to ways of life going back 150 years or more became apparent.

Commemoration thus came only after 1945, with Britain taking a pioneering role. The first European museum to concentrate exclusively on inland waterways opened in 1963, in a converted canal warehouse at Stoke Bruerne in the English Midlands. It was run by the British Waterways Board, an arm of the state, though the museum would not have been founded but for the intense political lobbying of waterways enthusiasts in the 1950s. It was part of a reorientation of the commercially moribund network of narrow canals towards leisure use. Such has been the success of this policy that there are now 11 waterways museums in Britain, including a National Waterways Museum which embraces the original development at Stoke

Bruerne as well as two more recent initiatives. Both of these involved partnerships with local government, which wished to see economic benefits from the rejuvenation of derelict land and buildings.[21]

Most other museums of inland transport concentrate on mechanically powered vehicles, although some (museums of urban public transport come to mind) trace a lineage back to the days of – quite literally – horse power. Similarly, motor museums often display bicycles (Colour plate 7) as one of the technologies that contributed to the evolution of cars and motorcycles. Personal motor vehicles were exhibited very early on, reflecting their high social esteem and rapid rate of technological obsolescence. Temporary exhibitions of 'historic' motor cars (the oldest was then barely a decade old) go back to at least 1909, when a display was mounted as part of the Imperial International Exhibition at London's White City; one of the vehicles passed the following year into the care of the Science Museum, the first in an important collection. But the earliest institutions with sizable collections of motor vehicles are as varied in their origins as other transport museums. The first in Europe, the Musée National de la Voiture et Tourisme at Compiègne, France, was opened in 1927 by the state. Other important European collections were started between the world wars, or even earlier, by private individuals or manufacturing firms, although many were not opened to the public until the 1950s or later (Colour plate 8).[22]

Private collectors were often passionate and idiosyncratic in their choices, and these characteristics can often still be detected in modern museums. One of the most important is the National Motor Museum in the south of England, originally the Montagu Motor Museum, a private affair opened to public viewing in 1952. The initial collection of just five cars was displayed as a tribute to the owner's father, a motoring pioneer. The present building, dating from the early 1970s and partly paid for by the European motor industry and private subscribers, contains hundreds of vehicles reflecting British motoring from 1895 to the present, rising to a climax in the achievements of speed record breakers. As with so many such collections, there is something of a bias towards the glamorous and unusual, and neglect of the mundane.[23] But none can compare in this respect with the most spectacular motor exhibition in Europe, the Musée National de l'Automobile (Collection Schlumpf) in Mulhouse, France. This collection, finally opened to public view in 1982, was built up by a pair of wealthy industrialists who were passionate about Bugattis and other famous marques of a sporting or luxurious kind.

Here the regional government played a large role in securing public access, and something similar was quite common in Britain in the 1950s and early 1960s. The reasons were different, however. Municipal museums in the famous motor-manufacturing cities of Coventry and Birmingham exhibited locally-made vehicles, many of which had been privately collected. The displays helped the postwar generation understand their cities' role in twentieth-century industrialisation.[24]

Elsewhere in Western Europe manufacturers' museums have helped with the same task – Munich's BMW Museum is an excellent example – as well as acting as a form of corporate memory. Indeed, corporate collections form the backbone of some of the oldest motor museums outside North America: Germany's Daimler-Benz Museum opened in 1936 with a collection dating back to the late nineteenth century and which had first been exhibited in 1911. Other corporate collections are as old, although few were put on permanent public display until after 1945. The richest in Britain is at the Heritage Motor Centre, opened in 1992 on its present rural site some little distance from the motor-manufacturing areas of the West Midlands; the collection was built up over decades by the numerous companies that became the Rover Group.[25]

It is easy to understand the fascination of private citizens with motor vehicles, since these have always been marketed as much in terms of social prestige as for their practical utility. Nor does it take much imagination to see the benefits to motor manufacturers of preserving and exhibiting their own products. Other kinds of road transport have never attracted quite such widespread esteem – even today, commercial vehicles, taxis and buses play only a small part in most motor museums. Nonetheless there are many museums of public passenger transport across Europe.

Public transport played a part in the expansion of towns and cities from the nineteenth century, making possible the spread of suburbs with their separation of residences from workplaces; trams (Colour plate 9), buses and local trains remain powerful and highly visible markers of civic identity in many European cities. It is therefore not surprising that municipal authorities, often cajoled or helped by enthusiasts, have played a large part in preserving public transport vehicles. Some of these collections date from well before 1939. This timing reflects the obsolescence of the electric vehicles at the core of many collections – trams started to disappear in some European countries from the 1920s, and even in those places that retained them modernisation took its toll of early vehicles. Munich, for example, has a comprehensive collection of tramcars built up by the transport authority over many decades.

Yet few transport authorities now seem willing or able to invest much in displaying their collections imaginatively. The Munich collection, still publicly owned, is cared for in a redundant depot by a society of enthusiasts and employees acting in a private capacity – but sadly it is not accessible, although the potential for a splendid museum of urban mobility and everyday life is there. The situation in Copenhagen is a little better. The city had one of the earliest and most comprehensive systems of municipally controlled public transport in

Europe, but the transport authority's collection of trams, buses and trolleybuses is crammed into a small hall attached to a suburban bus depot. Displayed like this the vehicles will never excite much interest, except among aficionados. But there are exceptions. The London Transport Museum, opened in the early 1970s, relocated in central London in 1980 and comprehensively redisplayed in the mid-1990s, is by comparison generously financed by London's transport authority. It is one of the finest museums of urban transport in the world, telling rich, multifaceted stories about not just public transport but also the great city that would stop without it.[26]

Elsewhere enthusiasts have made impressive contributions to saving and displaying urban transport. Museums with extensive collections in Vienna and Frankfurt, for instance, owe their existence largely to private societies. Indeed, the world's first dedicated streetcar museum (the Seashore Trolley Museum in the United States) was started in 1939 by such a group. It quickly developed into a working line, satisfying a desire for operation that I have already noted is widely found among railway enthusiasts. The success of the American enterprise inspired a similar initiative in Britain, where the rapid disappearance of city systems meant that there was little opportunity to emulate the practice still quite commonly found on mainland Europe, i.e. operating in the streets. The Tramway Museum Society, incorporated in 1955, dates back to the acquisition of a single tram in 1948 and a limited tramcar operation started at what is now the National Tramway Museum in the early 1960s. It is now arguably the most impressive tramway museum in the world, not least because it places the development of tramways firmly in the context of urban politics and living.[27]

Still, even this admirable museum betrays its origins. Tram enthusiasts wished to celebrate a type of vehicle heading for extinction in Britain, and the public transport successors to the tram – the motor and trolleybuses – were under no circumstances to be admitted. With the passing of time, and perhaps too with the resurgence of tramways in Britain, this policy has eased a little so that now a bus may be found sharing the museum's roadway on special occasions. But the general problem remains one faced by all sites dedicated to just one mode of transport: very few, if any, forms of transport entirely banish their rivals, and it is hard to tell histories of intermodal competition, or for that matter cooperation, in the single-mode museum. True, several European museums embrace several – but scarcely ever all – kinds of transport. Of the postwar examples, the Verkehrshaus der Schweiz (Swiss House of Transport and Communication) at Lucerne, opened in 1959, is the most comprehensive. Yet even this important institution separates the various modes so that the whole museum hardly adds up to any more than the sum of its often-impressive parts.[28]

The legacy of maritime and air transport

My final two categories of transport are a little different in that
they are capable of overseas communication. The earliest maritime
museums date from the nineteenth century, air museums from the
interwar years. Their legacy is mixed, reflecting the many and varied
uses to which the sea and air have been put.

Early displays of artefacts in state-sponsored maritime museums
often embodied narratives of the European domination of other
peoples, defining this in terms of the 'civilising' benefits of progress.
Until the last century, control of overseas dominions depended
entirely on maritime technologies – at first sailing ships and then the
steamship, which first emerged as a practical tool for long distances
from the 1860s. So these vessels, or, more commonly, models of
them, became symbols of Western power. Not surprisingly, early
maritime museums often betrayed a strong connection with naval
affairs. A good example is Britain's National Maritime Museum.
Although the museum did not open in anything like its present form
until 1937, its origins lay in naval collections dating back to the early
nineteenth century which had been assembled into a Naval Museum
in Greenwich in 1873.[29] In 1999 the museum tackled this naval–
imperial legacy in a critical manner by mounting an entirely new, and
somewhat controversial, exhibition based on modern historiography.

At least one early maritime museum was directed more towards the
display of state power in a domestic context. The core collection of the
modern Portuguese National Maritime Museum was founded by the
monarch as a naval academy and maritime museum in 1863, featuring
'the archives of glorious relics' – chiefly ceremonial royal barges.
Despite Portugal's long history as a commercial and naval maritime
power, this early collection seems to have had little to do directly with
overseas trade or colonies.[30]

The commemoration of pre-industrial folk customs associated with
fishing, whaling and other trading activities contrasts sharply with such
displays of state power. One of the earliest examples in Europe was
the tiny Museum of Fisheries and Shipping, opened in Hull, England,
in 1912; it included displays on whaling (a local industry until 1868)
as well as ship models, marine paintings and navigation instruments.
Elsewhere, museums at Elsinore, Gothenburg and Stockholm followed
before the First World War, displaying artefacts drawn from merchant
shipping, shipbuilding and maritime folklore.[31] In the last 20 years or
more this kind of museum has grown both in number and popularity,
reflecting the public's near-insatiable interest in the history of everyday
life. Now however, museums as often as not commemorate maritime
activities that were originally carried out on a small scale, were then
industrialised and are now threatened by economic or environmental
problems. A British example is the National Fishing Heritage Centre
at Grimsby.

The Vasamuseet in Stockholm (Colour plate 10) suggests what can be achieved in communicating about the history of a society through maritime artefacts.[32] The *Vasa* was a seventeenth-century warship which sank in 1628 and was raised in 1959. The impact of the display, which dates from around 1990, is amazing. One enters a relatively dark space to be dwarfed by the restored vessel. The ship and the achievement represented by its conservation and presentation are at first overwhelming. But it is the careful interpretation that continues to impress. One can take just so much of the spectacle of this wonderful vessel – yet whenever one turns away it is to find another smaller-scale but nevertheless engaging display that interprets some aspect of the wider story. There is a constant interplay between the object and these supporting narratives. The visitor is bounced continually to and fro; first captivated by the vessel itself, then turning to a smaller display that answers some questions but – at the same time – encourages the visitor to return again to the vessel to confirm new knowledge or test out learning.

Like other ship recoveries, the *Vasa* has yielded up large numbers of small objects, each of which contributes through its own fascinating story to the wider historical themes of the exhibitions. But the *Vasa*'s display offers powerful lessons for other types of transport exhibition. Most transport collections include supporting material beyond the vehicles themselves, but what is striking about the *Vasa*'s supporting displays is partly their variety – some object-rich, some multimedia or conventional film, some computer-based interactive. Each, however, uses the *Vasa* and its context to illuminate another aspect of seventeenth-century life. And herein lies the real achievement, for the visitor leaves with some understanding not just of seventeenth-century ships; international politics, mercantile trading patterns, shipbuilding skills, life in early modern Stockholm – all are revealed through the medium of the *Vasa* and its supporting material. In so doing, the object transcends its reality as a transport artefact and becomes a window on the wider world of the past.

The legacy of early aviation museums offers similar challenges to those of the maritime sector. This is scarcely surprising, for after the 1914–18 war all the major European powers cloaked civil aviation with the same mantle of nationalistic and imperial fervour they had previously reserved for their naval and merchant marines. National flag-carriers – Imperial Airways, Lufthansa and so on – were set up partly to resuscitate and prolong empires, and to defend and extend national spheres of influence in the European arena. Public enthusiasm between the world wars was fired largely through the adventure and technology of powered flight: sporting events such as speed and endurance trials satisfied the public thirst for spectacle that in the previous century had been satiated by exhibitions, expositions and museums.

This helps to explain why aviation museums did not appear in any number until after the Second World War. Nevertheless, by then state institutions had already started to commemorate the pioneering machines and military forebears of civil powered flight. The Musée des Arts et Métiers, for example, had, and still has, Clément Ader's extraordinary bat-like machine of 1897, which for very many years was displayed as a device that had been successfully flown; the claim is now much weaker, but does not entirely abandon French priority in this regard. The Musée de l'Air on the south-eastern outskirts of Paris (Colour plate 11) was the first institution in the world dedicated to the permanent exhibition of aircraft (the Smithsonian Institution had opened its first display a year earlier). Its collection goes back to 1919 and was opened to the public in 1921; the displays were wholly of a military nature, although now they embrace the gamut of aviation.[33]

The few private collectors of this period also tended to share the wider public interest in military and sporting endeavours. In Britain, for instance, the Shuttleworth Collection – started by Shuttleworth himself as a purely private venture and opened to the public as his memorial after the Second World War – includes many significant, and flyable, aircraft dating back to 1909. But ordinary passenger or freight carriers, even of small dimensions, are neglected; by way of compensation the museum's site, a small aerodrome, happily recalls the modest infrastructure needed by all aeroplanes in the 1920s. Since the Second World War private societies have set up several aviation museums at old airfields, although most of these, at least in Britain, have a military orientation.[34]

Business interests do not seem to have been involved in the early commemoration of flight, and nor are they greatly so today. The corporate museum of aircraft is almost unheard of, although Boeing has one in the United States. Like industrial-scale shipbuilders, aircraft manufacturers do not sell directly to the public (light planes aside), while the purchasers – that is, airlines – are unlikely to be impressed by the existence of a museum. Of course, experimental or prototype aircraft of great technological interest may be donated to an appropriate museum, and when there is a strong nationalistic dimension then considerable efforts may be expended on displaying the artefact. The British prototype of Concorde, a powerful symbol in the 1960s of state support for high technology, had in effect a new branch of the Science Museum created around it. By contrast the Zeppelin Museum, opened in Friedrichshafen, Germany, in the mid-1990s, lacked a complete example of its historical subject. Nevertheless the museum was sponsored heavily by the modern Zeppelin company; perhaps it thought that the airship's niche market might grow if the public was made aware of the technology's environmental and economic advantages.[35]

Commercial airlines are no more interested than manufacturers in commemorating the history of flight, probably because their markets are so dispersed. A museum in any one country can only appeal to a tiny fraction of the international clientele. Even now the minimum viable length of haul has fallen to just a couple of hundred miles, airlines seem no more convinced than most other modern transport operators that money spent on a museum is a worthwhile investment in terms of corporate image or memory. However, a few European airports – Frankfurt is an example – do have small displays as a diversion for waiting passengers.[36] It will be interesting to see what happens when the aviation industry comes under greater scrutiny as issues such as congestion and environmental damage rise up the political agenda. Perhaps then European airlines, airports and manufacturers will feel that it is in their interests to do more to mark the history of commercial flight.

Concluding remarks

This essay can do no more than indicate the rich variety in the origins of transport museums and their collections (Colour plate 12). Indeed, there is a good deal of scope for further research in this area, and I should not be at all surprised if it reveals an even more complex picture than the one sketched here. The main players will probably prove to be the same – the state (both national and local), businesses, professional groups, private citizens and their enthusiast societies – but different and changing historical circumstances have no doubt generated myriad forms of cooperation, competition and even indifference in the gathering and exhibition of transport artefacts.

What then of the narratives or stories told through artefacts when they are displayed? I have made the perhaps rather obvious point that in very broad terms it is possible to see links between the kinds of bodies or individuals responsible for museums, the wider historical context, and the content of exhibitions. But this needs to be qualified. Quite apart from the fact that one will always be able to find exceptions to the normal pattern – perhaps a corporate museum that gives significant space to the contributions of the labour force – there remains the problem that it is very hard, perhaps impossible, to know what contemporaries made of what they saw. This is an issue even today, for there is little research on what, if anything, modern visitors learn from transport exhibitions – the critic might 'read' artefacts one way while members of the public do so in another. At the very least then, a greater sensitivity is needed towards the needs and desires of the 'consumers' of transport exhibitions, past, present and future.

It is of course impossible to know in advance what such research will reveal. Still, it would be surprising indeed if citizens in the increasingly sophisticated consumer societies of Western Europe did not demonstrate a high level of interest in the kinds of choices open to transport users in the past, as well as in those faced by us all as we are forced to confront the worsening problems caused by our apparently insatiable appetite for transport. If I am right in any of this, then transport museums are entering another important phase in their evolution; it certainly seems to be the case that new exhibitions are incorporating consumer perspectives. The irony is that, whatever its origins, when a transport museum succeeds it ceases, in a sense, to be a transport museum: it becomes instead a place where transport melds with the rest of society and some of the most pressing political issues of historical and modern society may be informally debated.

Notes and references

1   Simmons, J, *Transport Museums in Britain and Western Europe* (London: 1970), p22; Fabijanska-Zurawska, T, 'Architecture and exhibitions of some European carriage museums', *Transport Museums*, 17 (1990), pp106–12; Piggott, S, *Wagon, Chariot and Carriage: Symbol and Status in the History of Transport* (London: 1992), pp152–63

2   Adas, M, *Machines as the Measure of Man: Science, Technology, and Ideologies of Western Dominance* (New York: 1989)

3   Simmons, J, note 1, pp189–97

4   Forward, E A, *Handbook of the Collections Illustrating Land Transport*, vol. 3, pt 2, *Railway Locomotives and Rolling Stock: Descriptive Catalogue* (London: HMSO, 1931), p3; Simmons, J, note 1, pp22–4, 29–49, 232–3; Hudson, K, *Museums of Influence* (Cambridge: 1987), pp96–103; Lindqvist, S, 'An Olympic stadium of technology: Deutsches Museum and Sweden's Tekniska Museet', in Schroeder-Gudehus, B (ed.), *Industrial Society and its Museums* (Chur: 1993), pp37–54

5   See pp47–60.

6   Atkins, P, 'The early British rolling stock inheritance', in Shorland-Ball, R (ed.), *Common Roots – Separate Branches: Railway History and Preservation* (London: Science Museum, 1994), pp88–94; Hopkin, D, 'A commentary on restoration, conservation and the National Railway Museum collection', in Shorland-Ball, R (ed.), *Common Roots – Separate Branches: Railway History and Preservation* (London: Science Museum, 1994), pp215–21; Anderson, R G W, '"What is technology?": education through museums in the mid-nineteenth century', *British Journal for the History of Science*, 25 (1992), pp169–84, at p181; Ferguson, E S, 'Technical museums and international exhibitions', *Technology and Culture*, 6 (1965), pp30–46, at p39

7   Jarvis, A, *Samuel Smiles and the Constructions of Victorian Values* (Stroud: 1997), pp69–91

8   Trevelyan, G M, *English Social History*, 2nd edn (London/New York/Toronto: 1946), p531

9   Hopkin, D, 'Railway preservation: railways, museums and enthusiasts', MA dissertation, Leicester University, 1987, pp3–5; Jeans, J S, *Jubilee Memorial*

of the Railway System: A History of the Stockton and Darlington Railway and a Record of its Results, 3rd edn (Newcastle upon Tyne: 1974), pp304–15

10 Greenhalgh, P, *Ephemeral Vistas: The Expositions Universelles, Great Exhibitions and World's Fairs, 1851-1939* (Manchester: 1988), pp23–4; Ashby, H, 'The great international exhibitions – railway prizewinners and the National Railway Collection', in Cossons, N, Patmore, A and Shorland-Ball, R (eds), *Perspectives on Railway History and Interpretation* (York: 1992), pp100–9; Wells, J, 'The Great Exhibition and the railways', part 1, *Backtrack*, 12 (1998), pp676–9; 'Railways and the exhibitions of 1851 and 1951', *Railway Magazine*, 97 (May 1951), pp299–302; 'Railway exhibits at the British Empire Exhibition', *Railway Magazine*, 54 (June 1924), pp468–474

11 Simmons, J, note 1, pp23–4; Hopkin, D, note 9, pp47, 88–99

12 Simmons, J, note 1, pp23–4, 149–158; Hopkin, D, 'Railway preservation in the 1920s and 1930s,' in Cossons, N, Patmore, A and Shorland-Ball, R (eds), *Perspectives on Railway History and Interpretation* (York: 1992), pp88–99; 'The preservation of relics and records', report to the British Transport Commission, (London: 1951), pp10–11

13 'The preservation of relics and records', note 12, pp9, 13

14 Simmons, J, note 1, pp245–53; Weber, W, 'The political history of museums of technology in Germany since the nineteenth century', in Schroeder-Gudehus (ed.), *Industrial Society and Its Museums* (Reading: 1993), pp13–25; Zeilinger, S and Hascher, M, 'Museums of technology in Germany', *Technology and Culture*, 41 (2000), pp525–9

15 Gottwaldt, A, 'The railway buildings of Berlin and the Museum für Verkehr und Technik', in Shorland-Ball, R (ed.), *Common Roots – Separate Branches: Railway History and Preservation* (London: Science Museum, 1994), pp37–42; Gottwaldt, A, 'A philosophy of display', in Shorland-Ball, R (ed.), *Common Roots – Separate Branches: Railway History and Preservation* (London: Science Museum, 1994), pp210–14; Zeilinger, S and Hascher, M, note 14

16 Simmons, J, note 1, pp198–201, 210–17, 227–31, 265–72; Angius, P and Farneti, A, *Guide to Railway and Tramway Museums in Europe* (Milan: 1990), pp182–9

17 Porcher, B, 'Vers un musée Français du chemin de fer: des amis motivés', *Chemins de fer*, 438 (August 1996), pp4–9

18 Porcher, B, note 17; Renaud, J, *Musée Français du Chemin de Fer, Mulhouse* (Mulhouse: 1993); Lee, C E, 'The Buddicom locomotive at South Bank', *Railway Magazine*, 97 (July 1951), pp487–9

19 The operation of so-called heritage railways is particularly common in Britain. See Divall, C and Scott, A, *Making Histories in Transport Museums* (London: 2001), chapter 5.

20 Kavanagh, G, *History Curatorship* (Leicester/London: 1990), pp14–31; Fabijanska-Zurawska, T, note 1; Lee, A, *American Transportation: Its History and Museums* (Charlottesville, VA: 1993), p48; Simmons, J, note 1, pp84–92, 202–4; Garvey, J, *A Guide to the Transport Museums of Great Britain* (London: 1982), pp62–4

21 'Other UK canal museums', http://www.canalmuseum.org.uk/canmusuk.htm,

2000; Simmons, J, note 1, pp115–121; Garvey, J, note 20, pp150–2, 161–3; Bolton, D, *Race Against Time: How Britain's Waterways Were Saved* (London: 1991), p39

22 Simmons, J, note 1, pp33–7, 108–9, 112–14; Nicholson, T R, *Automobile Treasures: An Introduction to the Open Motor-Car Collections of Britain and Europe* (London: n.d., *c.* 1963), pp16–120; Devauges, J-D, 'Le Musée de la Voiture et du Tourisme de Compiegne: 1927–1994. Histoire et perspectives', *Transport Museums*, 20 (1993), pp89–93; Cossons, N, 'Messages from motor museums', in Moore, J S (ed.), *World Forum of Motor Museums: Papers of the Fourth Forum* (Gaydon: 1996), pp7–13

23 Nicholson, T R, note 22, pp20–2, 25; Simmons, J, note 1, pp93–100; Garvey, J, note 20, pp57–9; Carter, G, *The National Motor Museum: A Pictorial Guide to Motoring History* (Beaulieu: 1995)

24 Simmons, J, note 1, pp130–5; Garvey, J, note 20, pp115–17, 130–3

25 von Pein, M-G, 'The new Daimler-Benz Museum: an invention sets the world in motion', *Transport Museums*, 13/14 (1986/87), pp14–18; Garvey, J, note 20, pp13–16; *Heritage Motor Centre Catalogue* (Gaydon: British Motor Industry Heritage Trust, 1997), pp3–5

26 Simmons, J, note 1, pp60–7; Garvey, J, note 20, pp21–6; Divall, C, 'Changing routes? the new London Transport Museum', *Technology and Culture*, 36 (1995), pp630–5

27 Kelly, R E, *A Guide to the Seashore Trolley Museum* (Kennebunkport, ME: 1997), p3; Yearsley, I, *Tramway Adventure: A Celebration of Tramcar Preservation, 1948–1998* (Crich: National Tramway Museum, 1998), pp2–12

28 For a comprehensive description of the present museum and its plans for the future see pp173–81.

29 Hicks, R D, 'The ideology of maritime museums, with particular reference to the interpretation of early modern navigation', PhD thesis, Exeter University, 2000, p17; Simmons, J, note 1, pp23, 77

30 Villarinho, M, 'Museu de Marinha: the Portuguese National Maritime Museum', *Transport Museums*, 9 (1982), pp19–35, at p20; Ramos Rocha, A, 'Exhibition of Portuguese traditional boats in a new environment', *Transport Museums*, 15/16 (1988/89), pp99–104, at p99

31 Hicks, R D, note 29, p32; Simmons, J, note 1, pp23, 144–5; Paget-Tomlinson, E, 'A maritime museum for Hull', *Transport Museums*, 3 (1976), pp9–17; Crumlin-Pedersen, O, 'The Viking Museum of Roskilde: a museum of nautical archaeology in Denmark', *Transport Museums*, 2 (1975), pp84–104

32 I am grateful to Andrew Scott for these paragraphs on the Vasamuseet.

33 'Musée de l'air et de l'espace', descriptive pack, *c.* 1998

34 Simmons, J, note 1, pp108–14; Garvey, J, note 20, pp105–10, 136–7

35 de Syon, G, 'The Zeppelin Museum in Friedrichshafen', *Technology and Culture*, 40 (1999), pp114-19

36 Wustrack, M K, 'The historical aviation collection of Flughafen Frankfurt Main AG', *Transport Museums*, 13/14 (1986/87), pp27–32

Bettina Gundler

Deutsches Museum Verkehrszentrum: a new museum for transport and mobility in Munich

The Deutsches Museum has been given the opportunity to open a new branch on the occasion of its 100th anniversary. Thus it can partly solve the problem of restricted space on the museum island and expand substantially its treatment of land transport. The city of Munich has donated three historical trade-fair halls (about 12,000 square metres of exhibition space) located in central Munich, close to the Oktoberfest grounds (Figures 1 and 2). These three halls, built in 1908, were among the earliest Bavarian examples of concrete construction and thus played an important role in Munich's architectural history. They are protected by law as historical buildings and are currently being renovated and restored. This renovation process is scheduled to be completed in 2005 and is financed by the state of Bavaria and the city of Munich.[1]

The Verkehrszentrum (transport centre) of the Deutsches Museum will be opened in stages, starting in 2003. The current land transport

Figure 1 The largest of the three trade-fair halls from 1908. (Deutsches Museum)

exhibitions will be abolished in this process. Most of the objects will be moved and redisplayed as part of the new exhibitions in the three trade-fair halls.

The overarching concept is formulated in the 'Vision 2003' report of the Deutsches Museum:[2]

- It is designed to be a place of education and information, where visitors can learn about both historical developments and current topical issues related to transport in all its complexity.

- It is to be a place of meeting and dialogue, a forum for topical discussions, where contemporary witnesses have an opportunity to be heard, where lectures are held, and where politicians, scientists and planners are invited to give talks and to debate.

- The exhibitions are considered places for entertainment and sensory experience as well as for the exploration of well-known and unusual objects. They are to satisfy the hunger for knowledge as well as simply to be fun. These goals will be reached through a mixed offering of conventional exhibits, animations, interactive media, demonstrations, period settings and artistic installations. Under current economic circumstances, not all of these goals can be reached at once, and indeed some may have to wait for a considerable time.

- Finally, the Verkehrszentrum is designed to 'open a window' through which visitors will see contextual backgrounds for the land transport collections of the Deutsches Museum. The exhibitions will present a comprehensive view of transport history and mobility. They will include social and technical systems of transport together with important political, economic, social and cultural forces that have led to their development.

The exhibits of the collections – bicycles, cars, coaches, rail vehicles, etc. – will thus be presented in contexts which go far beyond technology. The move to the new branch offers an opportunity to transfer the exhibits to a much larger space, where the former strict separation along the lines of transport modes can be converted into a system of interconnected exhibitions. An integrated presentation will be derived from contexts associated with transport and mobility. The development and importance of individual means of transport and vehicle categories will not be ignored, but the focus will have changed. The individual means of transport or the technical object will not be at the centre of the presentation, rather attention will be on the historical development of transport modes in a network of competing systems, including social implications and current perspectives. The main focus will lie in the nineteenth and twentieth centuries, in accordance with the collections and the special dynamics of history in this period.

Figure 2 Architectural models of the trade-fair halls. (Deutsches Museum)

As a first step, the contextualisation of exhibits requires thematic rearrangement, which we plan to accomplish with the help of transport scenes (a crossing, a square, a platform, a street). Each hall is assigned a topic. In this framework, the history of transport vehicles as well as the development of systems of transport and mobility can be presented as a series of case studies. Furthermore, this allows us to use existing collections, a factor of no small importance.

Hall 1: urban transport

The first and largest hall is dedicated to the field of urban transport. It deals with transport and mobility in urban agglomerations, their economic, political and social causes and the development of public transport systems in the nineteenth and twentieth centuries. In the centre, a part of the collection will be arranged to represent a highly frequented square in the 1950s. From there, sequences of exhibits form a time line to the past and the present. In the area around the square, important aspects of transport in urban centres are dealt with in so-called 'topic islands'. Topics range from the increase in commuter traffic and its historical roots to questions of city and traffic planning and rescue services. The design of the hall reflects the rhythm of urban transport.

Hall 2: travelling

The second hall deals with the development of mobility and transport technologies from the perspective of travelling and of travellers. The exhibits will be grouped around displays of coaches, cars, two-wheelers and rail vehicles. Two pairs of rails in the middle of the hall will run 'in competition' with two parallel 'streets', with each following a time line. This exhibition will show how different means of transport forged different cultures of travelling; it will also demonstrate that they affected mobility behaviour and the perception of the world, space and time. The development of railways and the automobile and the competition between them will be integral to the thematic treatment. The design of the hall will be inspired by the atmosphere of a large railway station, to give a suggestion of wanderlust.

Hall 3: mobility and technology

The last hall will deal with mobility in a physical sense, from both a human and a technical perspective. Starting off with human pleasure in movement and acceleration, it will show how people conceived of ways to move themselves and their goods in faster, more economical or more comfortable ways – from a skate made of bones to the basic innovations of rail and road which have revolutionised movement and transport in the last 200 years. Towards the end, the corresponding reactive developments in vehicle and transport technology and of the accelerated growth in mobility will be demonstrated through selected examples. It will be suggested that the reactive effects may have substantial limiting effects on the urge for mobility in future generations.

In our exhibits we want to appeal not only to those who have a special interest in the history and technology of transport, but also to reach out to new target groups. We want to attract visitors who are interested not only in technical details, but also in the usage,

further development and interpretational context of technical objects.[3]
We purposely do without a fixed path through the three exhibition
halls. Instead, we offer our visitors a range of thematic units that
complement but do not necessarily depend on each other. Variations in
the themes will show differences in perspectives and interpretations of
transport developments.

After this brief presentation of our concept, let us turn to questions
of special interest to readers of this volume: What is the role of
artefacts in context-orientated exhibitions? How can they convey our
messages? To what degree should we use period settings? How can we
communicate themes and messages without an overdependence on
photographs and charts and depictions of objects in graphic forms?

We have a fundamental belief that objects, from the impressively
huge complete machine to the intriguingly tiny fragment, can be very
effective as message carriers. Initially we want to try to convey the
central meaning of our exhibitions by using original objects either
alone or in special arrangements to tell stories. We will not try to create
exact historical or technical environments, but rather settings that
suggest these contexts.

For example the express train S 3/6 (Figure 3), which is currently
displayed under 'Locomotives', will in future be shown as a part of a
railway system carrying passengers and their luggage. It will be seen
as incorporating special technological advances compared to other

locomotives, but also as having been of particular importance in regional and cross-regional public transport in the first third of the twentieth century (it was, for example, used as a locomotive for the 'Rheingoldexpress'). Another example is the presentation of objects together with elements of the physical infrastructure, for instance, a train on tracks, with overhead cables and a station platform. In similar ways, equipping vehicles with luggage, goods and accessories from a specific time period will show the nature of its use, the era it was used in and the status of its users. These are, of course, not new methods of presentation in the museum world, but they are departures from the way exhibits on transport have been displayed in the Deutsches Museum.

Other exhibits describe the composition of traffic and the competition between methods of transport in specific time periods. The most important example of this is the 'Place and crossroads' scene in the 'Stadtverkehr' (city traffic) hall. The exhibits will be designed to suggest a congested area in the 1950s, the beginning of mass motorisation in Germany. The selection of vehicles – from bicycles, horse-drawn carriages, vans, two-wheelers, small cars and taxis of an earlier period, through trams from the late 1930s and luxury vehicles from the 1950s – will illustrate the composition of inner-city traffic in Germany during the postwar years and the broad spectrum of vehicles that filled the streets during the take-off phase of German mass motorisation. It permits conclusions about vehicles and the various vehicle types that this form of motorisation featured, and it also illustrates the different consumption patterns of the various road users.

This setting will portray the density of city traffic and show how shortage in capacity is a constantly recurring phenomenon, something that experts will recognise from their experience with both public and private transport systems. The display will highlight strengthening competition between public and private transport systems since the 1960s and the decline of trams as the 'automobile community' took shape. This historical representation will be contrasted with personal observations of current city traffic patterns, thus posing questions about further development (including city planning, changes in traffic volume and street capacity, effects of increasing use of the automobile on public transport, consequences for the environment, etc.). Certainly, not all visitors will comprehend the full spectrum of these messages. But the setting will offer a good starting point from which to deal with individual problems presented on the adjacent theme islands.

The displays of the Verkehrszentrum will depict objects from the various exhibition areas in different manners, in classical museum fashion: as unique icons, or as representative pieces that provide historically valuable information about a particular technology. But at the same time, many vehicles in our collection are representatives of general transport and mobility history, suitable to assist in telling broader stories. For example, from Switzerland we have the 'Pilatusbahn', as well as the 'Krokodil' from the Rhaetische Bahn, which includes a saloon wagon. In the exhibition we plan to have these vehicles tell the story of the development of transport in the alpine mountain region at a time of high tourism at the beginning of the twentieth century. They will be set in context by using background pictures, platforms and travel accessories. Other objects, such as a VW transporter, modified as a camping wagon and used by a German couple who travelled the world in the 1970s, present little stories; when put together, they will display the larger picture of the mobility culture of the last 200 years.

Relationships within exhibits will find creative expression in various ways: sometimes single objects will be emphasised, in other cases the objects will fuse with their surroundings, as in the above-mentioned scene. As the development of our ideas continues, additional choices will be made concerning the selection of objects and the context of their placement. This will be a complex process, involving reinterpretation of items currently on display as well as research on objects in storage.

The attempt to create a context-oriented exhibition of course includes new criteria for our collection policy, because the choices made in days gone by were focused more on technical characteristics and less on cultural aspects. We plan to broaden the collections by considering the specific needs of the Verkehrszentrum. Thus the locomotive collection will be complemented by travel carriages and the collection of street vehicles enhanced by adding mass-produced examples (including both two-wheelers and automobiles). Besides that, we are making an effort to expand our collections to include more objects related to public transport and to alternative energy. In addition to technical artefacts, we will pay more attention to objects which illustrate the sociocultural dimension of transport and mobility, including toys, tourist souvenirs, accessories, works of art, and objects that support exhibition themes.

Additional techniques are being planned which will illustrate in dramatic fashion some of the tensions inherent in our subject. An example is what we call an 'infrastructure cube', planned for the city traffic hall. It will take as its theme the underground traffic and communications network. One side of this large cube will be painted to represent a cross-section of space above and below street level, as if we had sliced through cars, concrete, cables, pipes and a subway tunnel. The sides of the cube will provide space for other visual information. The inside of the cube is designed to be accessible and will accommodate a showroom where themes related to the infrastructure of underground transport can be developed in detail.

As we only have limited funds for scenery and multimedia equipment during the first stage, we will rely on classical techniques, using photographs, graphics and motion pictures. Large pictures, especially moving pictures, are especially effective in bringing exhibits to life and engaging the attention of visitors. We expect to make extensive use of documentary films.

The rather restrained media effort has the salutary effect of being consistent with our overall thesis. In our view, museum exhibitions – in contrast to theme parks – must now more than ever focus on those treasures which can only be found in a museum: the artefacts. In the concept of the Verkehrszentrum, the various media and demonstrations are meant to have an additive, supporting, partly theme-referring, partly exhibit-referring function. The graphics, videos and computer games will enhance and give additional meaning to the machines.

In conclusion, we must consider how to create a balance between unbounded (and potentially meaningless) context versus narrowly construed (and interesting to only a few) technology (something that is also discussed by William Withuhn[4]). The concept of the traffic centre endeavours to solve this dilemma by combining the classical museum with a thematic approach, using an abundance of artefacts in conjunction with a number of techniques through which the visitor will have the opportunity to delve deeper into themes. Subsequent visitor-evaluation surveys will show us if this attempt is feasible and where we can make improvements. The step-by-step process by which we are developing the museum will provide us with the opportunity to make these changes.

Notes and references

1 In 2001 state and city approved a total sum of around €50 million. Close to 80 per cent of this sum is allocated to restoration of the three halls; the rest is for the interior architecture and exhibition project. In the future we plan to raise an additional sum of around €1.5 million from private partners, partly through in-kind contributions.

2 'Vision 2003. Grundsatzprogramm' (Munich: Deutsches Museum, 1995); 'Grundkonzept für das Deutsche Museum Verkehrszentrum. Zusammenfassung der Grundgedanken und konzeptionelle Leitlinien' (Munich: Deutsches Museum, 1998, published 2001).

3 The results of a research project dealing with visitors' interests confirm this approach in general and show differences between special target groups (e.g. male and female). See Klein, H-J *et al.*, 'Go West. Die Besucher des Deutschen Museums und ihre Meinungen über das Neue Verkehrszentrum' (Karlsruhe: 2000), pp29, 70f.

4 See pp167–72.

Bill Withuhn

Artefacts at the Smithsonian: a new long-term exhibition on the history of transport systems

Exhibit planners know that only a small fragment of their potential audiences have an intrinsic interest in specialised subjects – such as transport or transport systems. Automobile enthusiasts, for example, may come in sizable numbers to traditional automotive museums, but a very large part of the public ignores such institutions. Adding historical, cultural or other context is seen as the high road both to reaching larger audiences and to furthering a museum's educational mission.

Adding context, however, is a tricky business. A didactic overlay of 'system' incorporated in an exhibit of transport history may add cohesiveness but is likely to appeal to the same technologically inclined audiences that would have patronised the museum in any case. Taking other approaches that might be loosely tied to 'system', an auto museum may attempt to broaden its audience by treating automotive design or, as has frequently been done, by offering overt connections to nostalgia. 'Cars of the 1950s', with period advertising and 'road culture' included, may bring in new visitors for a while, but what of all those antique cars and their infrastructure beyond the direct memory of most people today? Appeals to nostalgia are inherently limiting, since they depend on visitors bringing into the museum an interpretive frame based on personal memory. Albeit powerful for some of us, the memories of one generation are not shared in the same way by people in different age groups, and such memories are simply not shared at all by people of different backgrounds. As to the concept of 'system', the problem is that it is in many ways an abstraction, and one obviously difficult to convey in a museum setting, with objects artificially excised from the complex interrelationships of which they were once a part.

In the mid-1990s, the Smithsonian's National Museum of American History (NMAH) began to take seriously the idea of renovating its existing halls devoted to road and rail transport – some 21,000 square feet of space. These areas had not been significantly altered since the museum opened in 1964 and desperately cried out for a 'contextual reinterpretation' and for rethinking in terms of historical transport systems. A breakthrough was an appropriation from the US Congress in 1998 for $3 million, which could be applied to building, caring for

167

and exhibiting NMAH's transportation collections. Since that time, a team of 15 curators and specialists has been assembled, designers have been contracted, exhibit content and floor plan have been created and vetted, and an additional $21 million has been raised from private corporations and trade groups to complete the required funding.

A word should be said about sources of funding, since it contrasts so dramatically with the usual European experience. With very rare exceptions, government money has not supported major exhibitions at NMAH since 1983; private funds have been essential. The explicit agreement with Congressional appropriators in the present case was that the $3 million, if applied to an exhibition, was a 'public down payment' against which the museum would raise funds from the private sector; no other federal support would be forthcoming. The initial federal backing proved crucial to the fundraising strategy in two ways: firstly, by allowing the museum time to set the exhibit's themes, storyline, content, floor plan and budget well *before* other fundraising began, and secondly, by investing the project with the institutional commitment needed to attract serious interest from potential contributors.

After some five years of work, the interpretive approach taken by the NMAH team (and it is very much a team collaboration) combines the following:

Upgrade of the maritime hall

A major upgrade of the adjacent maritime hall is planned, while merging into one space the existing road and rail halls, together with a portion of the existing civil engineering hall. The area currently under renovation is over 26,000 square feet.

Land and maritime time lines

The time line of the revised but separate maritime hall, *c.* 1600–2000, is quite different from the time line of the land transport exhibition, which is set at 1876–2000, based primarily on the strengths of our collections. The year 1876 is also the centenary of the United States and so gives a convenient starting point for what we are interpreting in the land transport exhibition as primarily a twentieth-century story (other planned or existing exhibitions at NMAH cover aspects of pre-1876 transport). The land and maritime time lines, though separated for the visitor, come together in key ways: for example, the land and maritime exhibitions each include at least two historical treatments of ports. The idea of 'system' is front-and-centre in these treatments.

Historical 'settings'

Time lines are divided into more or less immersive and discrete historical 'settings'. Each setting has an explicit time, place and limited set of themes. Wherever possible, each setting has one or a few central artefacts that fit precisely into the chosen time and locale. For instance, the first section of the land transport exhibition begins in the summer of 1876, in Santa Cruz, California. The themes are: the expectations in small American towns of the era that a railroad would ensure prosperity, the important new connections of mobility and commerce that were created, the unintended consequences that often ensued, and the great transformation in agriculture and agricultural distribution that railroads brought to the western US – and by extension to the entire country – during the final quarter of the nineteenth century. The central artefact is our locomotive *Jupiter* – which was built and delivered to the Santa Cruz Railroad in 1876. The themes are explicated by actual people and events: promoters of the railroad, Chinese who built the tracks and tended the new crops that came to the region, and the painful denouement of the railroad – founded as an independent line but taken over in a few years by the corporate colossus, the transcontinental Southern Pacific. Note that 'system' is an undercurrent throughout, but system in terms of the role of the railroad in changing human relationships. The story told of *Jupiter* is not its engineering details, nor its minor place in locomotive development, but its place in a much larger set of interconnected changes that directly altered lives. The Santa Cruz Railroad becomes a 'case study' that illuminates significant, nationwide themes of late-nineteenth-century economic and social history in the US.

Overlapping transport modes
All modes of transport – land, water; road, rail; public, private; horse-drawn, self-propelled – are included as overlapping and organic to an overall story of change in personal mobility and in the distribution and consumption of goods. For the first time at the Smithsonian, the story of transportation is given a central place in American history. To the team, it is a matter of 'following the travelers, the migrants, the immigrants, the commuters, and the stuff people produce and consume' rather than following the vehicles. The main idea is to reveal the ways in which Americans have chosen and built their transport systems and thus have changed their society.

Other settings
Other specific settings – each telling of nationwide trends – include:

- Washington DC at the turn of the twentieth century, with the impact of the trolley on urban and suburban development (an 1890s Washington streetcar is the central object) and the transition in urban diets as food distribution expands from regional to nationwide patterns

- New York city in 1920, with a look at aids to navigation in a busy port, and the growth of New York into a colossus of finance, manufacturing and marketing, while continuing to attract immigration

- a railway station in Salisbury, North Carolina, in the late 1920s, with a heavy Pacific-type locomotive of the Southern Railway of 1926 as the centrepiece – and with stories of travellers, of workers on passenger and freight trains, of the Jim Crow segregation[1] endemic to travel in the American South during that time, and illustrating the dependence of the nation's manufacturing, commercial distribution, and long-distance travel on the rail system

- a suite of exhibits on Americans' early adoption of the automobile

- a section on US Route 66 (complete with almost 50 feet of the highway's original concrete pavement from Oklahoma), the fabled road that connected Chicago with Los Angeles and in the Great Depression of the 1930s carried both migrants and increasing truck traffic

- a tourist cabin from US Route 1 in Maryland

- family tourism and camping by 'Trav-L-Coach' (i.e. caravan) at a vacation spot in Maine

- a 1939 school bus from Indiana and the transformation of rural education

- the new-car showroom of an actual Buick dealer in Portland, Oregon, in 1949, with a night-time street scene of a Portland 'strip' and a selection of late-1940s/early-1950s autos in the background

- the postwar Chicago suburb of Park Forest, Illinois, in 1955, followed by a large section on how expressways, buses, transit systems, and airport location decisions changed Chicago itself in the 1950s and 1960s (a walk-in exhibit of a recently retired Chicago transit car and on-board interpretation is featured)

- the story of containerisation and the ensuing radical changes to the ports of Oakland and San Francisco.

- two lanes of Interstate highway across the US South and Southwest in the 1970s–1980s (complete with a heavy freight truck and a variety of domestic- and foreign-built cars), with stories of truckers and tourists

The final section, 'Going Global', takes all the intertwined themes into the beginning of the twenty-first century – into our present world where systems of transport, personal mobility, communications, commerce, distribution, consumption, finance and marketing are truly international and inseparable.

A basic principle of museum design, we feel, is that visitors have a definite hierarchy of attraction regarding exhibit presentations. A museum is not a place conducive to deep intellectual enquiry. One is on one's feet, time is limited, and most visitors come in social or family groups. A museum's unique stock in trade is the genuine artefact. To tell meaningful stories with artefacts is the challenge.

Of least interest to museum visitors are abstractions, such as those we often try to convey with didactic labels. Of greater interest are subjects that meet a visitor's special interests. But such subjects, even with glitzy design, do not appeal to the majority who do not share those interests. One can imagine other steps ascending an 'interest hierarchy'. In transport museums, we know that big items (locomotives and airplanes, for example) can inspire awe. But that is usually all they do; the interest of most visitors is ephemeral. 'Interactive' exhibits are in fashion, and they appeal to both our sense of curiosity and our desire to take control of our learning activities.

Near the top of the hierarchy, I would argue, are exhibits in which stories of people are the touchstone. That is because all of us, as people, are innately interested in well-told stories of fellow human beings, especially in people with whom we can share some connection. At the peak of the hierarchy are stories of real and often ordinary individuals: every newspaper reporter knows this to be true. A story of a disaster, for example, may start with the simple facts: what, where, when, how serious. But within a few paragraphs, the reporter weaves in reactions and stories of individuals involved. Meaning is thus given, and the reader is absorbed in the story, seeking to discover how people dealt with the experiences described.

The team has thus chosen to convey most of the exhibition's content through human stories. Stories of migrants, promoters, workers, and travellers occur throughout. A story of Jim Crow is an example: Charlotte Hawkins Brown was a well-known African-American educator who frequently travelled through Salisbury, North Carolina, in the mid-1920s. Earlier in the decade, at a station in a different city, she was summarily evicted from her seat in a Pullman car by a gang of toughs who invaded the train; the Pullman Company officer aboard took no action to defend her rights. She later talked about her experience in lectures. We have her own words, and visitors to the new exhibition will meet Dr Brown and encounter Jim Crow through her eyes.

Added together, the team believes that the specific settings, artefacts and stories we have chosen add up to a provocative journey through a vital part of modern American social history. Our working definition of 'system' is stretched to include the places of our artefacts in sets of complex and dynamic human relationships. When the exhibition, called 'America on the Move', opens as scheduled for fall of 2003, our visitors will render a verdict.

Notes and references

1 Jim Crow was the common term for the legally enforced system of racial segregation in public accommodations in the southern and southeastern states of the US from the late nineteenth century until the mid-1960s.

Afterword

The new exhibition, entitled 'America on the Move', opens to the public on 22 November 2003. This is the largest exhibition to be mounted under a single banner in the history of NMAH, and occupies the full width of the east end of the museum's first floor. The design of the exhibition permits full access by unaccompanied persons in wheelchairs, and provisions are included for the sight- and hearing-impaired. An extensive Website open to all, as well as an education package for secondary schools, are part of the project. 'America on the Move' will remain open in the museum for a minimum of 20 years, with occasional refurbishments as budgets allow.

Henry Wydler

Verkehrshaus der Schweiz: Switzerland's different transport 'museum'

The Verkehrshaus: a special case

'Verkehrshaus' means 'house of transport', not 'museum of transport'. This small difference serves to define a different kind of institution: one that is a learning place with a leisurely atmosphere, where entertainment and enjoyment are permitted; one that focuses on the joy in watching and experiencing, and fosters curiosity for the unknown. A look back into history can explain this special case.

In 1897 a member of staff of the Jungfrau Railway Corporation sent out a call to all railway enterprises and 'interested circles' that they should keep historical material and provide public access to it. He stressed the pioneering role of the Swiss in building mountain railways. In 1902, the Society of Graduates from the Zurich Polytechnic University sent out a similar call. Neither initiative led to any further steps, and even the founding of the Swiss National Museum (Landesmuseum) in 1898 had no positive impact on the development of a transport museum.

Then, at the national exhibition in Bern in 1914, there were numerous exhibits of both contemporary and historical objects. Many of the rail-related items found their way into the museum of the Swiss Federal Railways, which was installed in the Zurich freight station in 1918.

The creation of a true transport museum can be said to have had its beginnings in the planning of the national exhibition of 1939 in Zurich. Corresponding museums in Budapest, Nuremberg, Berlin, Munich and Vienna were cited as examples. However, it is worth noting that R Cottier – Director of the Swiss Federal Railways, first President of the Verkehrshaus der Schweiz foundation, and the author of a letter promoting the idea of a transport museum – mentioned that none of the foreign museums devoted itself to all means of transport. Thus, the creation of a Swiss transport museum incorporating all areas of transport would mean something completely new in Europe.

Profits from the national exhibition were used to set up an office charged with making plans for the railway museum, and the engineer E Fontanellaz was appointed as executive officer. He made an initial sketch of the future transport museum: one building for each means of transport, interconnected by roofed corridors and with a central entrance. At the same time he had in mind two museums which were to influence the later Verkehrshaus: the Museum of Science and Industry in New York, which he called a 'hands-on' museum with all its buttons, films and models; and the Children's Gallery at the Science Museum in London, which had artificial rainbows and numerous light effects that made a strong impression on him.

On 27 February 1942 the 'Verkehrshaus der Schweiz' foundation came into being; in 1950 it moved to Lucerne, where it was given a building and grounds by the city authority in 1954.

The Verkehrshaus as a forerunner of science centres in Europe
On 1 July 1959 the museum was opened, nearly two years later than originally planned (Figures 1 and 2). The first Director, Alfred Waldis, who combined great enthusiasm for the topic with a fine feeling for public relations and the needs of the visitor, was responsible for an unprecedented construction phase, which resulted in a substantial increase in the museum's size.

Waldis's approach, incorporating texts in four languages, covering topics from local to global perspectives (planetarium, space travel) and employing numerous hands-on exhibits, helped to promote in Europe a new, Anglo-American style of museum and made the Verkehrshaus a forerunner of modern science centres. The focus on visitors' interests, the professional work by exhibition architects and designers, and good public relations efforts with the help of prominent persons from the transport field, added to the growing popularity of the museum.

There was a conference building dedicated to providing a forum for discussion of contemporary events, and spaces for special exhibitions on topical issues and multimedia presentations. The first large planetarium in Switzerland (1969), a multimedia show on the history of space travel (Cosmorama, 1972), the 'round' Swissorama cinema (1984) and the IMAX theatre (1996) can be seen as continuing efforts to incorporate the latest communications technologies into the museum complex.

The scope of many of these installations went far beyond the borders of canton or country, which was unusual for museums and collections in Switzerland. This was due in large part to the subject matter, which included mass motorisation and the rise of international aviation in the postwar period – a period which saw an opening towards foreign countries previously unknown, a kind of 'globalisation' focusing on the Western world. The topics covered by the Verkehrshaus were thus of great interest to a wide public for many years.

Unfortunately, the objects that served as hands-on teaching examples suffered as a result of the large number of visitors (120,000 in 1959, 700,000 in 1982 and since then an average of 500,000 per annum). Some objects were removed from exhibition; others were

Figure 1 Since its opening, the Verkehrshaus has owned a 1904 Oldsmobile. A collection of catalogues and 230 letters from the former owner provide documentary evidence of the life of this car, including accounts of the smallest breakdowns and other events. The history of the car is known in every detail. In contrast, however, several restorations of the car have erased all physical traces of this history. (Swiss Museum of Transport and Communication)

either replaced or restored with the help of sponsors. From today's perspective, these restorations were not done in a professional manner. Use of the artefacts within the exhibitions was given priority over their preservation. Therefore, knowledge about their operation or about their technical features (e.g. vehicle dynamics) was retained only in some exceptional cases. On the other hand, due to the lack of resources quite a number of objects remained in an unrestored state so that they still possessed substantial historical value.

The rapid expansion of the museum also saw an enlargement of the collection. Most of the objects were donated; today the collection has about 7000 items (excluding the archive). It does not have the completeness that one might expect in a national collection; on the other hand the museum is a private association, which guarantees an independent collection policy, free from political or economic interests.

New forms of education

In addition to the large multimedia shows, various projects have been accomplished since the late 1990s that are closely linked to the collection. They make use of the techniques of science centres used in the United States, but are based in history and on the knowledge gained from documents and objects. The following *mise en scène* gives

an idea of how the visitor is expected to view an exhibit and, hopefully, develop an emotional bond with the objects.

In *Nautirama* at the Vierwaldstätter lake, groups of visitors are guided with light and sound through the history of water transport and tourism (Figure 3). They experience a time journey in nine multimedia displays, which focus on changes in the perception of the Alps in the nineteenth century – from a barrier to a destination. Technical development from small freight ships to motorised transport is also shown. *Nautirama*, which opened in 1995, concentrates on the social and cultural effects of technology. The show tries to avoid being merely a presentation of fascinating technical milestones.

Outside *Nautirama*, there is a collection of about 70 ship models illustrating navigation on Swiss lakes and a panoramic picture of the lake; an architect's model makes clear the changes in the city architecture of Lucerne after the arrival of the steam ship and the railways.

When the railway exhibition was renewed and moved to a new building, it had to be confined to the same geometry, with the same vehicles on display. An increase of space was possible only in the basement of the IMAX theatre, which had replaced the previous buildings housing the railway exhibition. The concept developed by Geneva designer Roger Pfund in cooperation with the Verkehrshaus included: first, a red footbridge about 100 metres long connecting

Figure 2 Le Rhône, rotary engine from a Hanriot aircraft (1921/ 22). Traces of damage to several valve heads are still visible today. The damage undoubtedly dates back to an accident during a transfer flight in 1922, which was the reason why the engine was taken out of service and eventually ended up in the museum. (Swiss Museum of Transport and Communication)

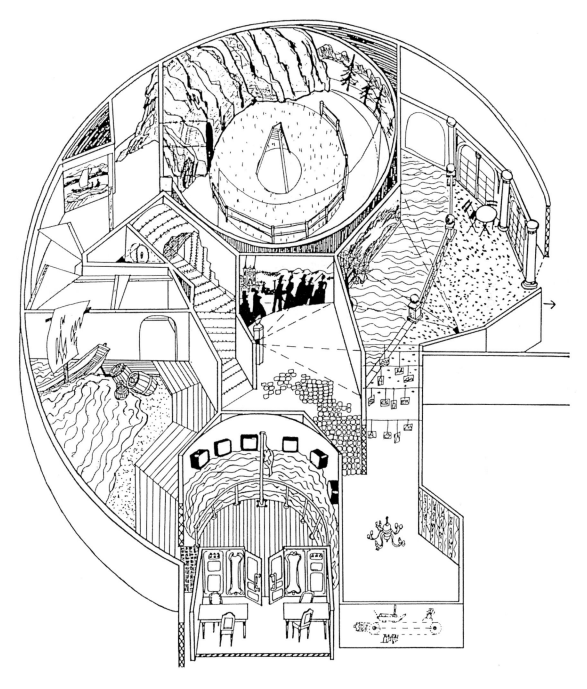

Figure 3 The history of water transport is displayed in a very small area in Nautirama. *Visitors pass through the saloon of a paddle-steamer and a scene depicting a shipping catastrophe in the Middle Ages, before arriving at Mount Rigi, which represents one of the most popular tourist destinations during the time of Enlightenment. Further along are experiences relating to industrialisation and the introduction of steamships, and a 'time theatre' which shows the effects of acceleration and speculation. The end of the exhibition is marked by a real shower of 'rain', at the point where visitors meet Queen Victoria, King Ludwig II of Bavaria and Kaiser Wilhelm II, who represent the heyday of tourism before the First World War. (Swiss Museum of Transport and Communication)*

the three existing halls with a 'classical' type of railway exhibition and, second, an opportunity for visitors to go on a train ride into the construction site of the St Gothard tunnel in 1875 (made possible by offering a vivid experience based on a thrilling yet historically accurate story).

The division of the exhibition into two parts makes it possible to address a large potential audience. The footbridge not only gives an overview and assists orientation, but also allows an unusual perspective on the vehicles, including both their interiors and their roofs. Furthermore, the show enables visitors to identify with human experiences and to find out more about tunnel construction, life in the mountain village of Göschenen and the political and economical context. The original drilling machines, stone samples and a theodolite give additional authenticity to the *mise en scène*.

Novel approaches were used as well for the newly designed exhibition *Cosmorama*, which opened in 1999, 30 years after the first moon landing. Crewed space flight was relatively new in 1972, at the initial opening of the exhibition. The few objects on display, mostly borrowed from the National Air and Space Museum in Washington, were of great interest to visitors at that time. By 1999 this interest had significantly diminished; the collection had grown hardly at all, and many exhibits had to be returned. On behalf of the Verkehrshaus, the ethnologist Jacqueline Milliet conceptualised an exhibition on the theme 'Life in Space'. It aimed to attract a wide, predominantly young audience and thus offered something different in terms of the media used, going beyond the existing IMAX theatre, planetarium and Gothard tunnel show.

The 700-square-metre exhibition is divided into three sections. The first deals with weightlessness in space in a playful way. The middle section of *Cosmorama* takes visitors on a journey to a mysterious asteroid field using video and laser effects. In the third section, authentic artefacts together with replicas and models illustrate the history of space flight and its significance for propaganda and international cooperation. In some showcases, Swiss companies present their latest contributions to space flight.

The ethnological approach mainly focuses on the effects of the exploration of space on human perceptions. This means that new and unexpected artefacts can be included. In the entrance section, for example, a reconstruction of the European ISS research laboratory Columbus is placed beside a children's merry-go-round. This unexpected exhibit can be seen as a perfect 'simulator' for space sickness.

The exhibition was designed as a succession of rooms which serve as exhibits by themselves. In the entrance, the visitor passes on an escalator through a familiar, homely environment: a bookshelf, a table and kitchen furniture arranged in a seemingly weightless and chaotic way, which introduces the concept of 'zero' gravity in space. Thus it becomes indirectly clear why sleeping areas and work stations in the space station are located under the roof and along the walls.

In the department of space archaeology the storage facilities in the museum's basement are integrated into the exhibitions. The attraction of storage facilities as an area usually not accessible to visitors and the desire to put on display as much as possible are thereby combined. Visitors can follow the traces of 30 years of space history, from a replica of Sputnik 1 to the Mercury space module and to the solar wind experiment by the University of Bern.

In the mausoleum, six spacesuits (originals and replicas) are displayed horizontally in individual niches (Colour plate 13). They suggest the architecture of a burial ground or of paintings of the Italian Renaissance, thus oscillating between tradition and provocation, between a reverence of heroes and a questioning of our relationships to the heroes of space travel. The spacesuits are viewed individually through small windows, instead of in a classical showcase, which limits access but at the same time increases attention.

In the rooms of the old *Cosmorama* a laser contact show is combined with a science-fiction video in six interactive sequences. Visitors can influence the action with the help of a programmable laser pointer, answering questions or 'destroying' space waste.

Apart from the conventional labels, quotations from prominent persons and astronauts about the history of space flight are displayed, close to specific objects or object groups. Visitors can quickly become acquainted with new and different contexts by reading just a few of these labels.

Balloons have often been used as an attraction in exhibitions. Modern materials and the use of helium now make possible long-term economical operation. The beautiful panorama of the Verkehrshaus, the city of Lucerne and the Vierwaldstätter lake, together with the view of the Alps of central Switzerland, constitute a perfect reason for the installation of such a tethered balloon as landmark and live experience. It is a special attraction in good weather, a time when visitors ordinarily avoid museums. After a postponement of the project due to local opposition, Hiflyer began operation in 2000. The distinctive white globe attracts tourists from the nearby city and provides extra fun for visitors.

Between vision and reality: the concept of 'Verkehrshaus 2002'

In preparation for the new road transport hall, an architectural contest was announced in 1999. The existing structure, built in 1959 (Figure 4), can no longer deal with the dramatically increased importance of road transport and will therefore be replaced by a larger new building. The winning architects, Gigon & Guyer (Zurich) have proposed a city development concept with several themed buildings

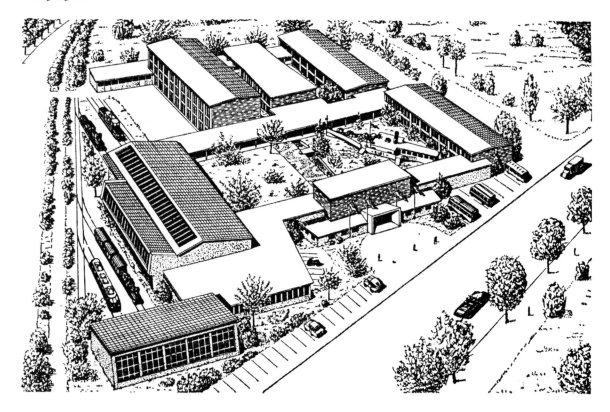

interconnected on several levels by small bridges (Figure 5). They symbolise transport and communication links and also divide the outside area. Existing buildings will be either integrated or replaced, depending on funding.

As a first step, a garden restaurant was completed in 2000, and in June 2001 the refurbished planetarium was opened, with a new hemispheric 'all-sky' video projection and a revised Zeiss projector. Currently, funds are being raised for the new road transport hall and plans are being developed for a new multipurpose entrance building.

Conclusion

The artefact, as a symbol of past reality, will forever remain fascinating, in part because of the number of ways it can be interpreted. However, the source of its attraction changes over time. It is in the power and imagination of curators, researchers and designers to adjust to those changes. The museum object will therefore continue to play an important role in the future planning of the Verkehrshaus.

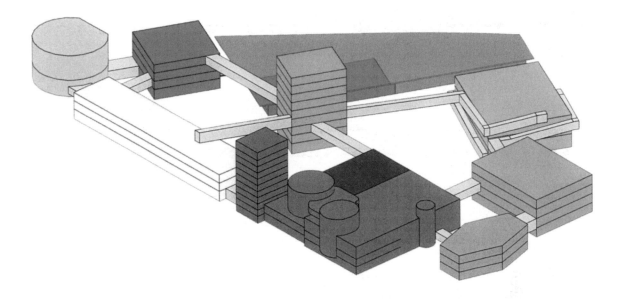

Figure 5 A vision of the Verkehrshaus in 2020. The architects A Gigon and M Guyer had to accept that the museum has grown in a heterogeneous manner, and that different architects, using different architectural styles, will probably add to the development of the museum in the future. The winners of the 1999 architects' contest do not speak of the 'Verkehrshaus' but of several houses, a contingent of topic-related buildings. (Swiss Museum of Transport and Communication)

Significant museums with relevant collections

Inland transport

Automobile and Road Museum – Mobilia, Kangasala, Finland

Automobile Museum, Belgrade, Yugoslavia

Auto Museum Wolfsburg, Germany

Auto & Technik Museum, Sinsheim, Germany

Baltimore and Ohio Railroad Museum, Baltimore, MD, USA

BMW Museum, Munich, Germany

Brooklands Museum, Weybridge, UK

California State Railroad Museum, Sacramento, CA, USA

Chemin de fer Musée Blonay-Chamby, Lausanne, Switzerland

DB Museum im Verkehrsmuseum Nürnberg, Germany

Deutsches Museum, Munich, Germany

Deutsches Technikmuseum Berlin, Germany

DSB Jernbanemuseet, Odense, Denmark

Finnish Railway Museum, Hyvinkää, Finland

Finnish Road Museum, Helsinki, Finland

Fundació Museu del Transport, Castellar de N'Hug, Spain

Fürst Thurn & Taxis – Marstall Museum, Regensburg, Germany

Heidelberg Motor Museum, South Africa

Henry Ford Museum and Greenfield Village, Dearborn, MI, USA

Heritage Motor Centre, Gaydon, UK

Közlekedési Múzeum Budapest, Hungary

Landesmuseum für Technik und Arbeit, Mannheim, Germany

Leonardo da Vinci Museum, Milan, Italy

London's Transport Museum, UK

Marcus Wallenberg Hallen, Södertälje, Sweden

Mercedes-Benz Museum, Stuttgart, Germany

Modern Transportation Museum, Osaka, Japan

Motor-Museum-Öhringen, Germany

Musée des Arts et Métiers, Paris, France

Musée des Transports Urbains, Colombes, France

Musée Francais du Chemin de Fer, Mulhouse, France

Musée National de l'Automobile, Mulhouse, France

Musée National de la Voiture et du Tourisme, Compiègne, France

Museo del Ejercito de Madrid, Spain

Museo del Ferrocarril, Madrid, Spain

Museo Nazionale Ferroviario, Naples, Italy

Museo Vasco del Ferrocarril, Azpeitia, Spain

Museum für Hamburgische Geschichte, Hamburg, Germany

Museum of Applied Arts & Sciences, Powerhouse Museum, Haymarket, NSW, Australia

Museum of British Road Transport, Coventry

Museum of Transport, Glasgow, UK

Museum of Transport & Technology, Auckland, New Zealand

Museum of Transportation, St Louis, MO, USA

Museum van de Belgische Spoorwegen, Brussels, Belgium

Museu Nacional dos Coches, Lisbon, Portugal

National Motorcycle Museum, Birmingham, UK

National Motor Museum, Beaulieu, UK

National Motor Museum, Birdwood, SA, Australia

National Museum of American History, Smithsonian Institution, Washington DC, USA

National Museum of Iceland, Reykjavik

National Museum of Science & Technology, Ottawa, Ont., Canada

National Rail Museum, New Delhi, India

National Railway Museum, York, UK

National Tramway Museum, Crich, UK

National Waterways Museum, Ellesmere Port, Gloucester and Stoke Bruerne, UK

New South Wales State Rail Museum, Thirlmere, Australia

New York Transit Museum, Brooklyn, NY, USA

Norrbottens Järnvägsmuseum, Lulea, Sweden

Norsk Jernbanemuseum, Hamar, Norway

Norsk Vegmuseum, Faberg, Norway

North Carolina Transportation Museum, Spencer, USA

Ofoten Museum, Narvik, Norway

Petersen Automotive Museum, Los Angeles, CA, USA

Porsche Museum, Stuttgart, Germany

Postal Museum of the Republic of China, Taipei, Taiwan

Postimuseo, Helsinki, Finland

Queensland Railways Historical Centre, Ipswich, Qld, Australia

Railroad Museum of Pennsylvania, Strasburg, USA

Riga Motor Museum, Latvia

Sam Tung Uk Museum – Hong Kong Railway Museum

Science Museum, London, UK

Seashore Trolley Museum, Kennebunkport, ME, USA

Spårvägsmuseet i Stockholm, Sweden
STEAM – Museum of the Great Western Railway, Swindon, UK
Stichting Nederlands Spoorweg Museum, Utrecht, Netherlands
Sveriges Järnvägsmuseum, Gävle, Sweden
Toyota Automobile Museum, Aichi, Japan

Tramsmusée, Luxembourg
Tyrwhitt-Drake Museum of Carriages, Maidstone, UK
Ulster Folk and Transport Museum, Cultra, UK
Verkehrshaus der Schweiz, Lucerne, Switzerland
Verkehrsmuseum Dresden, Germany

Aviation

Aeronautical Memorial Park, Tokyo, Japan
American Helicopter Museum and Education Center, West Chester, PA, USA
Aviodome – National Luchtvaart Museum, Schiphol, Netherlands
Brooklands Museum, Weybridge, UK
Central Finland Aviation Museum, Tikkakoski
Deutsches Technikmuseum Berlin, Germany
First Wing Historical Centre, Beauvechain, Belgium
Fleet Air Arm Museum, Yeovilton, UK
Flygvapenmuseum, Linköping, Sweden
Imperial War Museum Duxford, Cambridge, UK
Kalamazoo Aviation History Museum, MI, USA
Közlekedési Múzeum Budapest, Hungary
Lone Star Flight Museum, Galveston, TX, USA
Mag. Repülestörténeti Muzeum Alapitvány, Szolnok, Hungary
Musée de l'Air et de l'Espace, Le Bourget, France
Musée J A Bombardier, Valcourt, Que., Canada
Musée Royal de l'Armée et d'Histoire Militaire, Brussels, Belgium
Museo Aeronautico Gianni Caproni, Milan, Italy

Museu do Ar, Alverca, Portugal
Museum of Flight, Seattle, WA, USA
National Air and Space Museum, Smithsonian Institution, Washington DC, USA
National Museum of Science & Technology, Ottawa, Ont., Canada
Pima Air & Space Museum, Tucson, AZ, USA
RAAF Museum, Point Cook, Vic., Australia
Royal Air Force Museum, London, UK
Royal Netherlands Military Aviation Museum, Soesterberg, Netherlands
Science Museum, London, UK
Shuttleworth Collection, nr Biggleswade, UK
US Air Force Museum, Dayton, OH, USA
Verkehrshaus der Schweiz, Lucerne, Switzerland
Western Canada Aviation Museum, Winnipeg, Man., Canada
Wings Over Rockies Air & Space Museum, Greenwood Village, CO, USA
Yanks Air Museum, Chino, CA, USA
Zeppelin Museum, Friedrichshafen, Germany

Maritime

Altonaer Museum in Hamburg, Germany
Australian National Maritime Museum, Sydney, NSW
Bangsbo Museet, Frederikshavn, Denmark
Bergens Sjofartsmuseum, Bergen, Norway
Eesti Meremuuseum, Tallin, Estonia
Elbschifffahrtsmuseum Stadt Lauenburg, Lauenberg, Germany
Handels-og Sofartsmuseet pa Kronborg, Helsingor, Denmark
Maritiem Museum Rotterdam, Netherlands
Museu de Marinha, Lisbon, Portugal
Museu Maritimo de Macau, China

Museum für Hamburgische Geschichte, Hamburg, Germany
Mystic Seaport, CT, USA
National Fishing Heritage Centre, Grimsby, UK
National Maritime Museum, London, UK
National Museum of American History, Smithsonian Institution, Washington DC, USA
Norsk Sjofartsmuseum, Oslo, Norway
Science Museum, London, UK
Tamkang University Maritime Museum, Taipei Hsien, Taiwan
Vasamuseet, Stockholm, Sweden
Verkehrshaus der Schweiz, Lucerne, Switzerland

Index